# Women and Sexuality in China

# Women and Sexuality in China

Female Sexuality and Gender
Since 1949

# Harriet Evans

Continuum · New York

1997

The Continuum Publishing Company
370 Lexington Avenue
New York, NY 10017

Printed in Great Britain

**Library of Congress Cataloging-in-Publication Data**

Evans, Harriet.
    Women and sexuality in China : female sexuality and gender
since 1949 / Harriet Evans.
        p.   cm.
    Includes bibliographical references and index.
    ISBN 0-8264-0922-9 (hardcover: alk. paper)
    1. Women—China—Sexual behavior.    2. Sex instruction—China.
3. Sex—Political aspects—China.    4. Communism and sex—China.
5. Women and communism—China.    6. Discourse analysis—China.
I. Title.
HQ29.E93 1997                                                              96–8161
306.7′082—dc20                                                              CIP

# Contents

# Preface and Acknowledgements

Since I first went to China as a student more than twenty years ago, my friendships and relationships with Chinese women have changed and developed in diverse and often exciting ways. I have known a few of my friends since the early years of my acquaintance with China. I have come to know many more since then, through research and shared interests, through my students and through mutual connections, both in and outside China, in Europe and in the United States. My research interests have grown out of these friendships, out of the discussions and conversations they have generated, as well as out of my commitment to feminist ideas and goals. As the contexts in which we have maintained our discussions have changed, so old themes have been replaced by new ones, or have been interwoven into new approaches and analyses to produce different understandings. Some themes have returned to our conversations repeatedly: questions about how we see ourselves as women, how we conduct ourselves as daughters, mothers, partners and wives – questions about gender and sexual identity. Our responses to these questions have also, of course, been as diverse as the differences between us. Some of my friends strongly resist what they see as the negative gender implications of China's rapidly changing social and cultural environment. Others welcome the changes for the possibilities they give to explore new and empowering meanings associated with being a woman. Yet throughout the shifting ways in which the Chinese women I know have talked about their lives, a number of shared assumptions have emerged – for example, about notions of duty, obligation and pleasure, about the kinds of responsibilities having a female body implies, and about the links between women's reproductive role and gender practice. This book is an attempt to understand some of the dominant discourses within which these assumptions have been shaped; it is an attempt to try to formulate some ideas about why and how they are shared.

Even though the writing of this book has been of relatively short duration, the ideas and passions out of which it has emerged have been part of my life since I embarked on my career in Chinese studies. Many people have been indispensable to its completion. First are the women and men whose friendship has offered me an understanding of contemporary Chinese society rarely conveyed in academic writing: Bu Wei, Chang Xiangqun, Gao Changfan, Guo Yuhua, Huang Dian, Qian Wenbao, Shen Rui, Yang Lian and You You. In China, a number of academics have given me invaluable help and encouragement by sharing with me their ideas and research findings: Chen Yiyun, Fei Juanhong, Geng Wenxiu, Li Yinhe, Liu Dalin, Mu Aiping, Pan Suiming, Shan Guangnai, Shen Chonglin, Shen Yuan, Tan Shen, Tao Chunfang, Wang Xingjuan, Wei Zhangling, Xu Anqi and Zhang Ping. I would also like to thank Charles D'Orban, Jean Hung and Zhao Yiheng for their valuable suggestions about sources.

I am also indebted to many other friends and colleagues for reading parts of the work and discussing them with me. Elisabeth Croll was the first to encourage me to develop my interests into a research project; without her advice in its earlier stages, this book might never have come about. Felicity Edholm has been a constant source of critical and reflective ideas, as well as encouragement and support when the going got tough. Many stimulating discussions with Stephan Feuchtwang, Bronwyn Hipkin, Laura Marcus and Alex Warwick have given me new perspectives on my work, particularly at moments when confusion seemed to blur everything. Several others have also made specific and unique contributions to this work: Delia Davin, Frank Dikötter, John Gittings, Michael Palmer and Stuart Thompson.

Much of the research for this book was made possible by a grant from the British Academy and the Chinese Academy of Social Sciences to visit China during March and April 1993. A fellowship from the Leverhulme Foundation between October 1994 and February 1995 gave me the time to finish a substantial part of the first draft. I would also like to acknowledge the support of Hilary Footitt, of the University of Westminster, who generously reduced my teaching responsibilities at key moments during the project.

Others have also made unique contributions in different ways. Through the final stages of the draft, Nina Balogh provided essential and always entertaining childcare. My children, Rebecca and Gabriel, were both wonderful companions through the last stages of writing. Marilyn Young was always available with the right words at the right moments as I came near to completing the project. Finally I want to thank John Cayley for his rigorous and critical reading of every stage of the draft, for his generosity in looking after my needs during the last busy months of the project, and for his endlessly inspiring ideas about the issues discussed in the following pages.

A few paragraphs in chapters 1, 2, 3 and 5 originally appeared in an article 'Defining Difference: the scientific construction of sexuality and gender in the People's Republic of China' [*SIGNS*: Journal of Women in Culture and Society, Winter 1995, vol. 20, no. 2] copyright © 1995 by the University of Chicago. All rights reserved.

# Bibliographical Abbreviations

| | |
|---|---|
| AP | *Associated Press* |
| CND | *China News Digest* |
| DJJK | *Dajia jiankang (Health for everyone)* |
| DZJK | *Dazhong jiankang (Popular health)* |
| DZYX | *Dazhong yixue (Popular medicine)* |
| HNRB | *Henan ribao (Henan daily)* |
| HYYJT | *Hunyin yu jiating (Marriage and family)* |
| JTYS | *Jiating yisheng (Family doctor)* |
| MZYFZ | *Minzhu yu fazhi (Democracy and the legal system)* |
| NXYJ | *Nüxing yanjiu (Women's studies)* |
| NYZX | *Nüyou zhixin (Women's friend)* |
| XDJT | *Xiandai jiating (Modern Family)* |
| ZGFN | *Zhongguo funü (Women of China)* |
| ZGQN | *Zhongguo qingnian (China youth)* |

# 1 Introduction: Discourses of Sexuality Since 1949

Sex is a prominent feature of public life in China. Images of beautiful women in erotic poses cover the magazines found on corner newsstands and gaze down on passers-by from street billboards. Advice columns in local newspapers and weekly journals contain detailed information on topics that range from how to recognize the symptoms of the menarche to old people's need for sex and romance. Huge numbers of guides for newly-weds, self-help pamphlets on reproductive health, text-books on sexual hygiene, and encyclopaedic manuals on the management of modern family life testify to a flourishing market for publications about sex, catering for a diverse range of needs. After decades of exclusion from the classroom, sex education is commonly found on high school syllabuses; a 'scientific' understanding of sex is considered essential to the healthy development of the nation's future. Romantic scenes with erotic imagery are a recurring feature of literature and film, despite the watchful eye of the censors. More sensationalist materials, including pornography, often imported from abroad, are also widely available.

The view that sex has 'taken off' in China in the last decade appears to be borne out by the contrast between the liberalization of the 1980s and the constraints on sex-related discussions during the Maoist decades. Chinese and Western scholars commonly promulgate the idea that 'sex was a taboo subject during the period 1949–1980', when 'any materials relating to sex . . . were strictly forbidden' (Zha Bo and Geng Wenxiu 1992, 2). Attention to matters of love and sex was for decades treated either as the shameful expression of a warped mind or as evidence of bourgeois individualism and detrimental to collective welfare. Throughout the 1950s, principles of hard work, frugality, and collective enthusiasm for the 'new China' dominated images of marriage and family life. During the Cultural Revolution (1966–76), the slightest suggestion of sexual interest was considered so ideologically unsound that gendered tastes in hairstyle and dress were coerced into a monotonous uniformity of shape and colour. A kind of androgyny, a sexual sameness, based on the defeminization of female appearance and its approximation to male standards of dress, seemed to be the socialist ideal. By contrast, the current diversity of representations of sexuality in China suggests the explosion of a topic hitherto hidden from public view.

The argument that sex was a taboo subject in this period ignores the considerable range of materials published on sex-related issues during the 1950s and early 1960s (Evans 1991). Many articles and pamphlets focused on the requirements of the Marriage Law, introduced by the communist government in 1950, which outlawed arranged and venal marriages and ratified monogamy based on the free choice of partner as the only legal form of marriage. Between 1950 and 1953, numerous publications sought to educate the public about the new law, with particular emphasis on its importance for women, oppressed for centuries by the traditional system of arranged marriage and concubinage. With titles such as 'Establish a correct perspective on love' (*Jianli zhengque de lian'ai guan*) and 'Talking about my view of love' (*Tantan wode lian'ai guan*), articles devoted lengthy discussions to the meaning of love, now considered the necessary basis for the new model of conjugality (Cheng Jinwu 1950; Lei Ji 1950). Most issues of the official journals for women and youth, *Zhongguo funü* (Women of China) and *Zhongguo qingnian* (China youth), published in the 1950s and early 1960s, carried short pieces, often accompanied by readers' letters, on a particular aspect of sexuality, whether it was adolescent hygiene or women's anxieties about contraception. Some detailed the biological aspects of sexual difference and reproduction, for example, 'The hymen and love' (*Chunümo yu aiqing*) and 'Talking about the age of marriage from a physiological point of view' (*Cong shengli shang tan jiehun nianling wenti*) (Li Yang 1956; Lin Qiaozhi 1957). Others addressed the moral implications of sexual relationships outside marriage, as in a debate carried in a number of consecutive issues of *Zhongguo funü* in 1956, initiated by an autobiographical piece entitled 'Why did our marriage break down?' (*Women fufu guanxi weishenmo polie?*; Liu Lequn 1955). Written by doctors, lawyers, students, adolescent schoolchildren, teachers, young wives and mothers, these articles provided a regular public forum for discussion about a wide range of sex-related questions.

The pre-Cultural Revolution discourse on sexuality brought to the official vision of ideologically correct behaviour a code of normative sexual and gender expectations legitimized by so-called scientific authority. Medical experts claimed the authority of modern science to expound the view that biological differences in reproductive and sexual development determined all major distinctions between women and men in sexual and social behaviour. Experts also gave scientific status to opinions about sexual difference which reflected social and moral concerns as much as medical interests; the 'scientific knowledge about sex' legitimized practices that supported the state's interests in controlling young people's sexual conduct (Wang Wenbin, Zhao Zhiyi and Tan Mingxin 1956, 1). Equated with a 'modern', 'rational' and often Western-oriented approach to explanations of sex, 'scientific' knowledge produced and disseminated by the experts was widely contrasted with the mystifications of feudal superstition and popular distortions of the facts (Wang Peng 1993, 1–2).[1]

Discussion of sexuality since the early 1980s has encompassed a diversity of topics not included in the 1950s discourse. Recent writings make few direct references to the debates of the 1950s and tend to treat them as little more than the highly didactic and moralistic precursor of the later, less unified discourse of the reform period (Honig and Hershatter 1988, 6–7). However, despite what seem to be immense differences, the questions asked in the later period echoed many of the concerns of the former discourse. The 1950s approaches established the epistemic foundation grounding the assumptions, perspectives and parameters of the later debates. Indeed, the continuities between the two periods are sometimes so direct that the views of the 1950s are replicated almost verbatim in the later texts. For example, except for slight differences in wording, the warnings against masturbation in Shen Wenjiang's *A Manual for Young People's Hygiene* are identical to those of Huang Shuze's 'What should I do to get rid of the bad habit of masturbation?' (Shen Wenjiang et al. 1987, 22; Huang Shuze 1955). While in the changed social and intellectual climate of the reform period the more diverse tone of public discussion obscures many of the similarities between the different discourses, the assumption that women's gender characteristics are inseparable from their reproductive function and the use of science to legitimate fundamentally hierarchical gender relationships are as notable in contemporary approaches to sex-related issues as they were in the 1950s. Elucidating the discursive concerns of the 1950s, therefore, indicates the point of departure for the study of sexuality in China in the 1980s as well as some of the major assumptions and preoccupations informing the orientations of later debates.

This book analyses the dominant public discourses of sexuality produced since 1949 in the People's Republic of China in order to identify meanings associated with female gender that do not emerge from an analytical focus on socio-economic or political issues. Through such examination it identifies the discursive techniques which inscribed biologically determined sexual differences with hierarchical gender characteristics. It examines a range of narrative and some visual representations of women's sexuality publicized since 1949 with reference to distinct themes, outlining women's responsibilities and attributes in sexually implicated contexts and relationships. In exploring these themes, the book seeks to elucidate the tensions, contrasts and continuities between the apparently very different discourses of sexuality of the revolutionary and reform periods.

Some of the themes discussed in the pages that follow have been a consistent feature of official discourses since 1949; matters concerning adolescence, pre- and extra-marital relationships, marriage and divorce disappeared from public view only with the ban on women's and youth publications during the Cultural Revolution. Other themes have come to prominence in the last fifteen years; discussion about the commercial use of women's bodies, about the spread of sexually transmitted diseases and AIDS, and about homosexuality clearly corresponds with the current context of marketization of the economy. Many sections of this book reiterate hopes and fears which would be familiar to any reader of *Elle* or *Seventeen*; the debates about adolescent sex education, parental responsibilities for children's sexual understanding and behaviour, teenage pregnancy and the links between explicit sexual images and sexual violence are all familiar features of the contemporary Western media. Others touch on fundamental questions of women's human rights – questions which a book on discourses of sexuality cannot treat adequately. In formulating the terms of my analysis, I have attempted to identify the main themes and parameters of the dominant discourses of sexuality produced since the early years of the People's Republic.

## The political and ideological contexts

Before the radical changes that spread through China's cities in the late nineteenth and early twentieth centuries, a patrilineal system of inheritance and power governed matters concerning marriage and sexual conduct. The dominant form of marriage was arranged and patrilocal, contracted through negotiations between parents and marriage brokers.[2] Though uxorilocal marriages were quite common, they were generally a last resort in cases of extreme poverty or when the lack of sons threatened continuity of the male line of the bride's natal family. Female virginity was indispensable to the negotiations of marriage for its symbolic value as a signifier of sexual and reproductive ownership. The young wife entered her husband's household as a stranger, legally removed from the controls formerly exercised by her natal family and valued principally for her potential to reproduce male descendants for her husband's patrilineage. She had no rights of divorce or inheritance, even though she might receive some property via the dowry as a 'premortem inheritance' (Watson 1991a, 353–4), and ideally was not allowed to associate with men in public. So high a premium was attached to female chastity in the early Qing period that the 1646 rape law could compel the victims of rape 'to defend their chastity with their lives' (Ng 1987, 65). On the other hand, a man could have a number of wives or concubines, and enjoyed rights of divorce and free mobility. In formal terms, the husband and his family were the principal arbiters of a wife's fate.

As new social, economic and cultural forces began to alter urban family structures in the early twentieth century, social reformers increasingly identified free-choice monogamous marriage as the indispensable first step towards dismantling the system of oppressive patriarchal authority. Consensual unions became common practice for the educated urban elites in the early twentieth century (Dikötter 1995, 18–19). The Nationalist government's new Family Law of 1931 and the Communist Party's 1934 Constitution of the Jiangxi Soviet Republic both gave legal recognition to free-choice monogamous marriage, even though the formal procedures of the new form of marriage were far from offering an institutionalized alternative to parental arrangement, particularly in the rural areas (Croll 1981, 130–4). With the promulgation of the new Marriage Law in 1950, free-choice marriage became the main formal expression of the Communist Party's commitment to women's struggle for sexual equality. The model of marriage ratified by the law described a relationship between equal companions who shared responsibility for childcare and domestic tasks and who were 'in duty bound to love, respect, assist and look after each other' (*Marriage Law of the People's Republic of China* 1950, chapter 3; Meijer 1972). Combined with new rights of divorce, the right to choose a marriage partner now empowered women – in theory if still not in practice – to challenge the gender hierarchy on which patriarchal authority was premised. Disseminated through the media, women's and youth organizations and the education system, and folk operas and other dramatic forms revised to publicize the new communist message, the law received extensive coverage as the expression of the new form of marriage. By implication, it also indicated standards of sexual behaviour commensurate with the new model of monogamous marriage. Indeed, one main purpose of state intervention in debates about sex-related matters was to ensure that young people were educated in the principles of sexual morality deemed necessary for the successful implementation of free-choice marriage.

The social, moral and sexual requirements of the new Marriage Law thus established the immediate context for the 1950s discourse of sexuality. Free-choice monogamous marriage was publicized as a positive step to protect women from male abuse. It was presented as a means of empowering women to take control over their own lives and destinies, as the central pillar of the party's explicit goal of sexual equality. However, the law was premised on a naturalized and hierarchical view of gender relations that, by definition, limited the extent of the challenge that women could launch against the patriarchal system. Monogamous marriage was 'dictated not only by the physiological difference between the sexes, but also by the perpetuation of the species' (Chen Jianwei 1959). As the sole legitimate expression of a naturalized construction of heterosexuality, the monogamous relationship indicated clear boundaries of sexual behaviour, women's transgression of which signified a potential threat to female fertility as well as family stability. Monogamy was also represented as the wife's obligation to support her husband's interests and service his needs, whether as the self-sacrificing manager of his domestic affairs or as his moral guide. Women who went too far in questioning the implied gender constructs by postponing marriage, by 'refusing to see their husbands' for fear of becoming pregnant, or by spending too much time trying to acquire an education were described as the equivalent of gender deviationists – women who through betrayal of their proper gender attributes brought disruption and conflict to their marriages (Evans 1991, 176–80). Monogamy thus signified an emancipatory step away from the rigid controls of the feudal system at the same time as it reasserted hierarchical gender boundaries.

Within this context, official discussion marked the texts, themes and representational practices through which knowledge about sexual matters was produced and controlled – the nexus of knowledge and power – as a means of legitimizing certain values, practices and their exponents (Foucault 1984, 92–102). The official discourse regulated sexuality through the projection of norms and sanctions to accompany the more formal control of sexual conduct – for example, in matters of adultery or rape – exercised by the state's legal and political institutions. Discursive identification of a range of sexual practices offered a distinct technique for establishing mechanisms of control over the individual, exercised not by authoritarian denials but, as Weeks put it, by 'imposing a grid of definition on the possibilities of the body' (Weeks 1981, 7–8). Sanctions and rewards, associated with notions of physical and psychological health, indicated the boundaries between acceptable and unacceptable sexual conduct. The development of an official discourse of sexuality testified to the deployment of party-state power over individual, and particularly female, behaviour through the creation of uniform, normative standards of sexual conduct.

The materials that constituted the official discourse transmitted a view of sexuality and sexual difference as a set of biologically determined binary opposites that governed gender behaviour. Highly selective and explicitly didactic in its distinctions between right and wrong, normal and abnormal, this discourse aimed to regulate sexual practice in support of the project of social control and economic development formulated by the new government. Under the programme of national reconstruction in the 1950s, individual energies were to be channelled into working for the collective benefit. Expressions of individualistic interest in appearance or romance, for example, were to be contained by an ethic that stressed the superiority of selflessness and collective commitment.

Throughout the Cultural Revolution, any suggestion of sex in fiction, poetry or drama was enough to have the offending work removed from circulation and its author punished. Even when associated with a critique of feudal forms of exploitation, sex could not be mentioned in public. For example, the revision of the famous play *The White-Haired Girl* as a model revolutionary ballet contained no reference to the rape of the girl by the landlord's son.[3] Of course, the sexual attitudes and practices of many young people during the Cultural Revolution had little in common with the stringent standards of the official discourse. As personal accounts by women and men of the Red Guard generation have revealed, many young people found themselves free of parental supervision for the first time in their lives and able to explore sexual experiences that ridiculed the moral and ideological values of the time. Salacious stories were frequently copied out by hand (*shouchaoben*) and passed around clandestinely, giving many people their first introduction to descriptions of sex.[4] Fictional accounts of life as a student sent down to the countryside also suggest a range of experiences far removed from the realms of the officially acceptable (Ma Yuan 1993; Ah Cheng 1990; Min 1993). However, party-state control of publishing houses, the press and the mass media meant that popular discourses of sexuality were by definition not available in openly published form. Little information about 'unorthodox' practices reached the open press, and documentation of them was strictly classified.[5] Discussions with Chinese women and men acquainted with the popular texts of the Cultural Revolution suggest that the gender values they represented did not significantly challenge the naturalized heterosexist assumptions of the former official discourse. If anything, so some have indicated, they tended to reinforce the objectification of women for male pleasure and use.

The 1950s and the Cultural Revolution discourses shared common ground in their approach to love and marriage as issues of social, public importance. They also converged in the belief that removing such matters from identification with the private sphere served to protect women's interests. The view that marriage was 'not a matter of private enjoyment but a "cell" of the entire cause of revolution, something important to the interests of society as a whole' applied just as much to the 1960s as to the earlier period (Yu Ming, *Dagong bao*, 22 December 1956, quoted in Croll 1981, 6). However, the Cultural Revolution's discourse was one based on silence, even denial. Its defeminization of women's appearance, its gender-neutral encouragement to all young people to examine their political values by breaking with urban culture to go to the countryside, and its insistence on the possibility of developing a revolutionary outlook through working for the collective – all such representations signified the replacement of explicit advice by a discourse of 'no advice'.[6] There was virtually no public discussion about women's marital and sexual relationships, unless it was to extol the virtues of socialist comradeship. Even advice about basic contraceptive and reproductive needs was difficult to come by unless given by medical practitioners. Occasional publications such as *Qingchunqi weisheng* (Adolescent hygiene), initially published in 1974 and running to a circulation of half a million within the first year of publication, contained limited information about sexual development, reproduction and fertility (Xie Bozhang 1975). There was also a revival of discussion about discrimination against women in employment and political representation during the early 1970s, during the political campaign to criticize Confucian thought. As the Women's Federation began to re-establish local branches to develop women's political and gender interests, women were to be given improved access to information about contraception, childbirth and child-rearing, and attention was to be paid to their needs to combine work with domestic responsibilities (Croll 1978, 322–3). Until 1978, however, there were too few relevant publications to constitute a substantial discourse of sexuality. Even during the mid-1970s, when the 'later, more spaced, fewer' family planning policy was introduced to control population growth and actively disseminated by local cadres, public access to information about fertility and reproduction was still very limited.[7]

The diversity of images of women in sexually implicated contexts publicized since the early 1980s at first glance appears to repudiate the didactic constructions of the 1950s discourse. The entry of the commercial market into the production of recent discussions has imposed its own agenda on representations of sexuality. A rhetoric of 'privatization' has replaced the former insistence on the social significance of 'affairs of the heart'. Although still produced under official or semi-official auspices, representations of sexuality no longer subscribe to a unitary set of codes; sex has become an issue of debate and contestation, responsive to consumer interests and defying official attempts to regulate and control. Whether in advertising, biographical, fictional or documentary accounts, the gendered positions associated with being a woman do not seem to fit into any neat category, let alone one that is rooted in supposedly scientific arguments about sexual harmony and balance. The marketization of the economy, the increasing differentiation of social life, and the commodification of women in prostitution and sale into marriage have brought perspectives to the discussion of women's sexuality that are quite different from the concerns of the 1950s. The state's implementation since 1979 of a stringent birth limitation programme, its physical and psychological effects on women, and its implications for both challenging and reinforcing gender hierarchies signify an enormous divergence from the basically pronatalist orientation of the 1950s discourse.

Within this changed economic, social and cultural context, media approaches to sex mark evident departures from the didactic uniformity of the 1950s. One significant distinction is the greater prominence of discussion about women's sexual pleasure. Ordinary local newspapers carry articles encouraging women to enjoy their sexual relationships, to relax with their partners and to stop disguising feelings of sexual excitement. For too long, one such article in a Shanghai paper commented, women had been made to feel that expressing desire was in some way shameful and immoral (*Jiankang wenzhai bao*, 14 April 1993). In classes for newly-weds, instructors encourage women to approach their sexual relationship as a source of enjoyment and not simply a wifely duty. Sexual surveys suggest that increasing numbers of young women – even though they are still in a minority – are no longer willing to play the role of passive instrument of their husband's desire (Xu Anqi 1990a, 105–8). Women should take the initiative in expressing pleasure, and in saying 'no' to their excitable husbands. Some women have also told me that their under-graduate classes played a key role in introducing them to the notion of female sexual pleasure, including the suggestion that masturbation may enhance sexual enjoyment.[8] The fact that the press now publicizes references to homosexuality – however circumscribed these may be – is another new feature. While some of these approaches seem quite similar to those that used to emphasize a good sex life for marital harmony, they invest in the notion of female sexuality a degree of pleasure, even if not autonomous, that was absent in earlier discus-sions. Although representations of female pleasure are still firmly contained within a heterosexist discourse of conjugal responsibilities, the category of 'woman' – the representational practices and attributes associated with being female – is no longer an uncontested set of meanings that construct women as necessarily and always dependent on men.

Despite these changes, a fundamentally biological construction of male and female sexuality continues to inform current approaches.[9] Considerable evidence points to changes in young people's attitudes towards sexual morality, but little of this suggests any real challenge to the active-male/passive-female model generally explained through natural biological structures (Shi Yubin 1989). Expert opinion about women's sexual characteristics continues to assume natural parallels between sexual passivity and gender subservience. Educational texts on the physiological aspects of sex continue to stress the 'power' and 'strength' of the active, autonomous male who must restrain his unstoppable energy to preserve health and elicit a favourable response from his 'weaker' female partner (Li Xingchun and Wang Liru 1991, 109; Gao Fang and Zeng Rong 1991, 35–7). Whether in warning young women against the evils of masturbation or arguing that pre-marital sex leads to sickness and even cervical cancer, the advice literature continues to construct female sexuality according to either reproductive or male needs. The privileged model of monogamous heterosexuality has not yet been seriously disturbed. The comparative diversity of approaches to sexuality in recent years thus converges in what is, if not an official discourse in the same unitary sense as before, a dominant discourse sustained by official, semi-official and popular interests.

## Materials of the discourses of sexuality

This book analyses non-literary publications produced by official, semi-official and popular agencies since 1949 for a general and, to a lesser extent, professional and academic readership. Under party control of the press, media and publishing between the 1950s and the 1970s, relatively few titles appeared on specifically sex-related matters. The first that was not translated from a European language was a collection of eighteen articles initially written for a special issue on sexuality of the journal *Popular Medicine* (*Dazhong yixue*), edited by the Shanghai dermatologist Yu Guangyuan (Ruan 1991, 172). Probably the most influential, commonly available at this time, was *Knowledge about Sex* (*Xing de zhishi*), a sex education booklet written by two gynaecologists and a neurologist, and first published in 1956 (173–4).[10] Titles about female hygiene, reproduction, contraception and childbirth also appeared, some of which were translations of Soviet works; a handful of other publications addressed matters of sexual and marital morality (Zhang Lihua, Ru Haitao and Dong Naiqiang 1992, 592–602). National, regional and provincial newspapers – most notably *Renmin ribao*, *Guangming ribao*, *Gongren ribao* and *Nanfang ribao* – carried pieces on related issues, such as marriage and divorce, often because of their significance for broader policy reasons. However, most texts about specifically sexual matters appeared in the national journals that targeted women and young people – *Zhongguo funü* and *Zhongguo qingnian*. But by late 1966, conflict over the political control of the Women's Federation led to the closure of *Zhongguo funü*, and by early 1967, as the Cultural Revolution moved into radical swing, both the Women's Federation and the Communist Youth League disbanded. Works such as *Knowledge about Sex* were attacked and their authors criticized, and it was not until the late 1970s that similar materials again became readily available to the public (Ruan 1991, 173).

Between the 1950s and the 1970s, the party-state's control of channels of public information and the educational, medical and legal establishments gave the discourses it generated a strikingly unified character. Key members of the editorial boards were more often than not members of the local party committee. Editorial authority was more or less synonymous with political supervision. The information about sex selected for publication in these years depended on editorial/political identification of what was appropriate for publication and public education. In determining the parameters and content of the public discourse, and in legitimizing specific attitudes and practices, the official committees responsible for publicizing the relevant materials in effect became the ideological and moral overseers of sexual behaviour. As publicists of the party-state's approach to establishing new sexual standards they granted party and state institutions the possibility of intervening in the articulation of sexual relationships as part of the broad process of planned social change.

The themes identified for discussion in the women's and youth journals of the pre-Cultural Revolution period demonstrated a striking chronological and discursive convergence. Different publications not infrequently carried similar debates to review different opinions about particular problems. For example, a discussion about divorce initiated by an article in the *People's Daily* appeared in *Zhongguo funü*, the legal journal *Faxue* (Legal studies) and in a book published in the same year.[11] Identical articles were sometimes reproduced, more or less concurrently, in the publications of different organizations. A letter written by a young woman about the dangers of deciding to marry someone on the basis of initial impressions was printed in *Zhongguo qingnian* and in a book published at the same time on problems of marriage and love (Zhong Dianbei 1955; Henan sheng quanguo minzhu funü lianhehui 1955, 18–25).

Much as was the case in other areas of official discourse, the main content and boundaries of discussion about sexuality were determined in response to central policy. The similarity in content across different journals at any one time was the result of editorial responses to changing emphases in policy within ideological parameters that were clearly delineated in party directives, official statements and newspaper editorials. It was not the consequence of any tightly supervised plan guiding the selection of topics. Much less was it the result of direct censorship aimed at excluding potentially threatening materials.[12] Within the overall framework of political/editorial policy, the unified character of the official discourse could also sometimes contain notable variety. Sex educators, medical and legal specialists, party ideologues, high school teachers and university academics all participated in debates about sexuality. Readers – including anxious adolescents and despairing wives – made their views known in letters, often published as contributions to the magazine debates. While these commentators rarely challenged the views of the official editors, many of the issues about which they expressed concern did not fit into any clear ideological agenda. Articles about breast-binding and masturbation, for example, which occasionally appeared in response to readers' requests for advice, seemed to have only the most tenuous bearing on state policy. It may have been no coincidence that such topics were publicized during the relative relaxation of editorial controls during the movement to Let a Hundred Flowers Bloom in late 1955 and early 1956. However, the relatively *ad hoc* nature of some of the topics did not disturb the principal function of the discourse. None of the more unusual contributions selected for publication contradicted the norms ratified by official agencies. Rather, they represented a kind of limited spontaneity within an overall strategy designed to uphold standards of sexual morality defined by the party-state apparatus. The 1950s discourse was not therefore a totally homogenous practice, but rather one which was modified in accordance with the changes in central policy emphasis, while retaining certain key elements.

With the beginning of the reform in 1978, journals which had been forced to interrupt publication at the beginning of the Cultural Revolution reappeared, rapidly followed by numerous new titles (Ma Youcai 1992, 394–5). Texts of different registers, popular and official, were disseminated through an increasingly bewildering array of publications. Journals with reassuring titles, such as *Marriage and the Family (Hunyin yu jiating)*, *Love, Marriage and the Family (Aiqing, hunyin yu jiating)*, *A Guide to Family Life (Jiating shenghuo zhinan)* and *Modern Family (Xiandai jiating)*, dealt with a wide range of matters, including sexual morality, sexual problems, sexually transmitted diseases, and the joys and perils of romantic love and marriage. Marriage guides and pamphlets on childbirth, self-help guides on sexual hygiene, sex education books and texts on female psychology and physiology all targeted a popular readership looking for advice in matters considered by the experts to be vital to the healthy physical and moral development of young people. Legal publishing houses produced numerous publications on sexual crime. Made accessible to the consumer in very cheap editions, many of these publications quickly built up an enormous circulation; within a few months after the appearance of its new edition in 1980, there had been four reprintings of *Knowledge about Sex*, totalling more than two million copies.

In the first years after the introduction of economic reform, the market availability of more publications for women and young people did not, in itself, signify much noticeable modification to the basic themes and principles of the earlier discourse. Indeed, articles on love and marriage published in the early 1980s show an evident continuity with pre-Cultural Revolution constructions. However, as urban reform introduced new opportunities for commercial exchange, private property ownership and private entrepreneurial activities, the unitary moral didacticism of the former discourse began to give way to a new flexibility. In a social and moral culture which seemed to share little with the orientations of the 1950s and 1960s, the decentred structures of editorial authority that began to emerge in the mid-1980s contributed to a diversity of representations about sexuality unprecedented in the People's Republic. Official control of publishing houses and magazines was mediated by the delegation of budgetary power to the directors of the relevant concerns, permitting a new intellectual and commercial vitality. The boundaries defining the limits of acceptable intellectual and artistic endeavour were relaxed; the themes selected for publication no longer fitted into a totally coherent ideological framework. Though still responsible to state organizations, and often bound by ideological rules of editorial etiquette, intellectuals started producing works which departed radically from former standards. Encouraged by opportunities for travel and research abroad, and by the translation of foreign works into Chinese, their opinions not infrequently explicitly subverted the interests of the party-state. Hence, state-affiliated intellectuals could produce defences of homosexuals' rights even though homosexuality was – and remains – subject to a series of penalties (Li Yinhe and Wang Xiaobo 1992).

Though the vast majority of the publications used for this book are formally official, in as much as their production is financed – either partially or entirely – by state funds, the diversity of publication, register and theme brings a new dimension to the definition of official discourse. While still employees of state concerns, editorial and publishing directors make their own decisions about how to respond to the market. The lack of tight party control over the media and the lack of formal organs of press censorship permit editors considerable space for experimentation.[13] Serious journals, such as *Women's Studies* (*Nüxing yanjiu*), have brought into public debate issues over which silence reigned before the Cultural Revolution, such as marital rape, sexual problems and women's sexual needs. More specialist 'scientific' approaches to disseminating information about sexuality are found in sexological publications. Often closely based on the Kinsey model, surveys conducted in the past few years have produced a vast quantity of data about marriage and divorce, sexual behaviour in different age groups, the different characteristics of female and male sexuality, premarital sexual behaviour, and homosexuality.[14] Academic works on prostitution and homosexuality have focused attention on a range of issues concerning sexual rights in China (Li Yinhe and Wang Xiaobo 1992; Shan Guangnai 1995). Numerous titles about sexually transmitted diseases have made their appearance, often accompanied by lurid photographs. Stories about the sexual habits of foreign cultures cater for prurient tastes. Pornographic materials circulate in large quantities, particularly in the commercial zones of the south and south-east, often in totally unassuming-looking magazines which contain stories of sexual brutality alongside knitting patterns and advice about childcare.

The relaxation of financial and editorial controls over the press and publishing makes the convergence between different materials, registers and representations in recent discourses particularly striking. The directors of publishing houses have been quick to package their products in ways that are attractive to the young consumer. Hence serious journals such as *Nüxing yanjiu* sport cover images of beautiful white models in alluring poses, promising excitement and titillation on the inner pages. However, despite the use of more varied linguistic registers, more colourful references and a much diluted didactic message, the texts accompanying the glossy covers often sustain the standards of earlier discourses. Furthermore, in many ways the popular orientation of many recent discussions about sexuality has reinforced some of the gendered messages associated principally with the pre-reform regime. From this perspective, the proliferation of publications and debates in recent years has functioned not so much to encourage new voices and opinions as to reinforce key aspects of what is still a dominant discourse.

## Dominant discourses and their readers

The repeated production of cultural discourses of gender establishes the range of meanings which position women and men as different kinds of persons. In Henrietta Moore's words, the categories 'woman' and 'man' employed by these discourses 'have something to do with the representations, self-representations and day-to-day practices of individual women and men'. They 'participate in the production and reproduction of engendered subjects who use them . . . as part of the process of constructing themselves as persons and agents' (1994, 51). Of course, as Moore points out, this does not resolve questions about the kinds of self-representations that dominant discourses determine, nor why these discourses continue to be reproduced despite the many challenges to them. What it does do, however, is indicate the importance of examining the subject positions established by them. The sense of being a woman or man is formed within the context of dominant discourses and categorizations, regardless of how individual women and men consciously articulate their responses to them.

Before the reform policies, the dominant discourse offered a tightly unified view of normative sexual behaviour applicable to both women and men. It showed little interest in the mundane experiences of ordinary individuals, except in so far as these served as exemplars or models of some ideological message. Nor did it claim to identify the range of behaviours and attitudes available in contemporary Chinese society. This is not to say that many articles did not give interesting insights into the concerns and lives of the readers. Rather it is to suggest that, despite noticeable changes in emphasis at different moments of the Maoist years, and the occasional appearance of positional tensions within texts that disturbed the discourse's absolute homogeneity, the purpose of the official construction of sexuality was not to represent ordinary practices, but to mediate the behaviour, experience and self-representations of all women and men. As components of an explicitly didactic discourse, the texts of the 1950s and 1960s were concerned only incidentally with the day-to-day processes of how individual women and men experienced their sexual identities. Conversely, ordinary men and women did not conduct their sexual lives according to these texts any more than they necessarily supported or believed in the subject positions they offered.

The diversity of materials published in recent years makes the issue of the relationship between the dominant discourse and its subjects more complex. The boundaries of recent discussions about sexuality are much more fluid and changeable than in the earlier period. Texts published under official auspices often suggest themes and perspectives that subvert the notion of an identifiable official discourse. As a result, there is no easy way of defining what actually constitutes the official discourse, at least with reference to the themes of this book. In a political context in which the party is clearly concerned about its loss of popular legitimacy, the relaxation of controls over the media and publishing permits an extensive overlap between popular and official practices. However, just as we cannot assume that the official categories and interests of the 1950s and early 1960s operated in a realm entirely removed from the lives of ordinary women and men, so we cannot make any assumptions about the relationship between the dominant discourse and day-to-day attitudes and practices in more recent years. Whatever the moment and characteristics of their publication, the texts analysed in this book have constituted the main discursive framework within which, or in resistance against which, women and men have identified their own sexual and gendered identities over the past few decades.

My main interest in analysing these texts is to identify the ranges of gendered meanings associated with the category of 'woman' produced in dominant discourses of sexuality since 1949. It is not to analyse the effects of these meanings in persuading readers to identify with or challenge the subject positions they offer; nor is it to examine other, more popular meanings produced in the daily practices of ordinary women and men. An examination of the relationship between text and reader, between the dominant discourse and the individual subjects positioned by and responding to it, must be left to further research. Nevertheless, a few comments about the relationship between texts and readers will provide some indication about the former's effectiveness as narratives of political power.

By early 1957, the monthly print-run of *Zhongguo funü* was about 850,000. *Zhongguo qingnian*'s print-run increased from about half a million in mid-1952 to more than 1.8 million in early 1956. The principal targeted readership of these journals were the members of their parent organizations, the All China Women's Federation and the Young Communist Youth League. Copies of the journals were also on sale in local post offices and bookstores, and through collective and institutional subscriptions. Local broadcasting systems in urban work units and rural collectives commonly publicized their more important contents. Selected texts were also used as study material in meetings convened by the mass organizations, and key articles were often displayed on public notice boards. Thus, students, teachers and lecturers, legal specialists, health-workers and doctors, as well as local cadres and Women's Federation personnel working in village communities, all had easy access to these materials, whether through their organization, their school or university or their work unit. The biographical details accompanying readers' letters further suggest that many readers were housewives and adolescents who looked to these journals for advice on matters such as childcare and basic hygiene. The ideological configurations assumed in these texts reached a potentially enormous audience.

Since the early 1980s, the total print-run figures for the official youth and women's journals has vastly increased. The greater diversity of their contents has significantly augmented their circulation among younger readers not specifically motivated by professional or political concerns. However, the public availability of a much wider and more varied range of publications in a climate of widespread political cynicism makes the question of who reads what much more complex. Young city-dwellers commonly indicate an interest in the more popular, new-look magazines. By the same token, they often dismiss the official journals as instruments of an older generation's interests in maintaining political control. Readers of the Red Guard generation often belittle the standard publications as mouthpieces of an out-of-touch and repressive government, even though they may still consult them for specific purposes. The more serious women's publications, such as *Nüxing yanjiu*, attract a mainly professional and socially committed readership, concerned about the theoretical as well as empirical aspects of gender inequalities in China.[15]

However, the question of the variable effects of the dominant discourses on their readers remains. Urban sexual culture in China has undergone some extraordinary changes over the past decade or so. Young people's aspirations and expectations of love and marriage no longer assume the principles upheld by their parents. The language they use to discuss such matters has also changed. However, my own close acquaintance with China over the last twenty years would indicate that many people, including those who were students in the 1950s, Cultural Revolution Red Guards, and young women and men whose entire education has taken place since the death of Mao Zedong, share some key beliefs about matters expounded in the dominant discourses. Many women's ideas about masturbation fully coincide with the dominant views of medical experts expounded since the 1950s. Again, the idea that it is 'unscientific' and potentially harmful to have sexual intercourse during the menstrual period is held by women of different ages. Belief in a naturalized basis of heterosexuality is apparent in testimonies of active homosexuals, few of whom reportedly see even their own homosexual activity as 'legitimate' (*zhengdang*) (Li Yinhe and Wang Xiaobo 1992, 153). Many women and men of the thirty- to fifty-year-old generation seem to have entered marriage with minimal, and sometimes no, understanding of 'the facts of life'. With the taboo on public expressions of sexual interest between the 1950s and 1970s, it was difficult, if not impossible, to talk with parents, teachers or even friends about sex. And in an atmosphere in which sex was commonly considered illicit and shameful, it seems that few individuals considered engaging in any sexual activity before marriage. Evidence from the Beijing women's telephone hotline in the early 1990s would indicate that many young women have still not been able to benefit from the increased provision of information about sex.[16] While much of this kind of evidence is, by definition, personal, and cannot be explained by simple reference to the pervasive 'influence' of the dominant discourse, it does suggest a number of points of convergence between aspects of the dominant discourse and individual subject positions.

People form their gender and sexual identities through multiple processes, both conscious and unconscious, within the context of dominant discourses and categorizations and the differences within and between them (Moore 1994, 49–70). Discourses and their texts, set within particular historical and cultural structures, participate in the production of their readers as subjects through offering sets of positions to identify with and challenge, through the 'engagement of the subject in certain . . . positionalities of meaning and desire' (De Lauretis 1984, 196). Moreover, texts are effective not through their 'message', their 'content', but through the explicit and implicit, conscious and unconscious, positions they make available. The 'gaps and silences' are as important in shaping the interpretative possibilities as the explicit terms of the narrative. The factors explaining why readers assume different positions in relation to these texts are, of course, as varied and multiple as the readers themselves. However, if we accept, as Henrietta Moore put it, that the 'concept of the individual is only intelligible with reference to a culturally and historically specific set of categories' (Moore 1994, 51), then, even in cases when people reject the dominant gender and sexual categories of the discourses available to them, they are not totally removed from their effects. So, with particular reference to China, whether in the constrained ideological atmosphere of the 1950s to the early 1970s, or in the more consumer-oriented context of the last ten years, the dominant discourses and the practices they inform have established the broad parameters within which women and men become gendered and sexualized subjects. Whether or not individual persons consciously acknowledge the dominant gender categories of these discourses, they also participate in reproducing them by making representations and self-representations – both consciously and unconsciously – with reference to them. To use Henrietta Moore's words again:

> It is through engagement with and investment in the subject positions offered by discourses at this level that individual women and men succeed in reproducing the dominant discourse, whilst simultaneously standing at some remove from the categories of that discourse. (1994, 61)

Particular representations of sexuality may therefore be a point of mutual imbrication between the personal and the political, between individuated subject positions, understood as part of lived experience, and a political agenda formulated by external agencies, even when the apparent meanings in question are disavowed by the individual subject. Approaching the analysis in this way certainly helps us understand the presence of many points of convergence between the dominant discursive categories produced between the early 1950s and now, and between those categories and their audience, though the latter increasingly seems to challenge and resist them. So, although this study does not examine the nature of the relationship between the dominant discourses and everyday, lived experiences, an analysis of dominant discourses of sexuality grants access to meanings shared by more constituencies than the status of the 'dominant', particularly when associated with the official, would indicate.

## Derivations

The Communist Party's conceptualization of 'woman-work' that informed policies in the 1950s was shaped by the exigencies of war as much as by ideological principles. Under the siege conditions of the Jiangxi Soviet and the Yan'an base area, approaches to woman-work focused on ways to mobilize women to support the military struggle. While the CCP gave formal acknowledgement to the rights to free-choice marriage and divorce, evidence suggests that these were very imperfectly implemented. Conservative attitudes towards women among the rural populations of the liberated areas hindered systematic consideration of the tasks required to free women from subjection to 'male domination' (*nanzi de zhipei*). Coinciding with the CCP's ortho-dox Marxist position that the emancipation of women lay in participa-tion in social production, these limitations diminished the potential attention given to women's specific needs, unless these could be integrated into the broad definition of the tasks of social transforma-tion. Indeed, official commentaries on marriage reform suggested that the pursuit of free-choice marriage at the cost of other aspects of social reform was erroneous since the conflicts it provoked would disrupt the social and political unity needed to sustain the war effort (Davin 1976, 39). As the writer Ding Ling discovered in the communist liberated zone of Yan'an when she was harshly condemned for criticizing the party's negligence towards the needs of women's emancipation, the CCP's commitment to women's interests was defined within very tightly circumscribed limits and subordinated to other, more general considerations (Feuerwerker 1982, 1–18). In an atmosphere which proscribed suggestions that woman-work might deserve independent attention, and which condemned those who criticized the party's male bias for their 'narrow' feminism, it was perhaps hardly surprising that the potentially sensitive area of sexual relations and responses – at least *vis-à-vis* the issue of marriage reform – was absent from CCP discourse on women, youth and gender equality.

The materials on sex-related issues that appeared in the press in the early 1950s therefore had few direct points of reference in Chinese communist discourse. However, other cultural orientations had a determining influence. The *yin–yang* conceptualization of male–female sexual difference, discussed in detail by Robert van Gulik and Charlotte Furth, was particularly significant in shaping contemporary perceptions of sexual harmony, balance and moderation (Van Gulik 1974; Furth 1994). It was also just as important in contributing to the more baleful and dangerous constructions of female sexuality. The traditional cultural association between *yin* and the female contextualized some of the more negative representations of women in sexual relationships that did not conform to the standards of the official discourse.

Another aspect of the cultural legacy informing the production of the official discourse was the classical *lie nü* (virtuous women) tradition, according to which women were honoured for sexual chastity, loyalty to their betrothed and husbands and filiality to their parents-in-law (O'Hara 1971). Virtuous women whose houses were decorated with tablets testifying to their chastity brought respect and honour to the entire household. Conversely, women who violated Confucian standards of sexual morality were often severely penalized, and their relatives subjected to social humiliation and ostracism. As the Lie nü zhuan (Biographies of Chinese Women) testifies, physical beauty and expressions of femininity in dress and comportment were treated with suspicion; feminine beauty frequently signified immorality and danger to men (O'Hara 1971). Resonances of these views were not uncommon in communist discourse. As in the Youth League branch secretary's concerns about the ideological inclinations of a young woman in her factory who spent all her money on buying new clothes (Su Wen 1957), images of women who were interested in their appearance, who wore high-heeled shoes or who permed their hair were common signifiers of moral and social disorder.[17]

Self-sacrifice was a recurring theme in China's cultural history. Linked to the group orientation of the responsibilities which contributed to defining the individual, notions of selflessness and self-denial were commonly projected as superior moral virtues of universal validity. They continued to serve a valuable ideological purpose in the collectively oriented rhetoric of the CCP. However, when identified with women's sexual conduct, the concept of self-denial had particular significance. The normative expectations of female chastity central to the *lienü* tradition sometimes demanded specific and extreme forms of self-sacrifice, including self-mutilation and suicide. As Tien Ju-k'ang (1988, 17) argued, women's self-denial became the symbol of general standards of purity, courage and self-sacrifice, particularly at moments of extreme social and national crisis.

Dominant neo-Confucian ideology therefore projected onto women a vital function in the preservation of general moral standards. Female chastity – women's sexual self-denial – was, in effect, identified as the standard measuring sexual behaviour and morality in general. Whatever its expression, female sexuality had to be controlled to prevent domestic and social chaos. While, as the following chapters show, many notions about the dangers of female sexuality were condemned in communist discourse, the representation of women as the principal targets and agents of sexual morality and responsibility continued to be operative in a number of contexts. Women were subject to a gender-differentiated set of expectations and sanctions which converged in requirements of sexual self-restraint. The double standard implicit in the Confucian principle of female chastity was re-created in gender-specific identification of female responsibility for the maintenance of social and sexual morality. The practices of moral control and intervention that the Communist Party inherited from its Confucian past were associated with an economic and ideological system that it was committed to destroying. The practices themselves, however, were to be useful to the CCP's deployment of power after 1949.

Another aspect of the theme of self-denial in the communist construction of women invoked the traditional emphasis given to collective and familial interests over individual autonomy. Dominant discourses before the 1980s rejected the idea that love or marriage might refer to an individuated site of intimacy and desire, distinct from consideration for the group. The conceptualization of the person which informed the CCP's sexual discourse was bounded by moral and social obligations to the collective and the state (Evans 1991, 30–2). Western liberal constructions of the personal as a sphere of practice identified with individual identity and creativity did not form any significant affirmative part of the ideological and cultural perspective informing the CCP's view of women.[18] Despite echoes of the May Fourth slogans calling for 'freedom of love' and 'freedom of marriage', the individualistic bias of many of the May Fourth publicists of women's emancipation was explicitly repudiated in the CCP's programme for women. Individual (*siren*) enjoyment was invariably opposed to the 'public' or 'collective' interest precisely because it was, by definition, associated with selfishness, vulgarity and promiscuity. Liberal concepts of women's emancipation influenced by the feminist tendencies of the May Fourth period were unfamiliar and irrelevant to the majority of the population. They were also considered potentially divisive, particularly during a revolutionary period when unity of political purpose was given top priority. When associated with marriage and sexuality, they were also considered to be morally contentious, as the CCP's attack on Ding Ling demonstrated. Criticized in 1942 for her 'narrow' feminist outlook, Ding Ling was later further condemned for her unorthodox sexual behaviour in cohabiting with a man before marriage (Wales 1967, 190–221; Feuerwerker 1984). The fact that the sexual tastes of top party leaders were far from exemplifying socialist virtues escaped official attention (Cheo Ying 1980, 64–5). The gender bias in representations of selflessness and sexual propriety was repeated in references to 'individualistic' erotic pleasure. The absence of the individualized self as a category of analysis therefore had particular significance for the construction of female gender.

Since the early 1980s, the relationship between the individual, the family and the state has been considerably modified, with an evident relaxation of emphasis on the social orientation of sexual, marital and family matters. In formal terms, one expression of this was the inclusion of 'breakdown of affection' as a valid reason for divorce in the new Marriage Law of 1980. However, there are many indications that the recuperation of the notion of 'private' to categorize particular practices and relationships has by no means reduced attachment to former ideology. Michael Palmer (1986–7, 42, 44–5) has pointed to the continuing insistence by the state on the social usefulness of the family, the repeated practice of condemning a person's exercise of individual choice as 'bourgeois' conduct, and on the Leninist view of love as a social relationship with social duties. The difficulties that many couples continue to encounter in obtaining a divorce support his argument. Indeed, the reformist enactment of a plethora of laws, regulations and policies – the most obvious of which, of course, are those relating to the fertility control programme – testify to formal processes and possibilities of intervention in ordinary persons' 'private' lives on a scale unprecedented in the Maoist years (Palmer 1991, 342). They also testify to the leadership's concern to ensure family stability as the basis of social order and continuity (Palmer 1995, 110).

Despite the CCP's condemnation of the individualistic tendencies of Western liberal notions of women's rights, Western ideas were nevertheless instrumental in formulating dominant categories of the official discourse of sexuality. Their influence was evident in the official discourse's use of science to naturalize gender differences as biologically determined structures. Frank Dikötter argues that, though European medical concepts about sex introduced into China during the first decades of this century took root on the basis of cultural orientations in place possibly since the seventeenth century, modern biomedical science between the 1920s and the 1930s relied heavily on the approaches of Western sexologists in constructing sexuality as a bounded harmony of opposites governed by physiological structures (Dikötter, 1995, 10–13). Thus, while gender boundaries were thought until the end of the nineteenth century to be only partly dependent on biology, it was the modernizing science of the Republican period that fixed the grounding of gender in notions of natural sex difference (Dikötter 1995, 19–22).

The urban social forces out of which the model of consensual marriage emerged gave an evident urban bias to the major assumptions of the dominant discourse of sexuality as it appeared in the 1950s. Even now, in a radically different social and cultural context, the dominant discourse continues to privilege an urban orientation, with sometimes very limiting effects. In the 1950s, the standards of sexual morality considered consistent with the free-choice model of marriage generally presupposed access to the educational and social opportunities associated with urban living. The frequent warnings to young people against confusing friendship with love, for example, assumed possibilities of social contact between the sexes that were often considered outrageous in the villages and small towns. The representations of immoral behaviour in adulterous relationships invariably referred to urban practices, as did advice about clothing, hairstyles or contraceptives. The idealized relations and values of the official discourse therefore corresponded with practices that had little immediate meaning for its rural audience. As one informant from a peasant family in Shandong commented, there was little point in telling people about the 'oughts and ought nots' of falling in love when most people's understanding of marriage centred not on love but on basic material security.[19] Many of the difficulties encountered in popularizing the new law after 1950 were a consequence of the insensitive and threatening imposition of an urban-based model on a conservative rural population (Evans 1991, 35, n. 102; Croll 1981, 184–8). Despite official claims to uphold and transform the interests of the rural population, the tensions with the latter created by the urban orientation of the new model of marriage limited its effectiveness. Even now, in a social context in which free-choice marriage is much more common, though still far from universal, the urban bias of the dominant discourse continues to inflect many aspects of the sexual discourse. Visual images of beautiful women invariably assume an urban context; discussions about young couples' leisure activities prevalently assume access to urban entertainments. And, along the lines of the modernization argument used in socio-economic fields, a similar urban bias continues to assume higher degrees of knowledge about sex, higher levels of sexual enjoyment, and lower levels of sexual violence in the cities – in other words a higher sexual 'civilization' in the towns than in the countryside. The effect is to add another layer of hierarchization to the analysis of intra- as well as inter-gender relations.

The Communist Party's cultural legacy and its eclectic approach to Western ideas coincided with the precedents set by the Soviet Union in family reform. The Soviet, and particularly Stalinist, view of sexual morality emphasized the social commitments of the revolutionary person in a way that could easily be assimilated into the cultural and ideological orientations informing the CCP's discourse. The Chinese media made repeated references to the success of Soviet achievements in transforming popular notions of personal and family morality. Numerous short stories glorifying Soviet socialist morality were translated into Chinese and printed in the pages of *Zhongguo funü*; reports of visits to Soviet kindergartens and talks with Soviet teachers all conveyed a similar message (Deng Yingchao 1953).

As Minister of Social Welfare in the new Soviet republic, Alexandra Kollontai was the only major political figure of a socialist state to have formulated a comprehensive argument in favour of including sexuality on the agenda of women's emancipation. Accused of attempting to justify her own sexual indulgence, as well as provoking 'exploitative and irresponsible sexuality', Kollontai was publicly censured and removed from office in the Bolshevik government (Lapidus 1978, 85–9; Porter 1980, 180–1, 190–1). The early debates on sexuality and 'free love', and the liberalizing elements of the early decrees passed under Lenin and the family law of 1926, were increasingly overridden by the restrictive morality of Stalin's codes (Shreeves 1992, 132–3), and by 1936 harsh restrictions on abortion and divorce had been restored, penalties for homosexuality had been reintroduced and 'mistaking infatuation for love' had become a punishable offence (Millett 1971, 237). Policy towards the family witnessed similar revisions. The view of the family as a source of oppression embodied in the earlier legislation was replaced by a new conservatism. The new morality constructed sex as a degenerate and 'wasteful consumer of energies better devoted to the building of Communism' (Shreeves 1992, 133). The family was henceforth to be described as a 'micro-cosm of the new socialist society', and marital stability became the order of the day (Lapidus 1978, 82, 114). Within this context, efforts to incorporate sexuality into discussion about sexual equality were condemned, on the grounds that they encouraged sexual promiscuity and revolutionary decline.

The view of sexuality as a key site of women's emancipation was anathema as much to the exponents of China's discourse on women as to those of Stalin's family codes. Cultural and historical legacy combining Chinese and Western views and Soviet precedent together encouraged the production of a discourse in which the social orientation of personhood was clearly privileged over notions of individual identity and experience. As one commentator put it, 'in cases of conflict between individual and collective interests, a revolutionary must subordinate the former to the latter' (Henan sheng quanguo minzhu funü lianhehui 1955, 7). Marriage was to be regarded not as a private matter, but as a 'cell' of the entire cause of the revolution, of importance to the interests of society as a whole. While this emphasis applied to men and women alike in the CCP's discourse, the gendered history of women's subordination to family and group interest gave it a specific modality in the representation of female sexuality and gender.

## Chinese women's studies and the terms of analysis

Chinese research in the social sciences and humanities has given increasing attention to women and gender in recent years. The All China Women's Federation, the official national body responsible since 1949 for the organization and administration of women's affairs, has sponsored much of this discussion, particularly in areas concerning women's economic and social status. Women's employment, education, health and reproduction are now familiar topics in debates about women and the reform programme. Sociological research has produced important studies on changing structures of marriage and the family in the reform period. Women's studies centres have initiated major projects on women's history and related theoretical issues. One of the pioneers of such projects in China, Li Xiaojiang, Director of the Women's Studies Research Centre in Zhengzhou University, has already supervised the publication of several volumes of her *Women's Research Series* (*Funü yanjiu congshu*). Since the late 1980s, literary criticism, too, has taken up the linked themes of sexuality and gender, often to assert the liberatory aspects of an essentialist view of women against the apparent gender neutrality of representations of women of the Maoist era (e.g., Meng Yue and Dai Jinhua 1989; Meng Yue 1993).

Rey Chow recently noted that

> . . . in the study of a culture such as that of modern China (within and outside the PRC), the one critical paradigm that really has something genuinely new to say is, currently, feminism, which addresses from ground zero all the basic issues of sexuality and gender that forty-some years of patriarchal Communist rule have swept under the carpet (except, of course, when the state needs to control and police women's bodies against their will). (1993, 210)

Tani Barlow has also noted that Chinese women's studies have brought into academic discussion what, in very general terms, are clearly feminist issues (1994, 351–9), despite the resistance of many well-known women activists and scholars in China to being associated with the term 'feminism'.[20] Many women scholars have devoted their attention to exposing the multiple practices and discourses maintaining women's subordinate status in contemporary Chinese society. The idea that women should be responsible for defining their own needs and purposes – for creating their own subject positions – has begun to feature prominently in women's literature as well as social scientific and historical research.[21] In contrast with the officially sponsored project of women's liberation (*funü jiefang*), which, as Meng Yue (1993) has recently argued, appropriated women's lives for another political agenda, women's studies, as defined by key participants in the Chinese women's studies movement, should bridge the potential divide between the academic thrust of theory and the women's movement as political strategy by encompassing a range of themes identified on the basis of the interests of its massive audience.

Much of the recent narrative on women is premised on beliefs in a naturalized and essential sex difference. Meng Yue and Dai Jinhua (1989) argued that an essential sex difference may empower women through charting out specific sites where they may assert their equality with men through recognition of difference. Indeed, the view that the socialism of the Maoist period vitiated an essential, natural and yet liberatory sexual difference is widely held among Chinese literary theorists (Barlow 1993, 7). Recent legislation has adopted a similarly naturalized view of gender to argue for the 'protection' of women's different interests in the workplace (Woo 1994). However, the conflation of biological sex with gender – used in this immediate context to denote socially and culturally constructed fields of practice – echoed in these formulations is arguably much more powerfully used in the contemporary context to support fundamentally misogynist positions. The works of the controversial avant-garde writers such as Mo Yan, Su Tong and Ge Fei, for example, represent women as naturalized signifiers of weakness, submission and base animality (Zhao Yiheng, 1993). The assumption of a natural gender hierarchy that legitimizes the debasement of femininity is a common thread linking the different obsessions and projects of these authors (Lu Tonglin 1995, 19–22). Inscribed in law, assumptions of an originating, essentialist biological difference between women and men effectively serve to underpin women's inferior status in employment and wage structures through legitimizing employers' decisions to exclude women from the workforce (Woo 1994). Popular discourses, as represented in women's magazines or TV soaps, widely invoke a similar essentialism to suggest that women's natural interests may be best served by withdrawing from the labour market and returning home. And, as an indication of the tenacity of the perception of women as inferior to men, academic opinion, too, has adopted a similar position to argue that gender inequality should be recognized as a necessary condition of economic efficiency (Zheng Yefu 1994). Though the implication that difference necessarily means inequality is rejected by the feminist exponents of essentialist arguments, the latter's contribution to maintaining discriminatory practices against women is apparent in major areas of state policy and practice (Woo 1994).

The absence of a specific linguistic category for gender in contemporary Chinese language is often used to explain the prevalence of the essentialist conflation. While writers often prefer the term *xingbie* (literally, 'sexual difference') to denote gender, as opposed to biological sex, the issue of how to translate the Western term is still a matter of debate (Lin Chun 1995). The notion of sexuality is equally problematic in Chinese. *Xing yishi* (literally, 'sexual consciousness') cannot encompass those meanings associated with the Western concept that refer to the unconscious psychic structures contributing to the formation of the sexualized subject. Just to confuse matters, *xing* (sex) is commonly used to cover all three English concepts; its precise referent therefore depends on the interpretative understanding of the audience within the context of the meanings of the term that are already historically and culturally established. Though some women's studies scholars make explicit their use of gender as a social construct, to distinguish from sex as a biological marker, most of the arguments about what is considered to be appropriate behaviour for women in the materials used in this analysis assume a natural relationship between biology, in particular reproduction, and all the other meanings associated with the symbolic category 'woman'.

The meanings of and relationship between sex and gender continue to be the subject of extensive debate (Moore 1994, 8–27). Recent feminist critiques (Butler 1990) have suggested that the distinction between sex and gender, initially introduced as a means of explaining the social construction of women's subordination, in fact serves to reinforce the idea that there are 'two clearly differentiated and natural categories of the body' (Moore 1994, 38), linked via the sexual embodiment of gender identity (p. 39). According to this view, the insistence on binary sets of gender characteristics attached to two different kinds of bodies serves to reinforce the hegemony of reproduction and heterosexuality. In Judith Butler's words, it suggests a certain 'determinism of gender meanings inscribed on anatomically differentiated bodies, where those bodies are understood as passive recipients of an inexorable cultural law' (1990, 8). This approach to gender and sex does not allow recognition of biology and nature as culturally defined categories, nor does it explain how and why gender differences are so fixed in the physical body that the distinction between sexed bodies and socially constructed genders is collapsed altogether (Moore 1994, 13). However, while recognizing the fluidity of possible interpretations of the relationship between notions of sex, sexual difference and gender, an analytical distinction between them is essential in order to articulate the gendered associations between social practice and sexed bodies. The idea that gender behaviour – in this instance, social differences between women and men – can be evaluated according to the biological/sexual truth of bodies itself requires analytical distinction between the terms. Moreover, while the Chinese texts often conflate different meanings of sexuality and gender, they nevertheless demand the application of some conceptual category to refer to narrative representations of sexual experience, practice and desire. My use of the term 'sexuality' goes beyond, but includes, definitions of biological sex to encompass notions of sexual desire, practice, experience and identity associated with having a sexed body. As Jeffrey Weeks wrote in the opening paragraph of *Sexuality and its Discontents*, 'sexuality is as much about words, images, ritual and fantasy as it is about the body' (1985, 3). I use gender, by contrast, to refer to the multiple social constructions associated with the categories women and men, which, even if explained in the Chinese texts with reference to originating biological differences, identify social differences in other, non-sexualized arenas, such as education, domestic work, employment and so on.

Sexuality is a key site of the construction of gender differences and of the hierarchies inscribed in them. My aim in analysing modern and contemporary Chinese sexual discourses on the basis of theoretical insights located in a cultural context far removed from them is to attempt to unravel the specific modalities of meanings – particularly those that target and appropriate women – inscribed in their conflation of sex, sexuality and gender. For while under the pen of feminist writers, as Tani Barlow has suggested, an essentialist discourse of sexual difference temporarily proved to be a powerful tool of contestation against the CCP's implicitly masculinist standards of sexual equality, it has much more prevalently, and with greater effect, been used to sustain fundamentally hierarchical views about what women and men can and cannot do, in nearly all areas of social and sexual life. When associated with the regulatory powers of the party-state apparatus, through the medical, educational and legal establishments, the supposition of a determining biological mandate governing all gender behaviour assumes a dimension of control that makes the task of identifying the specific meanings inscribed in the Chinese use of the terms *xing* and *xingbie* a vital political project.

As a Western feminist academic, I am conscious of the distance of the theoretical terms of my analysis from those of the texts I examine, and of possible criticisms of using representations of intimate aspects of women's lives for elitist academic purposes. However, analysis of the dominant discourse through use of its own terms would do little to elucidate its mode of operation and effectiveness. The purposes served by the shifting interchangeability of the terms for sex, sexuality and gender – *xing, xingbie, xingyishi, nannü guanxi, xing guanxi* – cannot be adequately explained without establishing a distance from those terms. The discursive mechanisms of control of women's sexuality in China can be identified only through applying terms of analysis detached from them. To this end, I have used and applied a number of theoretical perspectives. Foucault's notion of sex as an effect rather than an originating essential unity has been a major influence shaping my thinking through the discussions that follow (1977, 1984, 1987). So too have his ideas about discourse, knowledge and power. Judith Butler's (1990) theoretical explorations of the meanings attached to sex, sexual difference and gender have been a consistent reminder of the need to question my own use of the terms with reference to the Chinese texts. Henrietta Moore's discussions about dominant cultural discourses, their texts and narratives, and individual subjects' positioning in relation to them have repeatedly reaffirmed for me the political importance of studying these texts (1988, 1993, 1994). They have also inspired many of the questions that run through this book.

An enormous amount of narrative has been produced about sexual attitudes and behaviour in China since the early 1980s. Women's autobiographical writings, fiction and film, academic research and the media have approached issues of sexuality in ways that signify a radical departure from the premises of the 1950s discourse. Nevertheless, public discussions about sex-related issues have generally been limited to a view of sexuality as a series of attitudes and practices permitted or denied expression at different moments of China's recent history. Little attention has been given to identifying the gender beliefs that inform 'expert' opinion about sexuality or to the gendered meanings inscribed in representations of sexuality. Other concerns have been more important, as the journalist and writer Dai Qing indicated:

Other conflicts are more severe. Chinese women are constituted of different groups. Divorced women are in a real predicament and women at the lower rungs of the social system are too sexually repressed. However, this is not a sexual issue, really, but an issue of poverty. Intellectual women like us are fortunate indeed. We feel no repression, and so for us there is no sexual oppression. (Dai Qing, in Barlow 1993, 205)

The idea that gender and sexual oppression are at root an economic issue is shared by many people in China, including theorists of the Women's Federation.[22] Moreover, as I noted before, the subordination of gender to the supposedly more substantial matters of economic development and political power has been a recurring feature of the party-state's approach to woman-work since the early days of communist control. However, at a time when the Chinese media give considerable publicity to practices such as the abduction and sale of women as prostitutes and wives, it is clear that such an approach obscures many sites and instances of gender conflict in China. It also obscures the ways in which gender ideology has maintained spaces for the appropriation and exploitation of women's lives through a naturalized gender hierarchy. While the reassertion of a natural femininity may, in part, be a response to the absence of erotic interest in previous decades, naturalized assumptions about gender and sexuality have fed into the perpetuation – and in many instances the augmentation – of gender hierarchy and conflict. The prevalent and frequently uncontested appeal of the essentialist construction of gender difference signifies that all arenas of society and the economy are potential sites of gender struggle.

Enormous numbers of Chinese women endure lives of extreme brutality. If they survive birth, abandonment and poor medical care, they may find themselves abducted and sold into prostitution or marriage, or coerced into making decisions about fertility and reproduction with devastating effects on themselves and their offspring. However, relatively few studies about women in China have focused on such issues. At a time when dominant academic interests in women and gender emphasize the impact of socio-economic change on Chinese women's lives and their contribution to the processes of economic reform, the importance of looking at textual and visual representations of women in sexually implicated contexts acquires a particular significance. First of all, analysis of the dominant discourses of women and sexuality establishes both the foundations and the parameters of the meanings associated with being female on which many practices and policies concerning women are constructed. It gives some idea of the range of gendered subject positions very specifically associated with beliefs about women's appropriate sexuality that are available to women in the construction of their self-identities. As Meng Yue has argued in her analysis of female sexuality in modern Chinese literature, it also indicates some of the ways in which women and women's bodies are used as metaphors for moral, ideological and political agendas (Meng Yue 1993). At a time when being female may invite threats to a girl's existence, and when the violation of women's rights is inseparable from culturally constructed views of women's sexual function, the contrasts between the official rhetoric of sexual equality and the lived experiences of women in every part of China are possibly greater than at any other time since 1949. Of course, this is not to deny that many Chinese women also enjoy rich lives, permitting multiple opportunities to explore diverse and fulfilling social and intellectual interests. However, the range of meanings associated with female gender in contemporary China that emerges from an analysis of discourses of sexuality makes the task of deconstructing the category 'woman' – what being a woman means in different contexts, in different discourses and representations – even more pressing.

# 2 The Scientific Construction of Sexual Difference

> The two sexes are characterized by different forms of sexual behaviour. Normal male behaviour is outwardly expressive and evident whereas in the female it is hidden and shy. This signifies a difference between the active and initiating male and the passive female, a difference that is determined by sexual physiology and psychology. (Wang Peng 1993, 97)

This definition of sexual difference set out in a recent encyclopedia of 'knowledge about sex' summarizes an approach that has been dominant in Chinese writings about sex and sexual difference since 1949. Sexuality commonly appears as a series of structures, functions, activities and attitudes characterized by a natural and fundamental difference between the female and male; sexual differences between female and male are, to a greater or lesser extent, the natural expression of biological needs, drives and responses. While in recent years expert opinion has somewhat modified this view with the suggestion that sexual behaviour is also determined by psychological, social and cultural factors, an essentialist understanding of sexuality continues to be prevalent in contemporary discourses. Psychological and social factors appear as accretions to, or modifiers of, *a priori* biological conditions; they contribute to 'socializing' sexual behaviour to make it acceptable to 'civilized society' (*wenming shehui*) and to increase its benefits to married life. Knowledge and education – the core features of the process of 'socialization' of the sexual 'instinct' – transmitted through familial, educational, medical and legal channels, are therefore vital to the control of natural sexual urges and desire.

The naturalization of sexual and gender differences on the basis of biological structures and functions is a key feature of post-1949 discourses of sexuality. In the name of science, it has legitimized a sometimes rigid code of normative sexual and gender conduct based on highly selective and didactic distinctions between right and wrong, normal and abnormal. Exponents of this view of sexuality have used the notion of 'scientific knowledge about sex' to support practices that accord with the party-state's interests in supervising young people's sexual and social activities. Medical experts have claimed the authority of modern science to argue that reproductive development, physiological structures and biological differences determine gender characteristics in social as well as sexual behaviour. By legitimizing fixed gender distinctions and hierarchies in sexual behaviour, the 'scientific' construction of sexuality corresponds with moral and social as much as scientific concerns.

In the 1950s, the biological essentialism of the official discourse of sexuality projected a particularly rigid view of binary sexual difference, according to which nature dictated an unchanging set of gendered attributes and expectations. Recent approaches are considerably less absolute in defining the status of nature. The greater significance now accorded psychological and social factors in the construction of sexual identities and subjectivities has given representations of sexual difference new dimensions not apparent in the 1950s. 'Expert' and official interests continue to appropriate science to channel potential sexual and gender diversity into the dominant model of monogamous marriage, but they do so in terms that are considerably more broadly and flexibly defined. 1990s texts, for example, may contest former 'scientifically based' assumptions about the passive character of female sexuality, even though such contestation is contained within parameters that naturalize monogamous marriage as a physiological as well as a social necessity. So though similar 'scientific' arguments continue to inform constructions of sex and sexual difference, they are contained within more fluid discursive boundaries, allowing for a much greater diversity of narrative representation.

## Sex and scientific education

Ever since the 1950s, arguments in support of sex education provision in schools have rested on the attribution of scientific status to the knowledge imparted. The views of the medical experts responsible for the production of educational texts are, by definition, presented to the reader as 'scientific' and 'correct', in contrast with other less systematically constructed discourses, such as film and literature, reportedly the most important sources of information about sex for young people. The representations subsumed under the category of sex education therefore constitute a dominant narrative form of the scientific construction of sexuality.

During the 1950s, in the absence of a formal programme of sex education, the publication of articles about sexuality explicitly addressed to a young readership indicated the provision of a public forum – limited though it was – for the elucidation of issues considered essential to young people's healthy development. In the words of the preface to the influential *Xing de zhishi* (Wang Wenbin, Zhao Zhiyi and Tan Mingxin 1956), it was to give young people a 'correct understanding of sex' as a basis for understanding 'questions of love, marriage and the family'. The appearance in *Zhongguo qingnian* and *Zhongguo funü* of articles about health, hygiene and sexual develop ment signified official recognition that young people's interest in such matters was legitimate. Traditional views of sex as 'obscene and shameful' created 'tensions and misunderstandings between two people and also impaired sexual satisfaction' (Wang Wenbin, Zhao Zhiyi and Tan Mingxin 1956, 1–2). 'Helping young people to gain a proper understanding of matters to do with sex, love and marriage' was, therefore, 'imperative'. Girls were informed about breast development and were encouraged to shed their embarrassment about mentioning menstrual problems. Mothers were told 'not to feel afraid or ashamed of explaining clearly to their daughters the biological processes of menstruation' (Chen Benzhen 1958). Boys were praised for bringing into the open anxieties about masturbation or facial hair. 'What should I do to get rid of the bad habit of masturbation?' asked one adolescent boy in a letter to *Zhongguo qingnian* (Huang Shuze 1955). Publicizing such matters also challenged conventional principles of sexual morality; the often detailed information provided could be interpreted as an attempt to destroy taboos and erode myths, whether about menstrual blood or the properties of semen, in the service of health and hygiene. However, this approach was extremely constrained and affected only a limited and principally urban-based audience; it is significant that the publication of such texts peaked during the brief period of political tolerance in the mid-1950s. Not even the reported support of Zhou Enlai for the provision of sex education could overcome the public treatment of sex as a 'forbidden zone' (Yao Peikuan 1992, 444).

The press began to feature debates about the pros and cons of sex education in the early 1980s, but conservative concern that public exposition of sex-related issues would encourage promiscuous behaviour continued to be widespread (Honig and Hershatter 1988, 53). Antipathy to public discussion about matters like masturbation or premarital sex was still considerable, and young people were given little encouragement to find out about issues still considered morally offensive. During the 1982–3 official campaign against 'spiritual pollution', overt signs of sexual interest in hairstyles or fashions were once again condemned for their association with bourgeois ideas imported from the West. In an ideological atmosphere dominated by conservative fears of contamination by the bourgeois West, open support for sex education was necessarily constrained.

If anxieties about the evils of sexual liberation fuelled the conservative fears of the early 1980s, they also encouraged support for a more systematic dissemination of knowledge about sex. At a time of increasing exposure to Western life styles through the mass media, commercial advertising and travel, general standards of ideological and moral education left much to be desired, and increasing numbers of young people were reportedly becoming sexually involved before marriage. The physical and emotional health of adolescents demanded a more 'scientific' approach to the discussion of sexual matters. Young people, the experts argued along lines very similar to those of contemporary Western debates, were becoming sexually experienced without really understanding what sex and love were about, and many were totally ignorant about sexual development. Girls who became sexually involved at a young age were often unable 'to distinguish between right and wrong'; many thought that sex was 'just natural' (Song Chu 1986). Without some basic knowledge about the physiological aspects of sexual development, young people, girls in particular, were vulnerable to abuse and suffering that could have ineradicable effects on their lives. Ignorance about sex could also lead the individual into criminal behaviour and homosexuality. Sex education thus appeared as a buffer against unacceptable forms of social and sexual conduct as well as a source of scientific information.

The experts' response to such concerns was on the one hand to address parents as parties who could be co-opted to assist in educating their children, and on the other to urge formal recognition of the need for sex education by the state's educational establishment (Song Chu 1986). Articles encouraging parents to be sensitive and timely in introducing their children to discussion about sex started appearing in the press. A sense of shame, it was acknowledged early on in the 1980s, had for too long prevented young people from asking the right kind of questions about matters that intimately affected their physical and psychological development (Yu Ronghe 1981). If parents were really concerned about their offspring's welfare, they needed to shed their embarrassment and provide the information their children required. A 1985 investigation showed that only 24 per cent of mothers discussed sexual matters with their daughters, and only 5 per cent of fathers broached the topic with their sons (Honig and Hershatter 1988, 55). By the mid-1990s, commentators continued to suggest that parents and teachers had a long way to go in providing their children with appropriate guidance. 'As soon as sex is mentioned, some parents and teachers react with wide-eyed astonishment, or move away in disgust, as if they had touched something really bad' (Zhang Yuan 1995). And, to guide parents in the right direction, editorial comments continue to praise parents for responding 'without evasion and without denunciation' to their young children's questions about 'natural phenomena' (Li Ruifen 1995). Parents were also urged to discourage and even penalize their children for behaving in ways that were inappropriate; most importantly, parents had a moral duty to distract their children from the perils of 'premature love' (zaolian). Such approaches found legal expression in September 1991 when a new law on minors' rights charged parents with major rights and duties to 'discipline and protect' their children and to promote their development as 'successors to the socialist cause' (Palmer 1995, 115).[1]

Attempts to incorporate sex education into the formal school curriculum gained more notable success. Various pilot projects were set up in 1982, most notably in Shanghai, where forty schools had sex education courses by 1986 (Ruan 1991, 175). Provincial and national conferences were held to advance the cause of sex education; educators and family planners met in the summer of 1985 to found the China Sex Education Research Association. Surveys about attitudes towards sex were also carried out, and extensive debates were held both in the press and in academic circles about the optimum timing and context for sex education. In recognition of its importance at the central governmental level, the State Family Planning Commission convened a meeting to plan for the training of high school sex-education teachers and decided to put sex education high on its agenda for key projects of the 7th Five Year Plan (1986–90). By February 1988, some six thousand middle schools all over China had sex education courses, and thirteen provinces included sex education as a formal part of the school curriculum (Ruan 1991, 173–7).

While the principle of sex education is, by and large, now accepted by the educational establishment in China, experts differ in their views both about the optimum age at which to introduce children to sex education, about whether the pedagogical approach should be coeducational or single sex, and about the precise nature of the information and advice that should be included. Against the dominant approach that recommends the introduction of sex education in junior high school (Chu Zhaorui 1994), some academics argue that sex education should begin at primary school, and informally from early childhood, on the grounds that the earlier children begin to think of sex as an integral part of life, the more likely they are to find sexual and marital satisfaction later on in life.[2] This view, however, does not seem to be particularly common. Founding masters of sex education in China, and notably the well-known sexologist Wu Jieping, suggest that introducing sex education at an early age, as occurs in 'the West', 'produces wanton and chaotic sexual behaviour', since it ignores the primary function of sex education 'firstly as a moral (renge) education and by no means simply as the acquisition of knowledge' (Chu Zhaorui 1994, 7). Articles and TV programmes may attempt to persuade parents that children's interest in sex is completely natural, but the idea that children experience sexual pleasure is far from being commonly accepted. Wu Jieping, for example, considered 'alarming' the idea that a child might find masturbation pleasurable (Wu Jieping et al. 1983, 52–3). Suggestions that sexuality – however defined – may be an aspect of childhood experience are popularly treated as indications of a somewhat suspect mentality (Wang Zhen 1986).[3] Professor Pan Suiming of Beijing's People's University, a pioneering researcher of sexual attitudes and practices, has written a number of popular articles about infantile sexual pleasure, describing the different aspects of children's sexual development and encouraging parents to respond to their small children's desire for bodily intimacy as well as to their questions about sex (Pan Suiming 1992). Given the infrequency of references, however, the concept of child sexuality does not seem to be widely accepted beyond the relatively small number of people acquainted with Freudian theories of child development (Chen Xueshi and Li Guorong 1992, 256; Chu Zhaorui 1994). Dominant views are also limited by fundamentally conservative assumptions defining the kinds of knowledge considered appropriate for an adolescent constituency. Hence discussion about sexual intercourse or contraceptive methods is not generally included in the syllabus for adolescents on the grounds that they should not be encouraged to acquire sexual experience. Sex education in high schools should concentrate mainly on the physiological aspects of sexual development, and move on to the moral issues at a later stage.

Already constrained by parents' lack of familiarity with liberal notions of child development, the conservative tendencies of the official approach are reinforced by the influence of the sexological theories favoured by the exponents of sex education. Since the early 1980s, a number of well-known sexologists have undertaken various studies and surveys about the sexual attitudes and activities of different social, generational and gender constituencies. The most ambitious of these, published in 1992 as *Sexual Behaviour in Modern China*, was a widely reported nationwide investigation carried out under the general supervision of Shanghai's famous sociologist and sexologist Liu Dalin. Praised for its commitment to the traditions of sexological research established by Kinsey, and dubbed the Chinese Kinsey report by *Time* magazine, its methodological links with its American mentor are evident, not least in its self-presentation as a science.[4] Its foreword notes that, despite the dissimilarities between the two studies, the Chinese investigation 'proves the correctness of Kinsey's basic approach, namely that human sexual behaviour is both a biological and social phenomenon; as a kind of energy it has to be released, and the main determinant of how it is released is cultural and social influence' (E. J. Haeberle in Foreword 1 (p. 2); Liu Dalin 1992b). The legitimacy that sexological theories give to biological and sociobiological constructions of sexuality simultaneously reinforces the naturalization of heterosexuality as the only 'normal' form of sexual relations and marginalizes other sexualities as deviant and perverse. While a number of the sexological surveys conducted in the 1980s include data on homosexual behaviour, celibacy and childlessness, they do not substantially challenge the representation of minority practices as abnormal and potentially harmful.

The provision of educational information about sex has made some significant changes in the last few years, though standard texts continue to emphasize the physiological aspects of sexual development and reproduction. A typical publication of the late 1980s starts with basic questions about 'What is puberty?', and goes on to give a brief guide to the stages and processes of adolescent development, physical changes, the characteristics of sexual difference, the problems that may occur during menstruation, and so on (Yan Ruizhen and Li Peifang 1989). Many texts present their contents as answers to typical questions adolescents might ask, such as 'Why do young men have seminal emissions?', 'What does premature sexual maturity mean?' (Shen Wenjiang et al. 1987, 19–21, 23–4), or 'Are delayed menarche and amenorrhea dangerous to the body?' (Yan Ruizhen and Li Peifang 1989, 20–2). However, increasing emphasis on 'psychological health' (*xinli weisheng*) since the mid-1980s has resulted in considerable attention to the emotional upheavals that accompany adolescence, often with specific reference to girls. Indeed, in recent years there has been an evident preponderance of titles targeted at a female readership that devote considerable discussion to psychological issues, like *Female Psychology and Physiology* (*Nüxing xinli he shengli*) (Zhang Mingyuan and Weng Zhonghua 1986), and *Encyclopedia for Young Women* (*Qingnian nüxing baike quanshu*) (Liu Luxian, Liu Nanxian and Huang Canheng, 1991). Sex education classes in schools also introduce discussion about the psychological aspects of adolescent development to the fifteen- to seventeen-year-old age group. However, the terms used tend to suggest a somewhat clinical, 'objective' approach far from the 'personal' appeal favoured by the agony aunts of women's journals and telephone hotlines. Indeed, one commentator recently observed that high-school-level classes are so couched in 'scientific' terminology – often on account of the embarrassment of the teacher – that they seem to have little meaning for young people for whom the experience of sexual development has some bodily and subjective import.[5]

The explicit aim of sex education, according to one of the pioneers of sex education in China, is to enable young people 'to respond to the needs of social development and the principles of social morality' and to help them 'to build up the correct outlook on sex, friendship and love, and to make them sound and developed in body and mind. Through education, students ... civilize their sexual instinct' (Yao Peikuan, 1992, 449). Wu Jieping has suggested that one of the main differences between sex education in China and in the West lies in the former's attention to the moral aspects of adolescent development. In his view, the West's focus on biology, sexual intercourse and contraception is a significant factor contributing to the 'recklessness and chaos of sexual behaviour' (*xing xingwei qingshuai hunluan*) of contemporary Western societies (Chu Zhaorui 1994, 7). By implication, the frequent omission of explicit references to sexual intercourse in Chinese booklets is dictated by a moral agenda. Sex education thus emerges as a means of guiding young people's social and moral development as well as a source of information about biological and psychological growth. Its explicit objective of safeguarding the physical and psychological health of the nation's future is inseparable from its use of scientific knowledge to support a moral and social purpose.

Legitimized in the name of scientific authority, sex education in China thus offers a code of normative sexual and gender expectations that amounts to a vision of 'correct' behaviour for young people. However, the gender focus of much of the educational information given in the name of science has particular implications for constructions of female sexuality. As one writer put it, 'the fact that their psychological level and cognitive experience is unable to keep up with the rapid physiological changes [of adolescence] means that girls often develop a series of psychological conflicts', making them vulnerable to influences which lead them into 'improper sexual relations' (Yan Ruizhen and Li Peifang 1989, 68). Indeed, the same commentators noted, 'the key to explaining young girls' degeneration into criminal behaviour is their loss of virginity and involvement in illicit relations.' A susceptibility to particular kinds of sexual behaviour not associated with the male problematizes female development in ways that attribute hierarchical values to the characteristics of sexual difference. Sex education thus emerges as a project that simultaneously seeks to educate young people and to modify their behaviour according to a series of asymmetrical gender assumptions.

## Sex and reproduction in 1950s perspective[6]

The conceptual starting point for the official discourse of sexuality in the 1950s was the view that sex was a collection of structures, functions and activities that corresponded with a biologically determined binary differentiation between female and male. The 1956 booklet *Knowledge about Sex* claimed scientific authority for defining human sexuality as a heterosexual 'instinct' (*benxing*) that was the 'natural result of biological development' designed to 'assure the existence of the species' (*baozheng zhongzu de shengcun*) (Wang Wenbin, Zhao Zhiyi and Tan Mingxin 1956, 5, 14; *Lun shehuizhuyi shehui de aiqing, hunyin he jiating* 1953, 17). In contrast with those of animals, this instinct could be influenced by subjective, psychological and social factors to stimulate and control sexual excitement (Wang Wenbin, Zhao Zhiyi and Tan Mingxin 1956, 14; Song Tingzhang 1955, 8, 16). Sexuality thus appeared as a natural process that had to be controlled in the interests of social morality and order.

The article 'Some questions about sexual knowledge' (*Guanyu xing zhishi de jige wenti*) in *Zhongguo qingnian* (1956) clearly set out the links between sex as a natural impulse and reproduction. It suggested that, since 'sexual intercourse is the means by which humanity propagates itself, therefore, in appropriate measure, it is not harmful to health' (p. 27). In this light, sexual activity was legitimized by its reproductive purpose; concerns with healthy reproduction determined the parameters defining acceptable sexual activity and provided the rationale for regulating sexual behaviour.

The conflation of sex with reproduction was explicit in official interpretations of the 1950 Marriage Law. Alongside impotence as grounds to withhold the right to marriage, hereditary diseases, mental disorders 'or any other disease which is regarded by medical science as rendering a person unfit for marriage' were stated as appropriate reasons to bar persons legally from marrying.[7] Eugenic concerns to ascertain the reproductive and sexual health of partners prior to marriage lay behind medical advice to young couples to have pre-marital medical check-ups (*hun qian jiankang jiancha*). Any impairment to reproductive capacity might be interpreted as reason to advise against marriage (Wang Bao'en 1953). Since sexual activity in the 1950s was considered morally and legally acceptable only within the context of marriage, this effectively denied legitimate opportunities for sexual relationships to women and men with physical defects considered to make them unfit for marriage and reproduction.

The view that sexual interest and activity were sanctioned by the requirements of propagation provided the subtext for many expert opinions about sexual behaviour. For example, the official discourse used medical opinion concerning the optimum physiological condition for childbirth to support arguments against early marriage and, by implication, pre-marital sex. Not until a woman reached the age of 25 – conveniently the same as the officially termed 'appropriate' (*shidu*) age of marriage for women – was her 'internal system' (*neifenmi xitong*) considered fully mature (Lin Qiaozhi 1957) and her pelvic capacity fully developed (Zhang Xijun 1957).[8] The duration of sexual desire was commonly described as more or less concurrent with the duration of an individual's reproductive capacity, although Wang, Zhao and Tan pointed out that the end of a woman's reproductive capacity did not necessarily signify the disappearance of sexual desire altogether (Wang Wenbin, Zhao Zhiyi and Tan Mingxin 1956, 24, 48, 61). Any possible damage to procreative function was treated as reason to warn women against sexual intercourse. As in Western medical opinion of the same period, experts advised women to refrain from sexual intercourse during menstruation and pregnancy on the grounds that the body's reduced defences at such moments increased the possibility of uterine and vaginal infection and, therefore, infertility (Wang Wenbin, Zhao Zhiyi and Tan Mingxin 1956, 47).[9] By the same token, sexual intercourse during periods of sickness and weakness was said to be likely further to impair women's reproductive health.

Advice on contraceptives reiterated the disapproval of non-reproductive and non-marital sex implicit in the above views. Despite the challenge to the link between sex and reproduction represented by the introduction of birth-control techniques, contraceptive methods were not recommended in contexts that questioned the priority attached to reproductive sex. Rather, they were recommended principally for women who already had children (Wu Yi 1956). In a letter about marital problems written to *Zhongguo funü* a young school-teacher in Henan clearly indicated that information about and access to contraceptives were not readily available to childless women. She wrote that, because she did not want to disrupt her work and studies by having a baby, she resorted to inventing excuses – 'I had meetings or was studying, or I had gone to visit my parents, or the weather was not good . . .' to explain to her husband why she could not see him (and therefore sleep with him) at weekends (Yu Ping 1957). An editorial about birth-control methods published in another issue of the same journal unequivocally disapproved of the use of contraceptives by women who were simply not interested in having children: 'of course, there are some men and women who, for the sake of idle pleasures, are unwilling to take on the responsibility of having children; such people should be educated in socialist morals, to make them understand that bringing up children is a parental responsibility, and also every citizen's duty to the state' ('Zenyang renshi biyun wenti' 1955).

The legitimation of sexual activity for its reproductive function corresponded with the assumption, evident in readers' letters, that most women wanted and would give birth to children. It also corresponded with concerns about women's health and hygiene, which sometimes echoed traditional injunctions against doing and absorbing certain things during periods of bodily weakness. Defining sexual activity in terms of reproduction further seems to have been motivated, at least in part, by interests in empowering women to protect themselves from excessive sexual demands by their husbands, particularly during so-called vulnerable moments of the female cycle. Restricting references to contraceptive methods to contexts featuring married women with at least one child similarly conformed to historically and culturally determined practices. To have focused such discussion on unmarried women would have implicitly challenged normative standards of pre-marital chastity, particularly in the countryside, where any public association with a man could expose an unmarried woman to severe punishment.[10] As the above quotation illustrates, the few women who did not want to have children were represented as failing in their natural duty. On the other hand, offering women contraceptives after one or more births was presented as a progressive measure giving women control over their own fertility and reproduction.

Alongside the reproductive emphasis on sex apparent in most texts, comments about the desirability of a 'good sex life [to] deepen the love between a couple and deepen their relationship' were briefly publicized during the mid-1950s. 'Sexual harmony' strengthened the foundations of the marital relationship, and thereby contributed to family and social stability ('Guanyu xing zhishi de jige wenti' 1956). Experts argued that an unsatisfactory sexual relationship could make a woman totally estranged from her husband; a 'perfunctory' sex life could have damaging effects on an otherwise harmonious marriage and therefore interfere with work (Wang Wenbin, Zhao Zhiyi and Tan Mingxin 1956, 41). As with other aspects of bodily experience, sexual activity had to be tempered in order to maintain harmony and health. The notion of a good sex life was accordingly identified with moderation as the key to tapping its health-giving potential. While it was recognized that 'couples want to have more sex in the first few months of marriage', the average frequency recommended was once or twice a week (Wang Shancheng 1956). With advancing age, as 'sexual desire diminishes', the recommended frequency dropped to once every one or two weeks (Wang Wenbin, Zhao Zhiyi and Tan Mingxin 1956, 46). If 'after sexual intercourse either partner shows signs of fatigue or lethargy', frequency had to be scaled down even further ('Guanyu xing zhishi de jige wenti' 1956).

In *Patriarchy and Socialist Revolution in China*, Judith Stacey argued that the 'new democratic morality linked sexuality not with procreation, but with felicitous marital relationships and, thereby, with the construction of socialism' (Stacey 1983, 188). Indeed, as a CCP document pointed out, 'the fact that there are no children does not mean that one cannot have marital life. This is not at all the same as having a physical defect and not being able to have sexual intercourse' (quoted in Meijer 1971, 219). Coinciding with the campaign to boost the image of the housewife and the introduction of birth-control policies during the period of rising unemployment in the mid-1950s, however, the short-lived emphasis on a good sex life and the rejection of infertility as a legitimate reason for marital separation did not question the identification of reproduction as the fundamental and natural purpose of sex. The appearance of comments about the benefits of sexual harmony for married life alongside articles insisting that women's first and natural duty to society was to bear children suggests that a harmonious sexual relationship and procreation were treated as complementary rather than contrasting aspects of marriage. As a commentator in 1953 suggested, having children was a social duty, failure to observe which 'should be severely criticized by the party' (Wei Junyi 1953).

## Sexual difference

As in other dominant aspects of the 1950s discourse of sexuality, views concerning sexual difference conformed to the biological model favoured by Wang, Zhao and Tan. Anonymous articles elaborating ideas from *Knowledge about Sex* appeared in the official press ('Guanyu xing zhishi de jige wenti' 1956). Named articles such as Wang Shancheng's 'Tan xing shenghuo' (Talking about sexual relations, 1956) contained views that clearly corresponded with the main principles of *Knowledge about Sex*. The uniformity of the views expressed and their repeated appearance in official publications clearly indicated official support for the model they expounded.

At first glance, the view of sexuality that accompanied the biological explanations of sexual development in the 1950s texts projected a model of harmonious balance and complementarity between male and female. Sexuality was constructed as a bounded harmony of binary opposites, governed by fixed physiological differences, echoing the approaches of the Western sexologists whose work was used by modern biomedical science in China during the 1920s and 1930s, as well as the *yin–yang* model of traditional Chinese views.[11] This construction was immediately apparent in the terminology used to describe the relationship between female and male. Reiterating ideas deeply embedded in classical culture, advocates of this view described the sexual balance between men and women as the 'mutual support of the *yin* and *yang*'; 'male is *yang*' (*nanzi wei yang*), strong and active; 'female is *yin*' (*nüzi wei yin*), yielding and passive (Tan Zhen 1956).[12] The action of the one on the other was described as strengthening to both women and men, through the absorption of the semen by the vagina and of female mucus by the penis (Tan Zhen 1956). Despite the experts' questioning of the unscientific basis of such views, narrative use of the *yin–yang* conceptualization indicated a persistent attachment to notions of complementarity in representations of the heterosexual relationship.

An analysis of the gender distinctions in explanations of sexual desire, however, indicated that the relationship between *yin* and *yang* was more asymmetrical than complementary. Male (*yang*) desire was associated with sudden and powerful excitement, expressed in words like '*chongdong*' (impetuous) and '*xingfen*' (excited). Female (*yin*) desire, on the few occasions that it was mentioned, was characterized as gentle and responsive.[13] In the male, the active physiological basis of the sex drive was described as a naturally spontaneous force, a kind of instinctual urge, that was 'easily aroused and satisfied' and demanded immediate gratification. Men reached orgasm within a few minutes, and then rapidly lost sexual desire. Female desire was more 'complex and generalized' because of the structure and functions of the female organs. More significantly, though, the female was passive and reluctant: 'even if she feels some sexual desire, it is for the most part very slight. It is not as strong as in the male' (Wang Wenbin, Zhao Zhiyi and Tan Mingxin 1956, 39). Female arousal was a gradual process, the reader was advised, and had to be patiently encouraged by the partner's 'verbal endearments and embraces' (Wang Shancheng 1956; Wang Wenbin, Zhao Zhiyi and Tan Mingxin 1956, 12–4). Occasional allusions to the physical specificity of female pleasure slightly diluted the active male/passive female opposition of this view of sexuality. References to the clitoris as 'the most sensitive part of the female genitalia' implied recognition of its independent place in the structure of female desire, unmediated by male initiative (Wang Shancheng 1956; Wang Wenbin, Zhao Zhiyi and Tan Mingxin 1956, 16). The dominant view stressed the autonomy of male desire, however, in contrast with the essentially contingent and dependent nature of female desire. Conditions such as 'physique, environment, age of marriage and sexual experience in marriage' had to be right for female desire to find expression (Wang Shancheng 1956). Indications that female desire might exist independently of male stimulation were commonly associated with danger, abnormality and harm. Wang, Zhao and Tan, for example, described a woman who, after years of marriage to a man ten years her senior whose 'sexual desire was average (*yiban*)', decided to have a clitoridectomy since she was 'unable to satisfy her own excessive (*wangsheng*) desire' (1956, 41).[14] The woman's request for the operation was described as her response to the personal unhappiness and damage to her work caused by her inability to satisfy her sexual needs. By implication, had her husband been able to satisfy her needs, or had her own desire matched the cooler levels of her husband, there would have been no problem.

From the few materials available for the early 1970s, it would appear that two decades later there was no substantial modification to these views; if anything, in the purist ideological climate of the 'gang of four' years, the biologistic construction of sexual development was even more emphatic (Xie Bozhang 1975). In the early 1980s, educational booklets for 'newly-weds' made similarly dichotomized distinctions between the 'strong' (*qianglie*) and 'frequent and highly intense' (*wangsheng*) character of male sexual desire and the 'relatively weak' (*xiangdui jiao ruo*) quality of female desire that echoed the terms of earlier texts (*Xinhun weisheng bi du* editorial group 1984, 28–30). Biological explanations that represent sexual difference as a binary set of natural responses continue to be prominent in contemporary materials, as the introductory chapter indicated; the idea that 'women's passivity in sexual relations is clearly linked to physiological differences between the sexes' (Dai Wei 1991, 103) has enduring appeal. Some publications also continue to represent sexual difference in terms of the *yin–yang* complementarity, echoing the same asymmetry of earlier approaches. For example, 'male desire is strong, easily excitable and quick to reach orgasm . . .; female desire is gradual, slow to be excited and reach orgasm . . . only through intimate coordination can mutuality and harmony be maintained . . .' (Cao Hongxin, Mao Dexi and Ma Zhongxue 1992, 36).

However, as I suggested earlier on in this chapter, arguments that focus on the influence of culture and society in shaping sexual difference have become increasingly apparent in recent years. 'Modern sexological research which shows that women have no spontaneous sexual excitement has no scientific basis. In instances where this seems to be the case, it is due to cultural controls over female sexuality, and certainly not to physiological differences' (Fang Fang 1987, 80–1). Sociologists concerned with widespread evidence of women's lack of sexual enjoyment and interest attribute it not so much to biological as to social factors, such as cramped living conditions, lack of time, husbands' insensitivity and the need to be constantly vigilant against pregnancy (Xu Anqi 1990a; Dai Wei 1991, 104). A 1989 publication called *Men and Women* argued that 'normative practice in sexual behaviour is established through cultural influences' (Liu Minwen et al. 1989, 78) and, while biology establishes the physical possibility for the expression of sexual desire, the construction of sexual identities depends on a range of familial, cultural and social experiences and influences (pp. 79–88). Another publication launched an even more direct challenge against the biological model in arguing that 'some people mistakenly think that the [biological differences between men and women] are a simple matter that explains sexual differences in external appearance, bearing, expression and dress. In fact, this is absolutely not the case. Some men wear patterned clothes, rings and bracelets, and make-up, and speak and behave in a feminine manner . . .' (Li Wenhai and Liu Shuyu 1992, 2). Sex, the authors of the same book explained, 'is a complex concept that embraces physiological differences, sexual (*xingbie*) differences, sexual role (*xing jiaose*) and sexual conduct . . . and that 'can only be scientifically understood through physiology, biology, psychology, law, aesthetics, philosophy and ethics' (p. 6). Thus while 'for a long time people have maintained the view that there is a substantial difference between men and women in the intensity and strength of sexual desire, in fact the differences are next to nothing; the greatest difference is between people of the same sex' (p. 38).

New descriptions, metaphors and imagery have brought an unprecedented variety to public representations of sexual difference in the last decade or so. The dominant tendencies in public imagery of women in sexually implicated contexts at first glance share very little with their equivalents of earlier periods. However, we have seen that many, arguably most, contemporary commentators maintain a strong – but no longer uniform or exclusive – attachment to biological explanations of sexuality that do not substantially differ from those of the 1950s. The same heterosexist assumptions continue to bound discussions about the 'normal' characteristics of sexual difference. Indeed, the notion of difference applies only to sexual and (therefore) gender differences between women and men. The rigid heterosexism of the dominant discourses precludes the possibility of any more sensitive and shifting significations of ideas of difference. Evident continuities with the former discourse are also operative in the contrasts between the essentially contingent nature of female sexuality and the autonomous power of the male drive. The male orgasm is spontaneous and universal; the female orgasm has to be nurtured by the man. Female desire needs encouraging within a context of intimacy and tenderness provided by her (male) partner (Li Wenhai and Liu Shuyu 1992, 47–50). Female sexuality is defined principally in relation to masculinity; outside the context of the heterosexual relationship, female sexuality has no existence. In its presence and absence, female desire is constructed in response to the powerful male urge. Educational texts on the physiological aspects of sex continue to stress the power of the active, autonomous male who must restrain his unstoppable energy to preserve health and elicit a favourable response from his female partner.[15] While biology, psychology and culture dictate the gradual nature of female desire, its full expression depends on the consideration, care and sensitivity of the male.

Conversely, the overactive and demanding male has the capacity to destroy female desire altogether (Gao Fang and Zeng Rong 1991, 35–7). The concern with female indifference and frigidity, explicit in many references, corresponds just as much to possible threats to the power of male sexuality as to notions of female pleasure and sexual harmony. Inadequacies in a husband's sexual approaches – whether in being 'too hasty and rough on the night of the honeymoon' (Liu Changqing 1995) or in 'suffering from premature ejaculation and impotence' (Xu Zhong 1994) – appear as major reasons explaining women's lack of sexual enjoyment. From this perspective, the projection of mutual orgasm as the highest expression of sexual harmony indicates little more than the man's success in controlling his own and encouraging his wife's sexual pleasure. While, as Chapter 5 demonstrates, women are urged to abandon the 'ideological fetters' thwarting their own sexual pleasure, and are encouraged to take more initiative (zhudong) in lovemaking, the male standard implicit in this view of sexuality suggests that women's enjoyment of or antipathy towards sexual relations is almost entirely dependent on male action. The dominant male drive initiates and shapes the woman's orgasm; left to her own devices, she has little chance of experiencing or realizing any autonomous sexual pleasure. Within marriage, the only context condoning expression of sexual desire and experience, a woman has no sexual self until awakened by the man. Female sexuality was acknowledged only in contexts and relationships which subordinated it to the dominant male drive. As in the Western constructions of sexuality that formed part of the 1950s discursive legacy, 'female sexuality was seen as having no independent existence of its own' (Jackson 1987, 70).[16] In the words of the Dutch gynaecologist Theodore H. Van de Velde, writing in a different context in 1926, the husband was seen as the 'sexual educator and guide through whom the woman is educated to full proficiency in love'.[17] Chapter 8 argues that representations of potentially independent female sexual desire outside the boundaries of marriage are commonly categorized as a sign of some physical or mental abnormality.

## Reformist constructions of sex and reproduction

With the circulation of different theories about sex and sexual difference in recent years, the biologistic arguments of the 1950s have been somewhat modified. Standard explanations of sexual difference and sexual desire now attach much greater importance to the function of psychological, cultural and social factors in moulding sexual behaviour and its subjective experience, to the point that some writers challenge the primacy of physiological determination (e.g., Li Wenhai and Liu Shuyu 1992, 2–6). The categorization of topics and the terms used to present them also suggest a move away from the physiological emphasis of the former discourse. The breakdown of the single category of 'sex' (*xing*) into various items such as 'sexual physiology', 'sexual psychology' and 'sexual behaviour' has become a common way of introducing social and cultural influences into discussions about the determinants of sexual behaviour (Yan Ruizhen and Li Peifang 1989; Wang Peng 1993). However, despite occasional objections to the notion of sex as an instinct on the grounds that it is as erroneous as it is outdated, and has been responsible for diverse social problems (Li Wenhai and Liu Shuyu 1992, 5), commentators continue to stress the instinctual aspect of sexual need and desire (Wu Jieping et al. 1983, vi; Tang Dao 1986, 1; Li Xingchun and Wang Liru 1991, 105). The modifications to former approaches have not fundamentally altered the dominant discourse's attachment to the sociobiological construction of sexuality, according to which gender differences in sexual identity and practice are grounded in natural biological processes.

Texts that deal with sexual intercourse suggest a more noticeable departure from the earlier discourse. The near synonymity of sex with reproduction that was so evident in earlier discussions has been replaced by a significantly greater emphasis on the contribution of a felicitous sexual relationship towards making a happy marriage. Bookshops are now full of titles advising couples on techniques for marital satisfaction, such as *Encyclopedia of Marital Harmony* (*Fuqi hexie quanshu*, Li Xingchun and Wang Liru 1991) or *The Secret of Conjugal Feeling* (*Fuqi qingmi*, Zhang Biao 1991), to name but two. Advisors may warn against exaggerating the importance of sex in a couple's relationship (Zhang Biao 1991, 30–2) but the assumption that a 'good sex life' is a vital component of a happy marriage pervades all discussions about 'sexual knowledge', as Chapter 5 demonstrates. 'The harmony and beauty that result from intimate coordination and the use of appropriate methods in lovemaking (*fangshi*) increase a couple's bodily and psychological health' (Cao Hongxin, Mao Dexi and Ma Zhongxue 1992, 34). Texts about the sexual component of the conjugal relationship also pay considerable attention to the sexual problems that may disrupt an otherwise harmonious marriage. 'Even though sexual interest and desire are periodic, and several years of married life reduce a couple's sense of sexual excitement, the emotional intensity of sexual love is still a vital component of an interesting and energetic marriage' (Chen Xianguo 1993, 18). At a time when emotional and sexual fulfilment is acquiring greater significance in the criteria women and men use when selecting a marriage partner; when sexual incompatibility is increasingly cited as a reason for marital breakdown; and when one logical effect of the single-child family policy is to reduce – but not eliminate – the importance of reproductive sex within the marital relationship, attention to sex as a matter for pleasurable recreation contributing to marital satisfaction is unsurprising.

Alongside the message that – always within the context of marriage – sexual intercourse is a health-enhancing activity, professional advice about the appropriate conditions, times and frequency for sexual activity suggests a rather different construction. The continuing prevalence of eugenic concerns in official discourses about sexuality and marriage is apparent in the requirement, in operation since the 1980s, that all couples undergo a medical check-up prior to marriage, 'to guarantee superior births, domestic happiness and social stability' (Ju

Ming 1995, 5). Couples are still strongly advised against marrying – and by implication against having sexual intercourse – if they are discovered to be carrying some mental or hereditary condition deemed inappropriate by medical science for reproduction. Medical advice about the optimum age for sexual activity echoes that of the earlier period, with experts suggesting that women's reproductive capacity is fully developed only by the age of 23 or 24 (Shen Wenjiang et al. 1987, 157). Warnings against having sexual intercourse during menstruation and pregnancy continue to prioritize reproductive concerns over others, including considerations of pleasure. While the development of the commercial market in China has made it considerably easier for unmarried women to gain access to contraceptives, abortions and relevant professional advice, and though the media make frequent references to pre-marital pregnancies and abortions, the dominant discourse has maintained its focus in such matters on married women. Furthermore, the absence of contraceptive advice in school sex-education classes gives implicit confirmation to the assumption that women – it is not men who are principally targeted in such discussions – should not engage in sexual activities outside the legally recognized context legitimizing reproduction. The continuing discursive margin-alization of women who decide not to have children or remain single – whose gendered subjectivity is not synonymous with the subject positions of mother or wife – is indicative of similar assumptions.

While, since the early 1950s, medical experts as well as lay com-mentators have consistently maintained a conceptual distinction between sexuality and procreation, the assumption that the two naturally go together informs all dominant representations of sexuality and gender. 'The idea of being someone's lover . . . however passionate a relationship it might be, would never convince me to abandon women's natural instinct of wanting to get married and have a family' (A Che 1995). It also explains the prevalent antipathy to acknowl-edging the legitimacy of homosexuality in China. 'Homosexuality is to satisfy an individual's sexual desire, and cannot reproduce the next generation. Giving legal recognition to homosexuality would therefore destroy marriage and the family' (Wan Zi 1993, 46). From the point of view of the individual person, sexual satisfaction might be seen as a matter of personal and marital happiness. Repeated articles advise women about how to make their sex lives more satisfactory, how to achieve orgasm, and 'what kind of sexual signals' to give out to make sexual intercourse pleasurable (Liu Dalin 1995a, 42), without any direct reference to reproduction. However, this is not incompatible with a public construction of sexuality that both assumes and empha-sizes reproduction. A kind of natural equivalence between women's reproductive role and sexual attributes serves to define the physical and moral parameters for the appropriate expression of female sexuality. The biologically determined capacity to bear children dictates the main characteristics of women's sexual desires and needs, notably during menstruation and pregnancy. As later chapters show, women whose sexual behaviour challenges the predominance of the female reproductive role are still widely represented as immoral or unnatural. The naturalized link maintained between female sexuality and reproductive role remains fundamental to the dominant construction of gender distinctions.

The fusion of sexuality with procreation also defines the boundaries between constructions of 'normal' (zhengchang) and 'abnormal' (bu zhengchang) sexuality. Indeed, representations of sexual identity that did not conform to the model of procreative heterosexuality were all but totally absent from the 1950s discourse. As one article of the time put it, the idea that the 'cohabitation of man and woman' was biologically determined and 'would survive until the end of the human race' confirmed heterosexuality as the only 'normal' sexuality (Feng Ding 1958). The few references I have found to homosexuality in the 1950s occur in more recent publications written to condemn homosexuality as a physical and psychological 'perversion' (biantai) and 'violation of nature', if not simply an 'abysmal crime' (Chen Fan 1990, 107–8, 126–8). References to female celibacy, formerly the subject of prolonged and heated debate in China,[18] were also excluded from the discourse, marginalized by the dominant assumption of women's reproductive duty to society. Alongside the universally assumed correlation between sexuality, procreation and heterosexuality, the exclusion from public mention of what Foucault called 'peripheral sexualities' (1984, 42–3) implicitly constructed them as biological abnormalities, illnesses or signs of moral degeneracy. Between the 1950s and the 1970s, the taboo on public references to homosexuality, well known to have been common at earlier periods of China's history, reinforced the normative authority associated with the idea of a single natural sexuality.[19] Since the 1980s, the public attention to sexual 'abnormalities' may have encouraged greater tolerance and acceptance in some quarters. Indeed, one commentator has suggested that, at a time when 'people are facing the dangers of a soaring increase in population, popular attitudes towards homosexuality may become more tolerant' (Wan Zi 1993, 46). The dominant discourse, however, continues to resist what it sees as a challenge to its own authority. As Li Yinhe and Wang Xiaobo point out in their sympathetic survey of homosexual attitudes and relationships, symptomatic of this view is the tendency of most homosexuals to marry and have children, even though they may be totally hostile to the idea of married life (1992, 142–5).

Ever since 1949, dominant discourses of sexuality in the People's Republic have privileged science as the agent responsible for defining biological truth. In the 1950s the scientific views of the experts were situated within a specific paradigm that did not question the scientific status of gendered notions of strength, energy, weakness and passivity. The official discourse presented as scientific fact a series of assumptions about sexual difference that reflected moral and social as much as medical concerns. The privileging of the views of medical experts such as Wang, Zhao and Tan or Yan Renying and the pervasive influence of these views in non-specialist texts gave an authority to expert opinion that extended far beyond the boundaries of medical interest. Science enjoyed an authority in reinforcing gender values that corresponded with cultural and ideological interests more than with notions of scientific objectivity.

That the parameters defining what goes under the name of science have changed is evident from the scientific arguments about sexuality expounded over the last decade. The specific meanings inscribed in scientific definitions and expositions have been both modified and expanded to include approaches not considered in the 1950s. The invocation of Freud and other psychologists has legitimized the integration of psychologically based approaches to understanding sexuality. References to Kinsey, and to Masters and Johnson, have permitted a reappraisal of the characteristics of female sexual desire in ways that might seem to imply an empowerment of women. Suggestions that women assert themselves and take more initiative in expressing their desires and needs in sexual relationships had no equivalent in the materials of the earlier discourse. Greater recognition of cultural and social factors in the construction of sexuality and sexual identities signifies a challenge to the biological essentialism of the former discourse. However, this challenge is minimal, not only in quantitative terms, but also because the premises on which it is launched invoke sociobiological arguments that differ from former views more in tone and emphasis than in substance.

Whether presented in the form of sex education in schools or as professional advice in popular journals, scientific opinion about sexual development and behaviour in the People's Republic of China is rigidly grounded in heterosexist assumptions. Nature determines an absolute binary differentiation between the female and male that governs – establishes the boundaries for – sexual and gender conduct. The same differentiation establishes the discursive basis for controlling sexual practice through demanding conformity to standards of conduct on the grounds that they are, predominantly, naturally determined. Defined in terms of what are represented as complementary opposites of male initiative and energy versus female responsiveness and passivity, (hetero)sexual difference determines gender characteristics in sexual need, desire and response. Women naturally behave in a certain way because their physiological and reproductive structure so requires. Moreover, the biological arguments concerning sexual difference sustain a model of asymmetrical gender relations according to which the representation of the female, far from being associated with subject positions invoking autonomy and equality – ideas that are more consistent with official party rhetoric of sexual equality – are dominated by gender requirements of responsiveness to the male. While gender ideology has been modified in other areas of social practice, continuing adherence to the biological construction of sexuality severely restricts conceptual, as well as political, possibilities of change in gender relations. To use Charlotte Furth's words, 'as interpreters of biological fact, the medical authorities therefore had a privileged role in the transmission of views of women's subordination as a natural human condition' (Furth 1987, 7). The conflation of sexual and gender attributes legitimized by science and the party permits the naturalization of gender inequalities in all public contexts and relationships associated with women's position, whether as girlfriend, wife, mother or adulteress.

Dominant discourses of sexuality in the last decade or so have continued to construct sexuality primarily with reference to the power of the male drive – as Weeks described it, 'a driving, instinctual force, whose characteristics are built into the biology of the human animal' (Weeks 1981, 2–3). Recent opinion has attached considerable importance to the need for women to assert their sexual needs, and to the value of a 'good sex life' in marriage, but scientific views of sexuality have not substantially departed from the asymmetrical model of male penetration and ejaculation and female receptivity. The indomitable male urge has to be controlled to avoid alienating the woman; women's desire has to be awakened by the man. The medical and educational authorities therefore lend their weight to legitimizing a representation of female sexuality that is defined by its dependency on the male initiator and by the requirements of reproduction. Later chapters argue that sex during moments of the female cycle or in social contexts that challenge this model are discounted as an appropriate expression of female sexuality; in so far as they subvert the dominant model, exceptions to the norm drive female sexuality beyond the bounds of acceptability.

Formulated and disseminated under the general auspices of the state's educational establishment, sex education is by definition accorded a unique and privileged rank in the hierarchy of discourses of sexuality. The moral and ideological principles that sex education explicitly serves receive the backing both of the medical experts and of the state. Sex education is the axis along which medical, moral and political projects of control converge in a formal discourse; it is central to the institutional, group and individual production of the dominant discourse. Whatever the effects of sex education, it makes a significant contribution to constituting the gendered subject positions available to ordinary young women and men in schools and colleges. Inseparable from the scientifically legitimized conflation of sex and gender noted above, the provision of sex education in schools signifies the dissemination of views about sexuality that invoke a clear gender hierarchy. The expansion of sex education and therefore of the sites and subjects affected by it in the last fifteen years has offered the state the opportunity for systematic intervention in ordinary persons' construction of their sexual and gender identities in ways that clearly contrast with the rhetoric of sexual equality.

# 3 Advice to Adolescents

In the social and political conditions of the newly established People's Republic of China, the question of how to channel young people's energies in the service of national progress caused state agencies to pay assiduous attention to issues of youth development. Officially sponsored discussion about adolescence indicated that the new opportunities available to young people were creating demands and practices that, from the party's perspective, had to be carefully supervised in the interests of their own and society's well-being. Official publication of articles about adolescent sexuality signified the construction of adolescence as a vehicle for state intervention to control young people's development in intimate aspects of daily life and via means not offered by other discourses.

Texts about teenagers published in the past decade or so suggest a problematization of adolescence that has both gone beyond and altered the concerns of the 1950s. Young people's attitudes towards sex have radically changed over the past fifteen years in China. In a context of increasing social mobility and changing urban values, aggressive exposure to information about Western life styles and unprecedented opportunities for travel abroad, young people in China's cities and towns now live in a sexual culture which has little in common with that of their parents' generation. Cursory observation of social behaviour in shopping malls, urban streets or university campuses suggests an ease of social contact between young women and men which was unthinkable a couple of decades ago and indeed is still considered shameful in many rural communities.[1] Television shows and popular magazines for teenage readers address sexual matters with a candour and humour which is far from customary among older age groups. Surveys about sexual behaviour indicate an extent of teenage sexual experience that is by many accounts the cause of considerable concern among parents and professionals. Liu Dalin's nationwide survey conducted between 1990 and 1992 concluded that, 'with the continuing lowering in age of sexual maturity and the increasingly earlier development of sexual consciousness (*xing yishi*), many middle school students hanker after social contact with the other sex and . . . some already have some sexual experience. In matters of sex, they are wavering at a crossroads' (Liu Dalin 1992b, 125). Some commentators further claim that there is a significant link between the lowering of the age of puberty, the lower median age of sexual maturity and experience, and increased rates of teenage pregnancies and juvenile crime (Yan Ruizhen and Li Peifang 1989, 93).

Advice contained in official publications of the 1950s about the sexual and emotional aspects of young people's development represented adolescence as a period of preparation for adulthood and reproduction. As part of the project to supervise young people's development, discussion of adolescent sexuality in the articles published in *Zhongguo qingnian* introduced young people to knowledge considered indispensable to their healthy development. The enormous quantity of materials targeted at teenage schoolchildren and college students since the early 1980s has shared a similar objective, despite its diversity. As we have seen, one of the explicit objectives behind 1980s proposals to expand the provision of sex education in schools was to enable young people to make decisions about their lives based on knowledge and understanding, rather than ignorance. In this light, 'sexual knowledge' emerges as an instrument to assist the establishment of 'healthy practices' in preparation for courtship, marriage and reproduction. Adolescence is discursively constructed as young people's initiation as sexual beings.

In the 1950s, the notion of a 'correct' understanding was postulated on the view that sexual conduct and ideology could be homogeneously categorized as 'wrong' and 'right'. The 'correct' signified a uniform mode of practice, premised on established views about the boundaries of the sexed and gendered body during adolescence. By contrast, more recent representations of 'correctness' have been built on shifting interests and referents that – depending on the specific site of concern – sometimes blur distinctions between 'wrong' and 'right'. While the outer parameters of 'correctness' may be identical to earlier definitions, recent discussions about adolescent sexuality include a range of questions which were simply absent from the former discourse. How to treat a girl on a first date, for example, or what kind of clothes to wear when you go out with a boyfriend, or how to acquire the confidence to ask someone out all suggest experiences and choices – potential or already lived – among adolescents that were unacknowledged – indeed, deemed improper – in the public discourse of the earlier period. Nevertheless, evident preoccupations on the part of parents, teachers and legal specialists about adolescent behaviour have sustained an attachment to the idea that there is a 'correct' approach to sexual matters. This chapter argues that contemporary representations of 'wrong' and 'right' in adolescence indicate various points of convergence with older assumptions about how adolescents should – and should not – be deploying their energies.

Premised on principles of self-control and conservation of bodily and mental strength, the single most prominent aspect of advice to adolescents is that premature sexual interest and involvement dissipate young people's energies (Wu Zhangming, Zhu Xiaolan and Lang Ying 1990, 73). Girls and boys alike are instructed to direct their developing physical and psychological energies away from sexual concerns to intellectual, political or social ones. While commentators note that adolescents' concern about sex is quite legitimate, even to the point of advising parents not to be too hard on their adolescent children if they are in a relationship of 'early love', the unvarying message of these texts is that sexual self-restraint is the condition of health and strength in adult life (Shu Zhe 1995). Given the discursive prohibitions on sexual involvement during adolescence, sanctions in support of control and vigilance focus on the individual person, female or male – on the individual's control of self – rather than on the relationship between two people of the opposite sex. As the following discussion shows, the gender distinctions that emerge in the process correspond in many important aspects to the naturalized sexual differences established by the biological account of sexuality.

In insisting on the social importance of a conventionally hidden area of practice, the agents of the official discourse were potentially opening the doors to a radical reassessment of the responses, needs and desires embraced by the meaning of sexuality. Appropriating a hitherto taboo topic for public examination potentially exposed it to diverse interpretations and constructions that did not automatically conform to the norms of the official discourse. Indeed, the party-state took a calculated risk in inviting discussion – circumscribed though it was – about adolescent sexuality for, as occasional references indicated, alternative discourses were available – even if only to a limited extent – in film or literature, for example, that suggested other constructions of sexual behaviour and desire (Wang Wenbin, Zhao Zhiyi and Tan Mingxin

1956, 37). However, the reassessment that took place was constrained from the start by the way in which it was channelled along lines determined by the state's experts. Far from being designed to present sexuality as an unbounded site for critical reflection, the state's redefinitions of adolescence and sexuality formed part of a project to liberate a socially useful force – youth – from its 'feudal fetters' by reconstructing it as an agent of the new socialist moral order. The concerns informing the official approach to adolescent sexuality indicated that it would be subject to ideological and moral constraints no less than had been the case under the traditional feudal order; the difference was that socialist constraints were to replace feudal ones. The provision of information about adolescent issues was a distinct aspect of a broader project to transform the private sphere of knowledge into a public discourse legitimizing a particular social and moral order.

While the relationship between private and public as constructed in Chinese texts about sex-related topics has again shifted in favour of reasserting a private realm – 'Love is our own matter' was the title of a recent article in a popular journal (Li Guixia 1993) – a substantial body of the materials distributed for adolescents' and young adults' consumption in the past fifteen years shares the ordering objectives of the 1950s discourse. Contemporary representations introduce individual persons' experiences as discrete cases, and not simply as clear-cut examples substantiating or rejecting a dominant view. They attempt to convey some understanding about the turbulence, excitement and pain of adolescence, even if the terms they use are far from those of popular teenage conversation. They also clearly demonstrate that in terms of public discourses young people now enjoy a measure of choice and experimentation denied them in the 1950s. However, approaches to adolescence are by no means open-ended; the common inclusion of guidelines about how to behave in particular situations indicates a didactic purpose that shares many features of the former discourse. As in the earlier period, the discursive construction of adolescent problems tends to exclude the possibility that they might refer to varying meanings and effects depending on individual experience. Individual experiences – the formation of individual identity and self-identity – continue to be subsumed under a series of general propositions about adolescence formulated as part of the official programme of education and control. Though the terms and boundaries have changed, discursive representations of adolescent behaviour continue to serve the interests of science, morality and the social order. The specificities of adolescence as a period of sexual and gender maturation continue to be defined principally with reference to the requirements of the political system to discipline the development of young people.

## Definitions of adolescence

In late imperial China, the term *qingnian* (youth) referred to males between the ages of sixteen or seventeen and thirty. By the late Qing dynasty (1644–1911), it was used less to designate age than the increasing independence of sons from paternal discipline and the period when men from rich families first experienced sexual relations (Levy 1949, 84–6); it excluded girls, because marriage was assumed to be concurrent with physical and sexual maturity (p. 89).[2] The appearance of 'adolescence' (*qingchunqi*) as a social category during the New Culture movement accompanied the transformation of 'youth' into a symbol of modernity, progress and science (Dikötter 1995, 147). The term was universalized to include young women as well as men, of all social classes, and to encompass distinct physiological and psychological characteristics that defined adolescence as a 'natural' process. The transformation of the young person into a mature adult was culturally constructed in biomedical terms that identified fixed sexual and gender differences (1995, 150–79) and that shaped the discursive approaches to adolescent sexuality developed by the official experts in the 1950s.

The stipulation of a legal minimum age for marriage in the 1950 Marriage Law signified the prolongation of the time between puberty (*fayu shiqi*) and marriage during which young people were considered sexually mature but without legitimate outlet for their sexual desires and energies. Imposing delays on the age of marriage and sexual activity – the term 'marriage' is still widely used as a synonym for sexual intercourse – foregrounded adolescence as a potential social problem. Wang, Zhao and Tan concurred with this problematization of the 'spring period' (*qingchunqi*) in their definition of its major characteristics. They suggested that the physiological and sexual changes occurring in adolescence created interests in young people which, if not properly disciplined, could lead to morally and sexually undesirable consequences.

Adolescence defines the period between thirteen and eighteen years of age, and is characterized by continuing physical growth and the rapid development of the reproductive system. With this a feeling of attraction for the opposite sex arises. This is natural, since it has a biological foundation. Inevitably, it gradually gives rise to the requirement for love and marriage. It is not appropriate for young people to fall in love too early, because this period is of great importance for studying ... Adolescence is a period for laying foundations, and falling in love too early is bound to disperse one's energy and impair one's studies. However, this is not to say that young people of the opposite sex should not engage in appropriate contact and friendship. (Wang Wenbin, Zhao Zhiyi and Tan Mingxin 1956, 22)

Defined in these terms, adolescence emerged as a stage when the speed and extent of the physiological and psychological changes affecting young people demanded vigilance, caution, and the adoption of a 'proper and serious' attitude towards the physical and moral issues implicated by sexual maturation. In its key role of establishing the healthy foundations for adult life, adolescence was also linked to the maintenance of standards of health and cleanliness, summed up in Chinese texts as 'adolescent hygiene'. In the words of one commentator, 'adolescence is a key period in determining a person's physique, psychology and intellectual development. Even though the body's defences during adolescence are stronger than in childhood, [many diseases] still occur and nervous disorders are much more common. Hygiene during this period should not, therefore, be neglected' (Shen Wenjiang et al. 1987, 3–4). Ideally, young people should use this 'golden period' to find an appropriate balance between the social, intellectual and emotional aspects of their lives; success in doing so is the indispensable condition for making mature choices in courtship and marriage. Adolescence is thus constructed as the first stage of initiation of young people as sexual subjects in anticipation of later marriage. Forming a 'correct' outlook on sexual matters at this stage of life acquires long-term significance for the individual person, their future spouse and children, and therefore for society. Adolescence becomes a symbol for the health of the nation's future.

Sex, however, 'is a complex phenomenon about which everyone has different views' and articulating a 'correct' approach is necessarily complicated (Li Wenhai and Liu Shuyu 1992, 2). Rather than confront the complexities of creating a single affirmative definition, dominant discourses about adolescence have sought to identify the 'correct' by reference to the negative consequences of inappropriate behaviour. Whether in texts of the 1950s or the 1990s, a whole catalogue of ills, physical and psychological, accompany advice about adolescent hygiene. Failure to exercise sexual self-restraint visits a sliding scale of repercussions on the individual girl or boy concerned, depending on the specific nature of the indulgence. In girls, these range from simple exhaustion to infertility and moral degeneration, as a later section in this chapter shows. In boys, they are the masculine equivalent, ranging from fatigue to impotence and nervous debilitation. Failure to comply with the experts' guidelines for healthy living during adolescence thus threatens to destroy all possibilities for a healthy and happy future. Even worse, it may lead to 'sexually perverse (*biantai*) activities' such as homosexuality and criminal behaviour, including rape and other forms of sexual abuse (Zhao Rongfa, October 1989, 14).

From these perspectives, adolescence appears not first and foremost as a period of positive growth, when intellectual and creative vitality promise a healthy and happy future; rather it emerges as a state of susceptibility to degenerate behaviour and to potentially irreversible psychological and physical damage. The extension of the period between puberty and adulthood signified by the drop in the average age of puberty in the last two decades adds to the problematization of adolescence in temporal terms as well (Shen Wenjiang et al. 1987, 3–4).[3] The inescapable implication is that, left to their own devices, unaquainted with the appropriate responses to sexual matters advised by the experts, young people may be tempted to give in to powerful cravings and lustful instincts incompatible with socially acceptable conduct.

Despite the general applicability of much of the 1950s advice for adolescents, many of its assumptions and preoccupations constructed it as 'more of a problem' for girls than boys ('Liuda zenmo la?' 1954). That adolescence began about two years earlier in girls than in boys (Wang Wenbin, Zhao Zhiyi and Tan Mingxin 1956, 28) by definition prolonged the period of vulnerability to the vicissitudes of sexual development. Physiological changes in the female were seen to be 'much more complex' than in the male, owing to the particularities of the female reproductive system, and as a result made girls more vulnerable to health problems than boys at a similar stage of maturation ('Xiang xie shenmo banfa lai zengjia xuesheng de jiankang?' 1950). The gender asymmetry in the construction of adolescence as a potentially problematic period was also associated with the particular ways in which premature sexual involvement on the part of girls would affect their future lives, most notably through becoming pregnant (Wang Wenbin, Zhao Zhiyi and Tan Mingxin 1956, 64). More significantly, it was attributed to girls' extreme susceptibility to irrational swings in mood. Warnings to girls to avoid 'emotional fluctuations' (*qingxu bodong*) and 'psychological tension, excitement or depression' (*jingshen jinzhang, xingfen huo yiyu*) during menstruation attributed an emotionality and sensitivity to adolescent girls that were not seen to affect boys (Wang Wenbin, Zhao Zhiyi and Tan Mingxin 1956, 32–3). The naturalization of the association between girls and the private sphere of the emotions made their 'extremely unpredictable and irritable' (*feichang bu zhengchang he jizao*) swings an irreversible fact of life ('Liuda zenmo la?' 1954; Li Xiaofeng 1959). Advice to young girls to take rest and avoid strain during the menstrual period invoked a vulnerability and potential weakness that had no equivalence in references to the specifically masculine issues of adolescence. Furthermore, professional opinion was that teenage girls 'are interested in everything that corresponds with their sexual development', including their 'appearance' and 'boys' ('Liuda zenmo la?' 1954). In naturalizing the gendered ascription of interest in emotional and sexual matters as private, feminine concerns, in contrast with the masculine, public domain of professional, political and intellectual life, physiological development subjected girls to the rule of their reproductive organs.

Recent representations of adolescence indicate many continuities with the gender imbalance of the 1950s materials. A 1987 publication on *Female Physiology and Psychology*, for example, argued that 'due to the particular biological changes affecting girls during adolescence, specific psychological tendencies [also occur], in addition to the general features of young people's psychology' (Fang Fang 1987, 41). The specificities of the physiological and psychological changes occurring during adolescence make girls much more emotionally sensitive than boys, much more prone to fantasizing about the ideal boyfriend, and much more susceptible to rapid swings in mood (pp. 45–62). An expression of this is their tendency to blush more than boys in situations of embarrassment or anger (Lu Shumin and Tang Jianhua 1991, 41). Girls' greater sensitivity attracts them to 'matters to do with interpersonal relations', which 'if they live in a narrow context, and lack good taste may easily draw them into a whirlpool of trivia' (*Gei shaonü de xin* 1984, 93).

It would be mistaken, however, to read these examples as mere reiterations of their 1950s precedents. As indicated in Chapter 1, the gender ideology to which the 1950s representations corresponded emphasized a kind of masculinization of feminine conduct and appearance as part of the attempt to bring women into the public sphere. Since the beginning of the reform period, a commitment to recovering women's sexual and gender specificity has informed many of the texts about adolescence; characteristics such as feminine sensitivity and emotionality are now consistent with the gendered subject positions present in naturalized definitions of the 'modern woman' (*xiandai nüxing*) (Fang Fang 1987, 1). Indeed, as Tani Barlow has demonstrated in her analysis of the different linguistic and discursive categories, positioning women in China, the inscription of distinctive gender characteristics into particular words for 'woman', formed a powerful part of the 1980s contestation of the androgynous representations of the Maoist discourse. Use of the terms *nüxing* (literally, female sex) and *nüren* (female person, woman) signified the reclamation of an essentialist meaning of woman. They reinforced the idea of an essential sexual and gender difference as the condition of full gender equality, replacing the earlier officially dominated category, *funü* (woman) and the masculine standards associated with it (Barlow 1994, 346–52).

Another, just as persuasive, argument is that the continued construction of adolescence as a particularly, though not exclusively, female problem is the consequence of an uncritical and unreflexive conflation of sex with gender within a context of patriarchal modernity. The last chapter argued that dominant discourses since the early 1980s have with few exceptions maintained their attachment to the naturalization of sexual difference and gender hierarchy. Indeed, not so long ago experts devoted serious attention to explaining that hormonal changes are significant in understanding why female intelligence may seem inferior to that of boys (Shen Wenjiang et al. 1987, 48–9). The agents of these discourses – teachers, doctors, lawyers and parents – have no particular brief or stimulus to assert an interest in deconstructing gender hierarchies in terms that challenge their own authority. Legitimized by the biomedical wisdom of the medical establishment, the binary hierarchy ordering sexual and gender difference establishes a basis for an entire gender discourse which divides the feminine and the masculine into separate spheres of representation and practice. As the following chapters argue, the identification of the feminine with a cluster of characteristics, from the soft and gentle (*wenrou*), and the servicing and supportive, to the emotional and easily led astray, is consistent with a representation of the female as essentially situated in the sphere of private concerns and interests. The binary divide demarcating the boundaries between feminine and masculine is therefore even more clearly defined than in the 1950s, when, despite the natural status attributed to feminine emotionality and interest in 'affairs of the heart', the rhetoric of sexual equality suggested a commitment to 'liberating' it by fusing it with and drawing it into the public. In this sense, the gendered imbalance in the problematization of adolescence is another instance where, in Meng Yue's words, 'the female image is the allegorical place where the public fuses with the private' (Meng Yue, in Barlow 1993, 8). It is also the site for the state's appropriation of the private into the public.

## Menstruation and female weakness

Menstruation has long been constructed as a source of social and sexual danger in China. Anthropologists have described how menstrual blood was thought of as a polluting essence, capable of disrupting social relations governed by male authority and bringing disaster on entire families (Ahern 1976). Taboos against menstrual blood typically prevented menstruating women from coming into contact with men and gods, and barred women from a series of social activities, participation in which would have threatened collective livelihoods (pp. 269–75). In the sixteenth century, the famous medical theorist Li Shizhen (1518–93) wrote of the menstruating woman that 'her evil juices are full of stench and filth, hence the gentleman should keep his distance; as they are not clean, they will harm his male essence and invite disease' (Dikötter 1995, 41). As Charlotte Furth has also indicated, gynaecological texts of the Qing period related images of menstruation to notions of female depletion and disease (Furth 1987, 13–17). Medical treatises and self-help books of the early Republican period described menstruation as a pathological process characterized by instability, tiredness and irritability, emotionality, and proneness to mental disorders (Dikötter 1995, 41–2).

The explicit purpose behind the appearance of menstruation in public discourses in the 1950s was to contest its customary association with dirt and danger. Short articles written about menstrual hygiene under titles like 'When you menstruate for the first time' and 'Economical ways of folding menstrual paper' set out to convince their readership that menstruation was first and foremost a health issue and not the source of shame traditionally ascribed to it (Chen Benzhen 1958; Li Xiangjin 1958). Some of these texts detailed their advice with minute precision, from the foods a girl should eat during her menstrual period to the length of time and time of day that the cotton sanitary belt should be left out to dry in order to kill off the bacteria. Texts published during the early 1970s demonstrated similar detail (Xie Bozhang 1975, 77–84; Shanghai diyi yixue yuan fushu Zhongshan yiyuan fuchanke 1974, 1–6). Indeed, it is significant that menstruation was one of the few aspects of female sexuality permitted public discussion during the Cultural Revolution decade; the representation of menstruation as a matter of basic health and hygiene effectively dissociated the female body from erotic and sensual meaning (Xie Bozhang 1975; Hunan Changsha xian geming weiyuanhui weisheng ju 1975). Sex-education booklets published since the early 1980s contain lengthy and detailed sections on menstruation and menstrual problems. Women's magazines and books about women's health similarly devote considerable attention to, for example, how to identify the symptoms preceding the menarche, how to prevent colds during menstruation, and how to deal with menstrual problems (e.g., Lu Shumin and Tang Jianhua 1991, 16–25; Fu Caiying 1991, 6–11; Yi Ming 1995). The public monitoring of women's menstrual cycles as part of the official fertility-control programme further signifies a challenge to traditional menstrual avoidance taboos. Workplaces and neighbourhood committees have deliberately exposed menstruation to public scrutiny in lists noting the duration of each female employee's menstrual period, failure to menstruate, type of contraception used, etc.[4]

Narrative introductions to menstruation have consistently emphasized that it is a 'normal biological phenomenon' which first occurs when girls are thirteen to fourteen years of age (Wang, Zhao and Tan 1956, 27; Shanghai diyi yixue yuan fushu Zhongshan yiyuan fuchanke 1974, 1; Shen Wenjiang et al. 1987, 12). Acknowledging the anxiety that menstruation generates in young girls, texts explicitly set out to quell fears of 'dirt' and 'shame' by explaining its function in women's reproductive cycle (Lu Shumin and Tang Jianhua 1991, 16) and by classifying such fears under the category 'feudal superstition' (*fengjian mixin*) (Hunan Changsha xian geming weiyuanhui weisheng ju 1975, 24). Mothers are advised of their particular responsibility to give their daughters a timely and 'correct understanding' of menstruation before the menarche, and to reassure them that menstruation is neither alarming nor degrading (Chen Benzhen 1958; Su Liwen and Lu Qiyi 1991, 1–2; *Jiankang wenzhai bao*, 14 April 1993). The explicit message, repeated over four decades, is that basic knowledge about menstrual health is essential to young girls' welfare. However, in so far as every affirmation invariably invokes its opposite, the implication is that menstruation is widely seen as a negative feature of women's lives, responses to which are dominated by fear and ignorance.[5]

Chinese texts about menstruation fall into two broad categories. Introductions to physiology and sex-educational texts cover the functions, properties and symptoms associated with menstruation – its function in the reproductive system, the colour and amount of menstrual blood, its normal duration, and symptoms commonly associated with it (e.g., Wang Wenbin, Zhao Zhiyi and Tan Mingxin 1956; Shanghai diyi yixue yuan fushu Zhongshan yiyuan fuchanke 1974, 1–4; Gao Fang and Zeng Rong 1991, 170–2). Other texts are oriented more to advising readers about what to do to maintain basic standards of hygiene and health. These may include diagrams of how to make menstrual pads, details about how to wash them, and advice about washing the genitals during menstruation (Yan Renying 1958; Lu Shumin and Tang Jianhua 1991, 18–25; *Jiankang wenzhai bao*, 14 April 1993). They advise girls about what kinds of activities they may or may not participate in during their period. They also give detailed advice about how to avoid menstrual irregularities. Hence, girls are warned against swimming during menstruation, against doing 'heavy manual labour and strenuous exercise', and against 'activities like dancing and running', since excessive movement may provoke irregularities in the flow of menstrual blood (Chen Benzhen 1956; Fu Caiying 1991, 10; Su Liwen and Lu Qiyi 1991, 24).[6] Drinking cold water, washing in cold water, sitting on cold or damp ground, and eating uncooked or cold foods during menstruation are considered to cause a heavy blood flow and diarrhoea, owing to the sudden shock to the abdomen (Zhou Efen 1955; Wang Wenbin, Zhao Zhiyi and Tan Mingxin 1956, 32; Su Liwen and Lu Qiyi 1991, 2). The weakening of the body's immunities against sickness during menstruation is also considered to make young women vulnerable to colds and exhaustion (Yan Renying 1958). Anger and 'emotional fluctuations', so young women are advised, are to be avoided during the menstrual period to prevent irregularities (Wang Wenbin, Zhao Zhiyi and Tan Mingxin 1956, 32–3; Shen Wenjiang et al. 1987, 16).

Advice about menstruation over the past four decades also converges in its representation of the menstruating adolescent as emotionally unstable. Mood changes, emotional unpredictability and irritability are all considered common symptoms of the menstrual cycle; warnings against getting angry and against 'psychological tension, excitement or depression' constitute an important part of advice about how to prevent menstrual problems (Wang Wenbin, Zhao Zhiyi and Tan Mingxin 1956, 32–3; Lu Shumin and Tang Jianhua 1991, 18). The proper management of menstrual blood in the service of reproductive health appears hand in hand with control of the emotions; the protection of women's reproductive potential depends on the preservation of emotional stability as much as physical well-being. A regular cycle, free of emotional turbulence, is the condition of reproductive health and fertility.

Notwithstanding the repeated references to the biological normality of menstruation, the approach used in standard texts is predominantly negative. A list of problems invariably follows introductory comments, suggesting a construction of menstruation as a medical liability as much as an indispensable requirement for procreation. '[During menstruation] the body's defences against sickness are reduced, making it vulnerable to colds and other sicknesses . . . some of the defensive capacities of the reproductive organs are also weakened, making them vulnerable to bacteria which, if one is not careful about hygiene and protection, can easily provoke inflammation of the reproductive organs, causing menstrual sickness, and even impairing general health and fertility' (Shanghai diyi yixue yuan fushu Zhongshan yiyuan fuchanke 1974, 4).

In drawing attention to the potential fears, difficulties and sufferings accompanying menstruation, advice to girls about menstrual health and hygiene centres on the dangers that lack of attention might provoke. Warnings against a range of physical activities and emotional states unequivocally convey the message that menstruation puts women in the category of the weak and feeble. Thus, though medical opinion since the 1950s has consistently rejected the popular view of menstruation as a sickness, on the grounds that such a view is unscientific and superstitious, the above descriptions leave no doubt about its debilitating properties. The use of terms like *shangkou*, *chuangshang* (wound or damaged place in the body) and *chuangmian* (wound) to describe the effects on the uterus of the loss its 'inner membranes' (*neimo*) during the menstrual period reinforces the representation of menstruation as a pathological process of damage, pain and loss (Yan Renying 1958; Chen Benzhen 1958; Fu Caiying 1991, 10).

The emphasis of most of these texts continues to be a dominant characteristic of contemporary approaches to menstruation. However, it is not universal; a number of works published in recent years challenge the implicit representation of menstruation as a state of incapacitating vulnerability verging on sickness. For example, arguments that appropriate activities such as playing ping-pong or practising the *taijiquan* are beneficial because of the gentle massaging they give to the uterus have somewhat relaxed prohibitions on physical exercise (Yan Ruizhen and Li Peifang 1989, 44; Lu Shumin and Tang Jianhua 1991, 25–6). Warnings against absorbing or touching cold substances are also less stringent, with experts suggesting that, while 'of course it is best' to avoid cold water, 'there is no need for fear or anxiety' if at times it has to be used 'for things like washing clothes or washing the face' (Shen Wenjiang et al. 1987, 16). Another notable feature of some of the more recent texts is the disappearance of the assumption that menstruation necessarily causes alarm in adolescent girls; the contrastive and often negating particle 'but' is no longer a standard sequel to the assertion that menstruation is 'quite normal' (Zhang Mingyuan and Weng Zhonghua 1986, 87–8). Criticisms of the views that persist in associating menstruation with dirt, shame and weakness, however, are offered in the name of scientific opinion and not gender. Moreover, they are very partial, for, as I argue later on, medical opinion continues to advise sexual abstinence during the menstrual period. The idea that representations of menstruation may constitute – in China as elsewhere – a specific site of gender hierarchy is absent from contemporary discourses.

Much of the advice about menstruation clearly echoes traditional medical beliefs that the introduction of cold substances during negative or 'cold' bodily conditions has deleterious effects on the organism. Warnings to women against stimulants like spicy foods and alcohol during menstruation are set within a context of dietary rules for 'nourishing life' (*yangsheng*) which articulate the dangers to women of *yang* or hot foods during *yin* moments of the cycle. Similarly, warnings against excessive physical exertion repeated traditional medical assumptions about the effect of physical stress on a weak organism. The reiteration of traditional advice, however, also coincided with the explicit health-giving objectives of such texts. In socio-economic conditions where basic knowledge about hygiene was, and often is, minimal, where the benefits of modern technology in drainage and water systems had not yet been felt, and where water was frequently contaminated, advice to young girls against, for example, sitting on cold and wet ground was sound. By the same token, 'scientific' advice to girls against over-exertion in manual labour offered momentary rest for girls otherwise constantly burdened with physical chores. Interpreted in this light, apparently constrictive and ideologically conservative advice acquires other meanings associated less with the pathologization of women subjected to the rule of their reproductive functions than with the protection of their specific interests.

Though of seemingly minor importance alongside the amount and detail of the discussion about menstruation, breast development – and breast-binding in particular – was a not infrequent theme of expert advice. Chinese women in the 1950s inherited an understanding of female beauty that emphasized slenderness and sleek grace above all else. As Esther Cheo Ying testified in her *Black Country Girl in Red China*, Chinese women whose breasts were even slightly prominent were commonly regarded as immoral, except when they were breast-feeding, and they often went to great lengths to appear flat-chested by binding themselves with strong cotton cloth (Cheo Ying 1980, 33). An article warning against the damage caused by breast-binding criticized the desire to appear slender and 'fine' (*xian*) as a reflection of the outdated view of the 'former exploiting class' that 'women were the accessory (*fushupin*) of men' (Huang Shuze 1953). Large breasts were not, as some people thought, a sign of 'immoral behaviour' (*zuofeng bu zhengpai*), and medical opinion warned that breast-binding was very damaging to normal breast development (Xu Linyue 1958). Mothers' timely advice was again recommended to encourage young girls to realize that breast development was neither shameful nor worrying (Xu Linyue 1958). Medical authority advised that excessive or insufficient breast development were both minor occurrences, so girls should not feel any particular anxiety about breast size (Wang Wenbin, Zhao Zhiyi and Tan Mingxin 1956, 33).

By contrast with the almost androgynous representations of the 1950s and 1960s, cleavages, prominent breasts and voluptuous curves have all become quite standard features of visual images of women in the last decade or so. While by no means as prevalent as in equivalent Western publications, the amply bosomed Chinese woman no longer appears as a figure of disdain, and women's magazines not infrequently carry articles about the 'protection of the breasts' – the 'symbol of femininity' (*nüxing de xiangzheng*) (Wang Yang and Xu Xiaolin 1991, 35, 76–7). However, breast size still appears to be a problem. Some texts suggest that young girls often worry that small breasts will cause complications in breast-feeding (Lu Shumin and Tang Jianhua 1991, 8–9). Others indicate that young girls are still ashamed about having what they consider to be large breasts (Su Liwen and Lu Qiyi 1991, 9–10). Moreover, standard publications about women's health contain warnings against the ill effects of breast-binding on the heart, the lungs and future breast-feeding, suggesting that traditional assumptions about the physical form of feminine beauty are far from having been eradicated (Lu Shumin and Tang Jianhua 1991, 8–9; Su Liwen and Lu Qiyi 1991, 9–10; Wu Zhangming, Zhu Xiaolan and Lang Ying 1990, 10).

## 'Evil habits' and the dangers of excess

Professional advice to young girls about how to prevent menstrual disorders signified the construction of women both as the 'weak sex' and as individuals responsible for self-regulation in the interests of reproductive health. The rational capacity to exercise self-restraint and self-discipline was also attributed to young men, with reference to the 'evil habit' (*e xi*) of masturbation. Advice to both the young woman and the young man centred on monitoring of the self. But if, in the female, self-regulation was associated with the nation through the protection of reproductive health, then, in the male, it was linked to notions of strength, intelligence and creativity as the foundation of social well-being.

The major problems of male adolescence as they have appeared in youth journals and papers, educational publications and popular advice columns since the 1950s have focused on the bodily and psychological effects of the loss of semen. Judging from the frequency of questions like 'Are emissions during a dream (*meng yi*) a sickness?' (Shen Wenjiang et al. 1987, 21–2), and 'How should we treat "losing essence" (*yi jing*)?' (Yan Ruizhen and Li Peifang 1989, 23–5) in advice books and informational pamphlets, many young men fear that the loss of semen depletes their 'vital energy' (*yuanqi*) and harms sexual development. Seminal emissions, an early text suggested, should be seen as the 'male equivalent of menstruation' – a natural phenomenon, 'which may result in feelings of tiredness, but [which] is totally normal and harmless' (Huang Shuze 1955). Wang Wenbin, Zhao Zhiyi and Tan Mingxin described involuntary seminal emissions as a 'reflex' response (*fanshexing*) to the 'accumulation of sperm in the seminal vesicles' which, 'after a long period, and stimulated by the external environment, particularly by sexual excitement and physical stimulation', naturally finds an outlet in ejaculation (1956, 34). More recent texts reinforce the message that seminal emissions are quite normal and to be expected; only if they become a frequent occurrence should medical advice be sought (Shen Wenjiang et al. 1987, 20).

Ejaculation induced by masturbation is treated with much greater gravity. As Frank Dikötter pointed out in his survey of approaches to masturbation in the biomedical literature of the Republican period, 'the medical distinction between "involuntary depletions" and "wilful masturbation" underlined the importance of self-regulation' (Dikötter 1995, 167). Sex-education publications devote entire sections to discussing the deleterious effects of habitual masturbation. Some texts simply condemn the 'evil practice' (*e xi*) outright as a source of physical harm and moral degeneration. Others adopt a more tolerant approach in acknowledging that it is a common experience among adolescent boys; more and more comments further recognize that it is also a female practice. Whatever the particular emphasis, masturbation emerges as one of the key concerns of adolescence, for, 'as every one knows, normal sexual activity refers to a man and a woman making love' (Su Fu and Huang Yuxian 1992, 38).

Experts since the 1950s have with few exceptions shared the view that, practised in moderation, masturbation has no harmful side effects. Outright condemnation along the lines that 'if it does not produce excessive excitement of the sexual nerves then it leads to neurasthenia (*shenjing shuairuo*)' (Xie Bozhang 1975, 94–5) has been much less common than the more tolerant approach that distinguished between habitual and occasional practice (Wang Wenbin, Zhao Zhiyi and Tan Mingxin 1956, 55). However, as in representations of menstruation, the reader is left in little doubt about the dominant opinion. Approaches which suggest that masturbation may be a source of comfort or 'consolation' (*ziwei*) and a 'buffer against sexual starvation for young criminals' do not fail to point out that, 'practised in excess, masturbation is harmful' (Chen Bin 1995). Lists of the harmful consequences of habitual masturbation repeatedly warn readers against the 'unpleasant consequences' of indulging 'bad habits' (*e xi*) (Shen Wenjiang et al. 1987, 22). A case history cited by Wang, Zhao and Tan in 1956 suggested that practising masturbation to satisfy sexual need during courtship could have disastrous effects; a young man could feel such extreme psychological pressure that he would find himself unable to get an erection and suffering from neurasthenia (*shenjing shuairuo*) (Wang Wengin, Zhao Zhiyi and Tan Mingxin 1956, 42). 'Confusion, tension and anxiety, self-recrimination and remorse, as well as premature ejaculation', were all the inevitable consequences (Wang Wenbin, Zhao Zhiyi and Tan Mingxin 1956, 35–6; Huang Shuze 1955). Medical opinion in the 1980s shared many of these views, summed up under the category of 'the masturbation terror' (*shouyin kongbu lun*) in Liu Dalin's nationwide survey (Yuan Fangfu 1985, 121, quoted in Geng Wenxiu 1991, 89; Liu Dalin 1992b, 94). 'Excessive masturbation makes people tense and anxious'; it may lead to 'impotence after marriage' and 'wastes the body's energy' (Yan Ruizhen and Li Peifang 1989, 26). In 'keeping the nerves in a state of over-excitement and tension', masturbation provokes 'headaches, insomnia, amnesia and lethargy' as well as 'involuntary and premature ejaculation and irregular menstruation' (Fu Caiying 1991, 22). Other commonly noted symptoms are excessive dreaming, dizziness, lack of concentration and breathlessness (*Xinhun weisheng bi du* editorial group 1984, 80). In much the same way as the earlier discourse, the dominant representation of masturbation as a shameful practice depends on the discursive deployment of negative sanctions to urge young men to exercise self-control. As an expression of an uncontrollable physiological urge which has no constructive purpose, masturbation remains the harbinger of a series of hidden effects that, left unchecked, will manifest themselves later on in adulthood. The findings of a survey among students in higher education, moreover, revealed that these opinions are not restricted to the experts alone. 31.3 per cent of the men surveyed and 41.8 per cent of the women thought that masturbation was 'degenerate, immoral and harmful to the body' (Geng Wenxiu 1991, 89–90). According to the same survey, more than 11 per cent of the men and 3.4 per cent of the women said that they felt severe psychological pressure (*jingshen yali*) as a result of their inability to stop the practice. And, according to Geng Wenxiu, such shame was associated with masturbation that more people were likely to admit to having had pre-marital sex than to having practised masturbation (p. 90).

Suggestions that early marriage could 'cure' involuntary emissions and masturbation were not considered an adequate response to the problem; 'education in hygiene' (*weisheng jiaoyu*) and 'medical measures' (*yiliao cuoshi*), including circumcision if necessary, were the appropriate methods to help young men overcome masturbation (Wang Wenbin, Zhao Zhiyi and Tan Mingxin 1956, 37).[7] 'Rest and psychological treatment could [also] be complemented by shortwave diathermatic methods, hydrotherapy and [the use of] natural springs' (p. 54). In tones reminiscent of those used by Baden-Powell to warn against 'evils of incontinence' and 'beastliness', young men have repeatedly been told to do physical exercise as soon as they get up in the morning, to lead a regulated life, to sleep and rise early, to avoid stimulants such as cigarettes, coffee and alcohol, to avoid wearing tight trousers, and to refrain from reading romantic literature (Baden-Powell 1954, 135; Wang Wenbin, Zhao Zhiyi and Tan Mingxin 1956, 36–7; Shen Wenjiang et al. 1987, 23). The most effective approach, however, is preventive action. As one text advised, 'when you realize that you want to masturbate, you should make a change of scene right away and find someone to talk to, or immerse yourself in the work or study that you most enjoy' (Yan Ruizhen and Li Peifang 1989, 26).

According to traditional medical and sexological theories in China, the loss of semen, particularly when dissociated from the possibility of conception, was seen to deplete the 'source not only of a man's health but of his very life' (Van Gulik 1974, 47). Masturbation was a particularly destructive waste of energy since it was interpreted as the loss of vital essence without any acquisition of the equivalent amount of *yin* essence from a woman and without any compensation deriving from the 'obtaining of children perfect in body and mind' (Van Gulik 1974, 47). While contemporary commentators declare their distance from such traditional approaches, notions concerning the debilitating effects of the 'excessive loss of semen' continue to inform the 'scientific' views of modern experts. Even if interest in sexual matters is considered a natural expression of a certain stage of biological development, self-restraint is indispensable to boys' healthy physical and moral development.

It would be mistaken, however, to read a simple repetition of old biases into current discussions about masturbation. There is considerable evidence that professional and popular attitudes towards masturbation are changing, slow though the change may be (Liu Dalin

1992b, 94–5). Masturbation is no longer identified solely as an adolescent aberration, a hidden vice of young boys unable to find any other outlet to their sexual energies. Child masturbation is occasionally acknowledged, and not always in oblique references to Western theories about infantile sexuality (Fu Caiying 1991, 21–2). Under the influence of liberal sexological theorists like Liu Dalin and Pan Suiming, greater emphasis is now attached to its 'normal' and 'harmless' aspects. And suggestions that masturbation may be an aid to promoting sexual enjoyment between two people signify an explicit challenge to former views (Wang Peng 1993, 135).

One particularly evident area of changing attitudes is in the acknowledgement of female masturbation, an aspect of female sexuality that was barely mentioned in the public discourses of earlier decades except in contexts dominated by concerns about female purity and reproductive health (Li Yang 1956). In identifying masturbation as a female practice, some commentators seem merely to shift the gender target of their condemnation. Indeed, some writers view it as a far worse aberration in women than in men: 'masturbation is the satisfaction of sexual desire through improper methods. There are some women who masturbate, although not too many, but female masturbation is far worse (*huai de duo*) than in men [because it] enlarges the clitoris and the labia and impairs sexual function after marriage and even produces frigidity' (Wu Zhangming, Zhu Xiaolan and Lang Ying 1990, 27).[8] A slightly less drastic argument is that habitual practice in women brings with it a series of effects equivalent to those in the male (Lu Shumin and Tang Jianhua 1991, 30). More liberal approaches, however, acknowledge that many women masturbate without causing any deleterious side effects; in the words of two commentators, 'masturbation is absolutely not the base expression of moral degeneracy, but is a particular manifestation of girls' sexual and psychological maturation and the growth of their sexual awareness' (Lu Shumin and Tang Jianhua 1991, 30). Analyses of changing sexual attitudes and practices make a deliberate point of referring to Western arguments about female masturbation as an aid to sexual intercourse with a partner (Li Wenhai and Liu Shuyu 1992, 32). Contemporary sex education texts also commonly recognize masturbation as a general practice, even though many still insist on its dominant association with male adolescents (Yan Ruizhen and Li Peifang 1989, 25).

However, as a number of Chinese commentators have implied, current discourse about masturbation continues to be dominated by a moralistic antipathy to a practice widely treated as a reprehensible diversion of energies away from the appropriate activities of adolescence (Liu Dalin 1992b, 95). The condemnatory tone of references to masturbation reveals a distaste that cannot be explained by anxieties about the clinical effects alone. In this light, masturbation emerges as a practice of the intemperate and ideologically unsound, the consequence of failing to adopt the 'correct' attitude to sex and love (Yu Jiu 1954), which visits a series of harmful effects on the male body and, by extension, on the marital relationship. As the expression of an uncontrollable physiological urge and a lustful mind, masturbation is replete with hidden dangers waiting to manifest themselves later on in adulthood. In the female, in causing the growth of the clitoris, it recalls the dangers, noted in 1916, of a kind of 'physical degeneration which brought the female closer to the hermaphrodite, a monstrous form of masculinization which disturbed gender boundaries' (Dikötter 1995, 177).[9] The sanctions and advice of the medical experts to exercise self-restraint thus support a strong moral message; masturbation emerges as a specific site where medical advice legitimizes standards of sexual morality.

## The moral and social supervision of adolescence

The need for self-restraint as a prophylactic remedy for harmful sexual practices during adolescence is represented as an ideological and moral responsibility as well as a precaution against disease and degeneration. Counsel to young people has consistently asserted that an 'exaggerated interest' in affective and sexual matters is wrong because it detracts attention from educational and social matters, or, as it was put in the 1950s, from the 'construction of socialism' (Chen Dong 1954). Any indication of wanting to extend the 'natural' sexual interest of adolescence into active desire for the opposite sex is unacceptable. Adolescents are seen as totally unprepared for emotional and sexual involvement, and even though they are understandably moved by the 'emotion of sexual love' (xing'ai de ganqing), their lack of experience and wisdom makes it totally inappropriate for them to engage in sexual activity. Youthful passions put young people in a vulnerable position, and, if not guided by the benevolent authority of their elders, they might well make choices they later regret. Even Ding Ling – whose tone in discussing such issues was considerably more tolerant than most – suggested that it was not just getting involved in love affairs, but 'thinking about' love, which was the main obstacle to concentrating on studies (Ding Ling 1950). In all, for both girls and boys, self-vigilance in all moral, social and bodily matters emerges as the means of ensuring that the path of youth development conforms to the terms of the dominant discourse. By the same token, disciplining the self becomes the condition of national vitality and strength.

The assumption that school years should be devoted to studies and personal development corresponds with an affirmative construction of adolescence. 'Adolescence is the golden period of life which young people should use to develop their bodies and their knowledge' (Wu Zhangming, Zhu Xiaolan and Lang Ying 1990, 73). The simultaneous characterization of the golden period as a 'time of many worries' (*duoshi de shiqi*) and when 'troublesome problems often occur' underlines the importance of using these years for personal development rather than sexual involvement (Zhang Mingyuan and Weng Zhonghua 1986, 80). In the 1950s, a number of factors gave this construction of adolescence special importance for girls. Comments to the effect that 'interest in sex and marriage is particularly widespread among schoolgirls' corresponded with girls' self-identification principally as wives and mothers, and explained the tendency of girls to become sexually involved considerably younger than boys (Xu Hua 1956). Pressure from older men anxious to find young wives without much education also signified the need for a vigilance on the part of young girls that their tender years had not prepared them for (Xu Hua 1956). The unworldly innocence of young girls made them particularly vulnerable to the unscrupulous behaviour of older men looking for sexual amusement (Zhou Xixian 1953; Yan Ruizhen and Li Peifang 1989, 93). For young women, advice against sexual involvement was not constructed principally as a repressive measure against certain attitudes and practices, except in so far as these affected women's freedom of choice. On the contrary, in the terms of the dominant discourse, it was given the progressive meaning of contributing towards women's rights and sexual equality, in a social and cultural context that was still dominated by patriarchal assumptions about women's primary duties in life.

Recent discussions about 'early love' (*zao lian*) share many of these views about the 'correct' approach to sexual and emotional involvement during adolescence. The evident focus on girls in relevant texts is consistent with the gendered problematization of adolescence. 'Early love' – an implicitly pejorative term that is specific to the post-Mao period – refers to the increasing tendency among adolescents to become prematurely sexually experienced. 'Surveys show that "early love" is currently very common in middle schools and the age of sexual involvement is decreasing' (Yan Ruizhen and Li Peifang 1989, 97). Authorial opinion generally coincides in constructing 'early love' as the immature, indulgent and invariably damaging expression of sexual desire at a time when biological growth has outstripped psychological and emotional development. 'External factors' such as 'television, films and many literary works' have their part to play in 'endlessly portraying love stories about young men and women'. The combined effect is often to exert pressure on young people to go along with 'love' because it is the fashion, or because they are afraid to say no (Yan Ruizhen and Li Peifang 1989, 100). Whatever the analysis of the cause, however, commentators agree that 'early love' is mistaken. As one text put it, 'getting prematurely involved in love affairs inevitably diminishes one's energy and badly affects one's study, and since adolescents lack experience and do not have an overall understanding of things, the consequences may be very unfortunate' (Wu Zhangming, Zhu Xiaolan and Lang Ying 1990, 73).

As in the earlier discourse, the gender specificity of many of the references to 'early love' corresponds with the aim to minimize girls' vulnerability to sexual exploitation by encouraging them to take their studies seriously. At a time when girls all over China are potentially threatened by traffickers whose profit depends on the sale of women and children, and when girls' attendance at school is in many regions seriously threatened by the interests of the patriarchal order of rural communities, cautionary notes against 'early love', often delivered in tragic tales of woe, warn of the possible consequences of premature sexual involvement.[10] Frequent stories tell of girls facing life as uneducated single mothers after being impregnated by boyfriends who then abandon them; readers' letters mention the suicidal thoughts of teenage girls who let their passions overcome them. A typical example was written by a seventeen-year-old girl who fell into the depths of despair because the thirty-year-old trainer of her basket-ball team did not reciprocate her love (Jun Qiu 1986). Another, more extreme, example was of an eighteen-year-old girl who died when her recently jilted boyfriend stabbed her fifteen times. This 'bloody lesson' appeared in a discussion about the importance of students adopting a 'stable view of life' to avoid lifelong suffering (Li Ping, Ou Xiaowei, Hou Hong and Dai Xiaojing 1985, 20).

Other readings of the gender distinctions in the problematization of adolescence suggest the ascription of specific attributes to female gender and sexuality that naturalize girls' tendency to become prematurely involved. There seems to be a general consensus that adolescent girls are by nature more easily drawn to affective and sexual involvement than boys of a similar age. Menstruation, and the menarche in particular, emerge as the key physiological phenomena that explain this. The universal desire to be loved (*bei ai*) becomes more pronounced in girls after the menarche, the 'first sign of maturity' (*chengren gan*), and is often tinged with sexual desire (Fang Fang

1987, 56–8). Although adolescence may be a time when girls develop a strong antipathy to boys, their tendency to 'hero worship' (*yingxiong chongbai*) and 'calf love' (*tongnianshi de lian'ai*) makes them particularly vulnerable to unscrupulous men (p. 61). Moreover, the desire to assert their independence from parents and teachers leads many young girls into sexual relationships that may end in personal tragedy, even suicide (Zhang Mingyuan and Weng Zhonghua 1986, 84). Other representations that draw on similar assumptions about the sexuality of adolescent girls go even further in suggesting that, when uncontrolled, adolescent female sexuality is a potential threat to marital, familial and social welfare. Girls' 'inability to exercise self-restraint', for example, is used to explain their loss of virginity and, by extension, a whole series of ills including 'chronic engorgement of the pelvis and heavy and prolonged menstruation which creates impediments to sexual function after marriage, such as frigidity' (Wu Zhangming, Zhu Xiaolan and Lang Ying 1990, 73). Two commentators further argued that, if not properly supervised by teachers and parents, young girls' natural inclinations could even lead them down the slippery slope to crime.

> Why does particular attention need to be given to girls' psychological hygiene? Because their psychological level and cognitive experience are unable to keep up with the rapid biological changes [of adolescence], a series of psychological conflicts may develop. For example, young girls may feel uneasy, confused or even frightened about their sexual development, and may become very sensitive as a result of their sexual psychology, pay excessive attention to the other sex and be obsessively interested in information about sex. All this may reduce girls' concentration on their studies, and lower their academic achievements, and . . . some girls even engage in improper sexual relations. Many research reports show that in the developmental process of juvenile female offenders, the loss of virginity and indulgence in improper sexual activities is the key to explaining their degeneration. (Yan Ruizhen and Li Peifang 1989, 68)

A recent article in *Nüxing yanjiu* (Women's research), a leading women's studies journal in China, pointed out that one of the difficulties in giving appropriate advice to young people about how to approach the problem of 'early love' is that parents, teachers and other authority figures invariably base their judgements on their own experience, without taking the feelings of the children into consideration (Wu Di 1993). Diaries and surveys of teenagers in middle schools make it clear that parents' concerns about 'early love' may be totally exaggerated. They may be about little more than their daughter walking home together with a boy or sharing food with him at lunchtime. The experience of 'talking about love' (*tan lian'ai*) enjoyed by high school students may be no different from ordinary friendships with the opposite sex in social contexts still heavily influenced by customary patriarchal requirements of sexual segregation.

While these criticisms may be very appropriate, the exaggerated responses of parents and teachers to indications of adolescents' 'improper' interests are consistent with the moral and sexual standards of the dominant discourse. The evident objective of many of the cautionary tales and notes of warning by the experts is to prevent adolescents, particularly girls, from engaging in any relationship that might pressurize, encourage or in any way lead to 'improper' sexual activity. Categorizing a young girl's love for an older man as a 'kind of muddled emotion' typical of the turbulence experienced by adolescent girls (Chen Yan 1986) is consistent with the avowed aim of protecting young girls from abuse by older men. However, it is also consistent with a view of sexual activity during adolescence as fundamentally illicit. In contrast with the pre-marital group examined in the following chapter – a group that is culturally and discursively constructed as legitimately preparing for eventual marriage – adolescents are enjoined to exercise self-discipline and control, to prevent chaotic sexual desires from endangering their own and society's health. The endless numbers of stories about the miserable fate awaiting young girls who disregard this advice and the educational and medical warnings against sexual excess can all be seen as informal sanctions imposed to reinforce the standards of the dominant discourse.

The party-state's supervision of youth welfare and education after 1949 inevitably brought issues of adolescent development into the orbit of its concerns, and in the process subjected young people to a series of medical, pedagogical and political controls for the sake of the country's future. Adolescence necessarily became an official concern because, newly defined by the communist authorities, it introduced a range of subject positions and practices into social discourse that needed to be channelled into the service of the new social order. The identification of adolescence as a distinct stage of life with specific sexual, moral and social characteristics facilitated the intervention of the agents of the state – doctors, teachers, other professionals and official cadres – in matters of young people's development. Public discourse about adolescence therefore signified more than recognition of an important aspect of social and cultural life; it also marked the identification of matters that, left uncontrolled, potentially threatened the new government's programme of social transformation. Representation of adolescence as a potentially problematic issue was coterminous with state mediation to harness it in the cause of socialist construction.

The redefinition of the relationship between public and private spheres permitted the party-state's intervention in aspects of personal experience hitherto considered too shameful to bring into the open. Indeed, it could be argued that tactical considerations about how to gain access to intimate aspects of individual lives informed official insistence on the public appropriation of the private, or, as Meng Yue suggested, the infiltration by the state's 'totalitarian incursions' of the 'field of the private conscious and unconscious' (Barlow 1993, 8). Located within an ideology of sexual equality, this reassessment of the public–private relationship had a potentially progressive significance for women. By the removal of issues of female development from the hidden controls of the patriarchal family, girls, it was hoped, would begin to identify with possibilities that belonged to the new era of public opportunity. Assimilating the private into the public also corresponded with an ideological position which rejected the conventional relegation of women to purely domestic and marital preoccupations. Suggesting that opportunities for educational and professional development would be available to girls as long as they rejected the path laid out by traditional gender expectations backed up official encouragement to girls to adopt a serious attitude to their studies. In this sense, they were offered an incentive to question traditional self-identities and subject positions; urging girls to restrain sexual interest during adolescence signified a critique of conventional sexual practice.

Since the 1980s the boundaries between public and private have again been redrawn, relocating issues of sexuality within the sphere of private and personal concerns. Public discussion about matters of personal development, whether this refers to adolescent anxieties about dating or about breast size, legitimates private interest in ways that were marginalized by the collective emphasis of the 1950s rhetoric. This, however, has not fundamentally interfered with the state's appropriation of adolescent sexuality as a site of supervision and control. Alongside continued references to the desirability of using these 'golden years' for educational and personal development are other concerns about familial and social stability that, in the context of the commercial opportunities and political uncertainties of the last decade, have acquired an even greater intensity. Alarmist references to the sexual permissiveness of today's youth – the evils of being exposed to Western ideas of sexual liberation – and its effects on the juvenile crime rate suggest that control of a potentially rebellious age group is just as, if not more, important to the authorities than promoting adolescents' educational achievements. Thus while the specific form and objective of the state's intervention in adolescents' lives has altered along with the changing socio-economic context, the fact of its pervasive influence in shaping the discourses constructing adolescents has not.

The model of health popularized in advice to adolescents is bounded by the notion that self-restraint is vital to the conservation of energies for adult married life. The principal issues of concern – masturbation, seminal emissions and self-control of natural urges in the male, menstruation and reproductive hygiene in the female – correspond to the characteristics of sexual difference examined in the last chapter. However, the particular significance accorded young girls in discussions about adolescent sexuality – whether in advice about reproductive hygiene or in warnings against premature sexual involvement – constructs the female as the key marker of general standards of sexual conduct. As we have seen, self-supervision in matters of health and hygiene is required of girls principally to protect their reproductive capacity, to ensure successful fulfilment of their responsibilities to society. The discursive contexts within which girls are enjoined to patrol their own sexual conduct suggest that the avoidance of premature sexual and emotional involvement is important for social stability – to guard against crime and disorder – as much as for self-advancement. As following chapters argue, the appropriation of the female as signifier of social and familial order is a dominant theme in representations of female sexuality.

# 4 Pre-Marital Preoccupations

The prevalence of romantic and erotic images in the Chinese media identifies one of the most evident changes in recent discourses of love and sexuality. Passion and romantic intimacy are widely represented as key features distinguishing the pre-marital experience from married love. Romantic stories published in seemingly limitless quantities hold out to young people the promise of sexual gratification as one of the great bonuses of the reform programme. Advertising and fashion foreground young women's beauty and sexual desirability as dominant characteristics of women's gender identity. Alongside such images, the sexual conduct of young couples has also come under intense scrutiny. Television chat shows, agony aunts' advice columns, family planning agencies and moralizing officials all devote considerable attention to debating the appropriate standards of sexual behaviour young unmarried couples should respect. In the process, a dual message has emerged, presenting romantic passion as a main signifier of pre-marital aspirations and, at the same time, restricting the boundaries of romantic experimentation to conform to standards established by professional and political interests. This message has particularly targeted young women's sexual behaviour, reinforcing the representation of the female as the key to upholding the moral and social terms of the dominant discourse.

Much of the commercial publicity given to sex and romance is deliberately encouraged by official agencies as a means of making money. Official publishing houses commonly print popular love stories or use soft-focus photographs of lovely young women to generate the funds to finance other, less popular publications.[1] Pictures of beautiful and sexy women, often the young white women of Western fashion magazines, are *de rigueur* on the front covers of different kinds of publications. The young, sexy female body has become the standard property of picture postcards and novels, popular magazines and advertising. Ostensibly responding to consumer demand, official sponsorship of sometimes quite salacious material is thus responsible for the transmission of gendered and sexual messages that seem to contradict those explicitly upheld in official discourse.

The narrative representations of young unmarried people reveal a series of tensions with these visual images. While many of the latter suggest a sexual permissiveness unrestrained by the realities of social pressure, the accompanying texts often indicate constraints and prohibitions that give very different meanings to representations of sexuality. Texts caution young people against the dangers of pre-marital sex alongside images that exude sexual desirability. Photographs of beautiful bodies and fashion models are followed by lengthy discussions about the importance of 'inner beauty' in selecting a partner. The disjunctures created by competing representations and the contrasts between these and the uniform representations of the 1950s and 1960s suggest that the category 'woman' is no longer associated with a unitary set of gender and sexual attributes.

In contrast with the prohibitions on amorous liaisons during adolescence, discussion targeted at the pre-marital group assumes that amorous interest in the other sex is legitimate. The principal subject of concern is no longer the single person, and control of the self, but the self in relation to the other. Exhortations to exercise restraint accordingly address the mode of response to the other rather than the needs of bodily health and strength. Despite the implications of the visual images noted above, active sexual involvement before marriage is still widely treated as a mark of immorality and irresponsibility, as it was in the 1950s. Texts written for this group are designed to provide the ideological, moral and social tools necessary to select a partner and construct a stable basis for marriage. Political and professional opinion about pre-marital conduct seeks to persuade its audience of the virtues of nurturing a moral outlook consistent with market socialism.

## Courtship and 'dating': the historical and social context

The Marriage Law established the main context for public references to pre-marital sexual relations in the 1950s. Monogamous marriage, conceived as an exclusive and life-long partnership based on the principle of free choice of spouse, provided the standard according to which pre-marital practices and courtship were judged. The official discourse upheld courtship as an indispensable aspect of the free-choice model of marriage. Often known as 'making friends' (*jiao pengyou*), it was explained as the appropriate way for young people to develop the mutual understanding and affection considered necessary to realize the new model of conjugal marriage. As Deng Yingchao, the Chairwoman of the All China Women's Federation, put it in 1942, 'Permitting free social contact between young men and women and giving young people the opportunity to get to know and make friends with the other sex is the necessary premise for making love and marriage satisfactory' (Deng Yingchao 1985, 3). Deng Yingchao's comment indicated that a key intention in representing courtship as the dominant pre-marital ritual was to provide young people with the opportunity to base their decisions about selection of marriage partner on affection and love. Courtship was publicized as a means of preparing young people for marriage by enabling them to discover the meaning of love via a process of mutual acquaintance, friendship and trust.

The repeated emphasis in the 1950s on the need to protect young people's rights freely to get to know potential marriage partners corresponded to China's specific history of marriage procedures. As an aspect of the system of arranged marriages, traditional imperatives governing sexual, and particularly female, propriety made sexual segregation one of the most striking features of social life before 1949 (Croll 1978, 15–18). Public proximity between an unmarried woman and a man was widely regarded as immoral, and girls were thought of as wanton and shameless if seen talking to boys (Ayscough 1937, 39; Chen 1973, 291). Courtship was virtually an unknown practice among the rural population, and, as with free choice of marriage partner after the May Fourth movement, it was practised only by women and men from the educated families of the cities. Before 1949, it was available as an individual rather than a social and institutional alternative to traditional procedures (Croll 1981, 59).[2]

Customary requirements of sexual segregation continued to impede both the popularization of courtship as a pre-marital practice and the successful implementation of the free-choice principle of marriage throughout the 1950s. The popular notion that freedom of marriage was little more than an invitation to promiscuity effectively prevented young women and men from engaging in ordinary day-to-day social contact. Sexual segregation was thought to be a major source of the ignorance and fear with which many young people approached marriage.[3] It was also widely considered responsible for the rash decisions about marriage that young people often made; such was the extent of social pressure against public contact between men and women that any public sign of mutual interest was often understood as a commitment to marry (Ren Kunru 1951).

Other related factors also worked against the extension of courtship as a pre-marital practice consistent with the free-choice model of marriage. As Croll has pointed out, part of the difficulty lay in its definition (1981, 54). The distinction between friendship and courtship was often difficult to grasp given that both were ideally based on mutual interests and understanding in work and study. A typical case published to initiate a debate in *Zhongguo qingnian* about attitudes towards friendship and love described a young woman who was vilified for rejecting the advances of a team leader and then falling in love with someone else (Su Yuan 1956). Despite the woman's reluctance to respond to the man's interest, the fact of her public contact with him made her as liable as him to social disapproval, and to imputations of 'loose' behaviour. Courtship was also seen more as a 'form of anticipatory socialization for marriage' than as recreation or experimentation. Even though biographical examples showed that a limited degree of experimentation was possible as long as it did not transgress normative boundaries of morality ('Zunzhong aiqing shenghuo zhong de ziyuan yuanze' 1956), the idea that 'love is a prelude to marriage' prohibited the possibility of seeing courtship as a preliminary to selection of a partner.

Another complication arose from the distance of the urban-based official discourse from rural practice. As an exhortatory – even idealized – representation of pre-marital gender relations, the identification of 'making friends' as a desirable mode of 'normal' (*zhengchang*) social contact between young women and men had little to do with standard practices in the countryside. It was only in the urban areas, where young people typically took more initiative in marriage negotiations, and where residential and employment structures offered real possibilities of getting to know potential partners, that courtship found a receptive audience. Indeed, the CCP's commitment to institutionalizing courtship contrasted sharply with the hostility shown it by the rural population. Parents and cadres were told that it was 'wrong' (*bu dui*) to forbid ordinary, healthy contact between the sexes on the grounds that it would lead to improper behaviour (Yu Jiu 1954). Any ridicule or rumour-mongering about a couple seen 'talking together or going for a stroll' was 'liable to accomplish nothing and spoil everything'! (*cheng shi bu zu, bai shi you yu*) (Deng Yingchao 1985, 3).

Local cadres, caught between the conflicting pressures of local custom and official policy, often bowed to the former in their mediations. As those considered responsible for upholding the law at the village level, they were frequently targeted for harsh criticism for effectively maintaining customary rules of sexual segregation, and for wrongly forcing young people to 'confess the crime' (*tanbai*) of illicit activities, frequently at tragic cost to both women and men.[4]

However, the most important factor explaining the barriers to popularizing courtship was the retention of controls over the procedures of marriage by the older generation in rural areas where household and family structures encouraged the economic interdependence of its members (Croll 1981, 127). The collective structures of economic organization under the commune system tended to prioritize the economic interests of the household over those of individual members; subject to the continuing authority of the household head, young women were still far from enjoying the possibility of conducting their own marriage negotiations. The reiteration of the principle of free choice in the first chapter of the new Marriage Law, put into practice on 1 January, 1981, gave implicit acknowledgement to the very partial success of the 1950s programme. And while, ever since the 1950s, scholars have recognized many of the impediments to universal practice of free-choice marriage in the countryside, recent studies show that in some rural areas high proportions of marriages continue to be arranged through the services of a matchmaker (*meiren*), 'signifying that the method of acquaintance [between a couple] is still restricted by traditional marriage customs' (Lei Jieqiong 1994, 174–6).[5] Since the early 1980s, the combination of decollectivization of agriculture, restoration of economic autonomy for the farming household, marketization of the economy and population control has contributed to the maintenance of marriage as an economic transaction between different interest groups. Marital arrangements may often be conducted for explicitly venal purposes, as in the case of young girls who are sold into betrothal or marriage with older men sometimes thousands of miles away from their natal home.[6] In a heavily patriarchal cultural environment, in which virilocal marriage is dominant, in which women's bodies have once again become the object of commercial gain, and in which the combined effects of population control and economic exigency have produced serious imbalances in sex ratio in many rural districts, the choice of marriage partner is not infrequently removed from the control of the younger generation.[7]

The main difference between rural and urban practices would appear to be of degree rather than of kind. Surveys conducted in the late 1970s among couples married since 1958 showed that more than half of them had met directly without going through any third-person introduction (Whyte and Parish 1984, 123). Since then, however, other studies have indicated that the proportion of marriages initiated through third-person introduction is still very high. In his study of courtship and 'dating' practices in Chengdu in the late 1980s, Whyte found that after the dramatic changes towards greater freedom of mate choice in the 1950s, only very minor shifts towards greater freedom occurred between 1957 and 1987 (Whyte 1992, 5–6). The dominant form of marriage was an intermediate one that combined introductions by third parties with individual choice, and in which many of the former controls enjoyed by the older generation had passed to bureaucratic agencies such as the work unit and the neighbourhood committee (pp. 6–7). In a survey conducted in Shanghai, Lei Jieqiong estimated some 73.7 per cent of the marriages contracted between 1979 and 1986 were similarly through third-person introductions (Lei Jieqiong 1994, 175). Professor Lei further pointed out that, over the same period, the proportion of marriages arranged through matchmakers in Shanghai had also increased from 2.5 per cent in the Cultural Revolution years to 10.5 per cent.

The main features of these changes suggest that, while by the mid-1980s the characteristics of parental involvement were evidently very different from traditional forms, courtship was still far from the norm as an experimental practice of pre-marital relations. The diminution of parental intervention in the negotiations of marriage by no means signified a simple increase in arrangements which depended on young people's 'free' initiative. The official discourse of sexuality of the 1950s demonstrated that the state was far from indifferent to the private lives and sexual choices of the young. Between the 1950s and the late 1970s, a range of informal and formal sanctions were deployed to prevent school and college students and young workers from engaging in romantic liaisons, with the effect that the reduction of parental authority was not replaced by an increase in young people's controls over 'adult resources', such as housing and education. As Whyte points out, state and bureaucratic agencies – the work unit, the neighbourhood committee, colleges and universities and mass organizations – took over many of the advisory, counselling, introductory and proscriptive functions formerly associated with parental responsibility, imposing political, ideological and bureaucratic limits on courtship as a recreational practice. An atmosphere was created which made it difficult, if not totally impossible, for urban young people to experiment with different partners (Whyte 1992, 7).

Since the early 1980s, official agencies have taken various steps to provide young people with organizational opportunities to find a marriage partner (Honig and Hershatter 1988, 82–97). The Central Committee's attention first turned to encouraging the Women's Federation, the Communist Youth League and the trade unions to organize 'friendship activities' to enable singles to meet ('National concern for singles over 30' 1984, 8–9). Work units began to hold dances and discos, and by the mid-1980s marriage introduction agencies had been set up in most large towns under the auspices of official bodies (Zhang Lisheng 1984). Unofficial bureaus, organized by young people frustrated by the registration requirements and restrictions of the government-sponsored bureaus, have established their own centres in public parks. Computerized dating agencies and singles' bars have been set up in many large cities. The media have also become popular channels of information for people looking for a partner; lengthy personal columns publicizing the details of single women and men seeking mates are now standard features of youth and women's magazines.

## True socialist love

'Normal friendship is established on the basis of broad mutual ambitions, diligent study, hard work and mutual help; only the love which develops out of this is the healthy love which provides a firm foundation for a family' (Wang Wenbin, Zhao Zhiyi and Tan Mingxin 1956, 24). Given its new status under the free-choice principle of the Marriage Law, love – what it was, how to achieve it – was one of the central themes of official writings about the new model of marriage after 1950. However, identification of love as the foundation of a successful marriage did not enlighten the public as to how to recognize or define it. Suggestions that the 'objective of love is marriage and a marital relationship is for life' (Niu Zhi 1951, 29) clearly indicated that love was to be the key criterion in selecting a marriage partner, but they did not identify its various characteristics. Many young people welcomed the new model of marriage not because of its legitimation of a 'modern' approach to love, but because it represented the possibility of breaking away from parental controls.[8] In a social and cultural context in which the concept of conjugal love had little meaning for many people, in which economic and material considerations dominated the choice of marriage partner, and which put stringent limits on overt expressions of amorous interest, the meaning of love had literally to be spelled out.

One of the first problems was how to distinguish love from 'ordinary friendship', and how to explain the significance of love in the progressive steps of a relationship preceding marriage. Attaching definitions to the various stages of familiarity in a friendship offered a technique for marking the boundaries of permissible behaviour in courtship; progress from initial 'mutual acquaintance' (*huxiang renshi*), through friendship (*youyi*) to 'love' (*lian'ai*) signified the transition between qualitatively different degrees of commitment, implying the possibility of engaging in progressively intimate, although never overtly romantic or sexual, contact. The final stage beyond which expectations of marriage were legitimate and indeed morally required was the 'declaration of love' (*biaoshi aiqing*), withdrawal from which was considered the mark of a flippant, immoral and fundamentally bourgeois character. A woman should not feel free to look for another partner once 'love had been declared' with a man (Li Ruolin 1956), and a young woman who embarked on an amorous relationship with a suitor having already enjoyed a 'love relationship' with another would be creating a 'triangular relationship' that violated the monogamous requirements of the law (Wei Hua 1958). Before the point of no return, however, a certain measure of experimentation was permissible, as long as it did not lead to any sexual involvement or to false expectations. As the author of an article on 'friendship and love between young men and women' wrote, it would be 'wrong to think that friendship that does not develop into love is immoral simply because after it you may look for another intimate relationship', for such an attitude would restrict freedom of choice ('Zunzhong aiqing shenghuo zhong de ziyuan yuanze' 1956). On the other hand, freedom to choose a partner should not be interpreted as an invitation to irresponsible conduct, as in the case of the 'wanton' (*husan musi*) young Shanghai factory worker who reportedly had five or six boy friends in a year, or the nurse in Fuxun who had romantic affairs (*tan lian'ai*) with more than thirty men (Song Tingzhang 1955, 13).

Debates held in *Zhongguo qingnian* to air readers' views about friendship and love revealed considerable differences of opinion about precisely what kind of behaviour was acceptable before the 'declaration of love'. What were the limits on experimentation and selection? Some contributors to the debate suggested that absolute commitment was required only after a declaration or sign of love had been given and accepted; for example, in exchanging photographs, writing letters, or even showing extra attentiveness during sickness (Ren Yuan 1954). However, determining the appropriate boundaries could still be a very delicate matter, as when a young factory worker earned the disapproval of the authorities when she responded negatively to the young man she worked with 'when he expressed his love to her' (Qin Zhengru 1953). The editorial comment criticizing her 'ideological shortcomings' implied that her initially friendly behaviour towards the young man had led to certain expectations which could not, morally, be let down. Another girl who rejected a man's offer of marriage was similarly criticized for having misled him into imagining that a 'love relationship' was possible (Zhang Xiaoling, in Zhang Fan 1952, 17–18). Having had a long and close friendship with him during which she had discussed such matters as love and marriage, she had transgressed the boundaries of ordinary friendship. Marriage could thus reasonably be expected.

On the other hand, many case histories also attacked conservative tendencies thought responsible for wrongly castigating young women. One typical story, published under the title of 'What is it that hinders friendship and love between young people?', focused on a bright and outgoing girl who was interested in all sorts of activities including art, literature, music and dancing (Yu Minghua 1956). Her liveliness and friendliness attracted a number of suitors, but she was not interested in any of them, and rejected their advances, only to find herself shunned by her workmates, who accused her of 'immoral conduct' (*zuofeng bu zhengpai*) for 'leading [men] up the garden path' (*aiqing shang de pianzi*) (p. 33). The editorial comment suggested that friendship and love needed to be clearly distinguished in order to avoid making this type of error. A more serious case told of a peasant woman who, after the death of her first husband, fell in love with a man from her own village (Meng Changqian 1950). Her mother and mother-in-law both opposed her liaison, her mother principally because she thought it would jeopardize her chances of finding a wife for her son. To stop the marriage, she orchestrated a number of people to write reports to the district authorities, proving that the woman's lover had raped an innocent widow. As a result of the mother's machinations, the man was imprisoned for more than a month, and the woman tried to commit suicide. It was only at this point that the local leaders realized their mistake in uncritically accepting local gossip.

Stories illustrating the 'correct' approach to love during this period consistently put shared social and political commitment in pride of place in the hierarchy of criteria for selecting a partner. A highly idealized example of this was the heroine Zhao Yiman, who, as a Young Communist League member, met her future husband on a boat going to Moscow, where both had been sent to study (Yang Ge 1957). The couple's initial acquaintance came about because of mutual commitment to further the revolution. It developed on the basis of work and study, and, despite separation and suffering back in China during the struggle against the Nationalists, it survived as a source of inspiration to give even greater commitment to the cause. A more mundane example was a couple who first met in a model labour group in a factory in Jinan. Both were known for their exemplary attitude of cooperation and hard work, and established a friendship through work and study. As the woman began to show her affection through simple gestures – such as spending her last few pennies on buying him noodles and nice vegetables when he had a cold – so the man's love began to grow. Then, before the young woman left for a meeting in Shanghai, the two pledged their troth, and promised to stay together forever (Ren Yuan 1954). True socialist love could not be based on a fleeting acquaintance, even less on 'love at first sight' (*yi jian zhong qing*). Love had to grow gradually and steadily on the basis of friendship. Love which was not rooted in mutual familiarity and shared interests was considered inherently unstable, 'no good' (*bu hao*) and bound to fade, as exemplified by the case in 'Zhenshi de gushi' (True story), a story translated from the Russian and published in *Zhongguo qingnian* (Hua Ming 1952). The story told of a young woman's brief acquaintance with a young man who 'danced well' and was interested in art and books. The woman was initially quite interested in him, but when she discovered that he was a cement worker and not a graduate from the college of architecture, as she had hoped, she broke off the relationship. This kind of behaviour, so the reviewer argued, was mistaken, because it indicated that the girl had attached too much value to superficial talents like dancing without understanding the importance of establishing a friendship first. It also showed by negative example that 'sharing the same political and ideological outlook was the most basic condition of love'. The message was unmistakable; the 'true love' of the proletarian was inconsistent with interests which put private pleasure before the social good.

The overriding importance the official discourse attached to love as a social, political and moral response dictated the terms of its representation. The ideological values informing the discourse cancelled out possible descriptions of love as an emotional, romantic and erotic experience. Physical attraction, excitement and longing for the loved one came too close to the dangerous territory of bourgeois attitudes to be permitted explicit reference as aspects of love. However, they could be useful in negative relief. Constructing images of what was acceptable and desirable by reference to their opposite simultaneously offered a means of advising and encouraging certain modes of behaviour, while condemning others as immoral and harmful. Thus, articles which set out to inform their readers about what friendship was, or about how it differed from love, often did so by inverse reference to what it was not. Descriptions which started off on a positive note were interrupted by some contrasting word to introduce the necessary tone of admonishment, and to indicate the place in the hierarchy of social commitments and concerns where love should be situated.[9] The romantic, 'bourgeois' associations of love also contributed to the contrasting ideological labels used to identify acceptable and unacceptable behaviour; the use of binary sets of ideological opposites – 'feudal' and 'socialist', 'individualistic' and 'collective', 'private' and 'social' – offered a convenient technique – widely used in all other aspects of communist discourse, too – of registering the normative standards of the official discourse in the minds of its audience.

High up in the hierarchy of bourgeois evils was romantic attachment to the notion of 'love at first sight' (*yi jian zhong qing*). Individual indulgence in trivial fantasies was, by definition, incompatible with ideological commitment to the party and state. Love was important, and for too long had been subjected to imputations of shame and suspicion, but an exaggerated, abstract and individualistic view of the importance of love was the erroneous expression of a bourgeois mentality ('Bu yao gulide jinxing guanyu lian'ai wenti de jiaoyu' 1952). For example, two undergraduates who fell in love and thought it was wonderful to be engaged in the revolution together decided to go to the liberated zone, but on arrival there discovered that spending their time distributing land was monotonous and living conditions were harsh (Guo Su 1950). The magic of their love suddenly disappeared, and it was only by undergoing self-criticism for their 'bourgeois' attitudes that they learned to overcome their mistaken notions. Deng Yingchao made it clear that 'putting love and marriage before everything else' was dangerously close to 'bourgeois passion'; an individual affected by such a view might well show the 'cowardly behaviour' (*qienuo xingwei*) of 'no longer wanting to live' if obliged to confront rejection or the loss of a loved one (Deng Yingchao 1985, 4). Song Tingzhang also took pains to persuade young miners that the imbalance between work and private life implicit in the bourgeois notion that 'love was more important than work' could lead to disastrous consequences. 'Quite a number of mine workers who spend time with their girlfriends (*tan lian'ai*) go to sleep late, with the result that they yawn all the time at work, and, because they lose their concentration, have a finger cut off by a machine or produce poor quality material and damage the machinery. Some suffer from insomnia because they spend too much energy thinking about love' (Song Tingzhang 1955, 1). Left unchecked, romantic belief in 'love at first sight' could produce the 'selfishness and self-interest' (*zisi zili*) typical of an individualistic outlook (p. 13). The pejorative value of these terms obviated any need to spell out the erroneous, immoral and salacious connotations of the practices they identified. Condemnation of an approach to love which focused on gratification of the self instead of commitment to the other – to the group and the individual – reaffirmed the importance of self-denial and restraint in love relationships. A 'bourgeois outlook' in matters of love denoted all attitudes and actions that subordinated group or collective needs and interests to those of the individual, from the expression of passing fancies, jealousy and rivalry, to romantic fantasies of passionate love. The moral superiority of the true proletarian spirit was contrasted with the depraved desires of the bourgeois individualist. Logically, it was only in a socialist society that true love could be realized. 'Mutual trust, and therefore true love, cannot exist in bourgeois society', because the 'principal condition for marriage in the West is individual wealth', whereas under socialism it is 'shared ideological interests, mutual respect and trust' (Deng Yingchao 1953, 11; Xie Juezai 1953).

The collective appropriation of love for ideological purposes left little possibility for other renderings. The discursive exclusion of the individual person and the denial of the self prevented the representation of love as an exchange between two people. The occasional letter, or gesture, such as going out of one's way to deliver milk, symbolized the declaration rather than the texture and substance of love (Wang Yuling 1959). But few words or images indicated what it might *feel* like to love someone. Neither facial expressions nor references to the body and appearance – except when these were intended to praise an individual's revolutionary commitment or condemn her bourgeois indulgence – or to nature were part of the vocabulary used to describe love. 'Why is it not possible to describe love in literature?', asked the author of an article about reading literature (Cai Qun 1953).[10] Reticence about the emotional, sensual and romantic aspects of love was symptomatic of the party-state's interests in controlling sexual behaviour in an increasingly restrictive moral atmosphere. Public discussion of the sensual aspects of love would have implicitly invited readers to indulge in ideas about sexual matters which were inconsistent with the norms of the discourse. As such, it would have threatened the state's interests in representing love as a predominantly social responsibility.

This is not to suggest, however, that romantic imagery was entirely absent. Images and language that in other contexts might have belonged to descriptions of romantic and sexual love were reserved by the official discourse to express the nature of an individual's relationship to the party and state.[11] Hence, a young widow could be described as having given 'her whole heart to the party, and to the people', without a word about her feelings for her newly married second husband (Zhu Keyu 1951). Alternatively, a girl's love for Lenin and the party could give her the strength and determination she needed to overcome feelings of deep loneliness and despair (Zhu Li 1951). During the Cultural Revolution, this mode of representation reached its apogee. As examples of 'socialist realism' and 'socialist romanticism', films showed young men passionately declaring their devotion to the party as they joined forces in struggle, and young women's eyes burning with intensity as they turned in the direction of the rising sun.[12] Model operas and ballets transformed emotional ardour into revolutionary commitment. Of course, their message was to persuade the audience of the revolutionary virtues of working for the collective; they were not, first and foremost, constructed as statements about appropriate approaches to matters of the heart. However, read from another perspective, they suggested a displacement of personal emotion from the discursively forbidden zone of private experience to a sphere that could absorb the expression of sentimental attachment without incurring any ideological threat. The disembodiment and desexualization of desire in such images under the rhetoric of revolutionary romanticism left the party-state and/or its leader as the only possible focus of individual passion.

Expectations of love were limited for most people between the 1950s and the 1970s. Political considerations increasingly influenced the choice of marriage partner, and in both rural and urban areas the preferred partner combined the recommended ideological criteria as well as socio-economic status (Croll 1981, 80–107). Yu Luojin, a woman whose autobiographical accounts of her loveless marriages became the topic of heated debate when they were published in the early 1980s, demanded more of a marriage than just 'making do', and argued that love signified a special spiritual and emotional bond, not a political arrangement.[13] However, as Yu Luojin's critics implied in arguing that mutual affection could develop on the basis of daily cooperation in material matters, a marriage that offered basic companionship and support was enough to make many women feel that they had not done badly. Love was for many an irrelevance in which only the leisured and wealthy had the opportunity to indulge. Yu Luojin's view implicitly belittled the fact that, for many, marriage signified a mutual accommodation of basic needs. The contrast between the abstract ideals of the official discourse and the general day-to-day expectations of marriage was potentially immense, and fraught with dangerous attractions for dissatisfied readers. It is possible, therefore, that one consideration in minimizing the representation of love as a source of emotional experience and pleasure was realistic and pragmatic. It was to provide a practical response to concerns that 'marriage was the tomb of love' (Cheng Jinwu 1950), and to reduce the possibility of advice and encouragement being interpreted as an invitation to high (and unattainable) hopes and expectations. Romantic love was an illusion which obscured the mundanities, and difficulties, of true love. As a commentator reminded his readers in 1954:

> True love may make you anxious and jealous, as well as filling you with happiness and contentment. Love sometimes creates insurmountable difficulties in a person's life, and people sometimes have to endure tension and strife in order to make their partner the kind of person they want. ('Yao shanyu zhengui de aiqing' 1954)

In attacking notions of romantic and passionate love disengaged from social responsibility, the discursive politicization of love and sexual relations signified the textual excision of an aspect of love imagery that was associated with the gender inequalities of 'feudal' and 'bourgeois' behaviour. The romantic ideal was an ideologically unsound illusion. The girl who spent her time 'reading novels, watching American films, and listening to love songs', with the sole aim of becoming a 'beautiful and gentle young mother' (*meili wenrou de muqin*), could expect little sympathy when her fantasies were shattered by the rejection of a man with whom she had fallen in love (Meng Zheyin 1950). Love was now to embrace a series of new meanings which represented a commitment to social as well as personal responsibilities. In its new representation, love was explained as a means of enabling young women to take advantage of their new freedoms without risking subjection to new types of oppression in the form of sexual promiscuity. Integrating private issues into the public sphere was presented as giving women a leverage over issues long used to ensure their obedience to restrictive Confucian rules.

## Approaching love in the 1980s

With the introduction of policies that emphasized the importance of 'objective' economic principles against the ideological purism of the Cultural Revolution years, the constraints on public discussion of 'personal' matters began to relax. As Honig and Hershatter point out, legal specialists and possibly the government hoped to use Yu Luojin's plea for a redefinition of 'mutual affection' to discredit classist definitions of love as a relationship based on political ideals and revolutionary commitment (Honig and Hershatter 1988, 213). Love became a hot topic of public debate. A new tolerance in literature and the arts encouraged the use of romantic metaphor and imagery. Zhang Jie's approach to a hitherto forbidden subject in her story 'Love must not be forgotten' seemed to mark a turning point in recuperating the individual voice and subjectivity from the public realm. As the first tentative attempts to describe emotion and passion were replaced by bolder, more direct approaches, so discursive insistence on maintaining 'correct' standards of pre-marital behaviour was overtaken by an unprecedented diversity of descriptions, information and advice about love. The new status of love as a symbol of the young generation's dreams and aspirations was seemingly omnipresent – in film, novels, the mass media and advertising. Stories of passionate longing, abandonment and disappointed love, accompanied by illustrations of couples in intimate embraces and tearful, wistful young women, began to feature in the pages of popular magazines. And an endless stream of enquiries about love-related matters – how to ask a girl out, what to wear when meeting a girlfriend's parents, how to interpret a young man's advances on a first date, how to let a boyfriend know that he is not the first – gave ample evidence that the unitary didacticism of the 1950s was irrelevant as a response to the anxieties, hopes and desires experienced by young people of the post-Mao era.

Public discussion about love, however, was far from unanimous in approving the new status of romantic love and private experience. 'Social commitment without love', one writer intoned, 'may make you feel unfortunate, but love without social commitment will make you feel empty' (Xiao Dong 1981). Though the absence of love in marriage was now recognized as legitimate grounds for divorce under the new Marriage Law's clause concerning 'alienation of mutual affection', this did not mean encouragement of a less serious attitude towards love. 'Love has now become the basis of marriage and the family. Carrying out scientific discussion about it is of central importance to eliminate the many unscientific misunderstandings of it that abound and to establish a happy and harmonious home' (Ding Wen and Li Ying 1984). From the editorial columns of *Zhongguo qingnian* to the discussions in academic style of social science journals, young people continued to be told that love signified shared ideals and commitments as well as compatible personalities. Love that was not based on mutual interests was too fragile to sustain a lifelong commitment in marriage.

And, while 'some physical contact between partners is permissible, provided that desire is mutual' and 'between people who are in love', it should not go beyond certain boundaries (Dong Xijian and Fan Chongyao 1984, 49).

In retrospect, the continued assertion of the social significance of love in the early 1980s was in many ways a defence of an outdated ideological position in a rapidly changing and threatening social context. To many people, notably of the older generation, the invasion of urban culture by dubious Western values exacerbated the ideological and moral confusion created in the wake of the Cultural Revolution. As millions of rusticated youth flooded back to China's cities after years spent in the countryside, and as the eloquent appeals for democratization – the 'fifth modernization' – of China's political structure gathered momentum during the Democracy Wall movement of 1979 and 1980, so the nation's revolutionary guardians gave voice to their anxieties about the moral credentials of the younger generation.[14] By the time a nationwide campaign was launched against 'spiritual pollution' in 1983, official reiteration of a view of love which sought to reinforce its function in family life clearly corresponded with interests in maintaining social order.

By the mid-1980s, the imagery and language used in dominant representations of pre-marital love seemed to indicate a total abandonment of principles that only a few years before had been a matter of revolutionary orthodoxy. The new approaches to love and the premarital relationship signified a conscious distancing from the dominant discourse of the preceding three decades. This was particularly evident in the new legitimacy given to love and sexual desire as sites of individuated experience. The view that 'in modern life . . . people treat love as a personal matter' (*ziji de shi*) permitted the expression of a wide variety of views (Gu Shi 1983, 31). Readers' letters printed in the growing number of women's and youth journals revealed approaches to emotional and sexual matters that the collective emphasis of the former discourse had obscured. Although many young readers described feelings of shame, embarrassment and fear about matters that had long been hidden from public scrutiny, they needed little bidding to give voice to their experiences, and in so doing to challenge the taboos with which they had grown up. Gone was the need to disguise individual experiences in representations that invoked the good of the country. Suggestions that 'love for an individual is only true love when combined with love for the country' soon became an anachronism, ridiculed for its revolutionary connotations (Lin Dong 1955). Romantic imagery could now idealize love as an all-consuming attachment of individual souls. The new exclusivity of romantic love seemed to signal the expulsion of the former social, collectivist ethic to an unwanted past.

References to physical attraction and sexual excitement further added a tone of permissiveness to the post-Cultural Revolution discourse that marked it off from the intolerance of its precursor. Images of couples in close embrace, or of beautiful young women looking longingly into the distance, brought to the new constructions of love suggestions of sexual desire that were unprecedented in public discourses since 1949. A new language of love could now approach feelings and emotions in imagery that had been totally circumscribed under the collective ethic of the former period. The movement of the body, the look in the eyes and the touch of the hand became part of a diverse vocabulary used to celebrate and explore the new possibilities of pre-marital love. A focus on fashion and adornment in texts about pre-marital conduct made the sexualized body, particularly the female body, a recurring feature of reformist constructions of pre-marital love.

Since the late 1980s, and in particular in the last few years, the ideological struggle over love and sexuality would appear to have been resolved. In a social context governed by market emphasis on consumer interests, individual initiative and enrichment, the legitimation of the individual person's needs and desires effectively protects representations of love and sexuality against any collectivist reappropriation. The demarcation of individual spaces of emotional and sensual interest, removed from necessary association with the public sphere, would seem to parallel the creation of individual opportunities heralded by commercial expansion and economic privatization.

However, the discursive rejection of the public emphases of the past does not indicate the withdrawal of the state from concerns about young people's sexual conduct, any more than the abolition of the post of party chairman in 1982 indicated the disappearance of vertical command from China's political structure. Rather, alongside the redefinition of the individual person's collective responsibilities to suit the ideological emphases of the new period, the relocation of issues of love and sexuality in the private sphere indicated a tactical modification in official approaches to the control of youth behaviour. The earlier discursive emphasis on the public orientation of 'affairs of the heart' has been absorbed into a new approach in which the balance between public and private fluctuates, depending on the party-state's valuation of the specific theme addressed. Attention to the public significance of pre-marital experiences of love and sex has not disappeared, but is embedded in a grid of public–private relationships which are constantly being modified in response to policy and changing practice. As the following section shows, behaviour that is thought to endanger social stability – whether through association with disease or immorality – is no more acceptable to the professional exponents of the dominant discourse than it was in former times.

## Pre-marital passion

The 1950s discourse condemned the passionate individual's disengagement from social responsibilities as anathema to an ideological project that aimed to appropriate the private and personal for the public sphere. The imputed dangers of individualistic indulgence and excess – the core of bourgeois evil – reached their peak in representations of passion, the point at which an individual could 'lose self-control' (*sangshile kongzhi ziji de liliang*) ('Lun shehuizhuyi shehui de aiqing, hunyin he jiating' 1953, 9). Love was not to be confused with passion and sex, so young people were told. Passion signified all that was most unstable and impure to the communist moralist. It was unequivocally dismissed as socially divisive, injurious to the individual, and base. Similar to the technique of linking dire physical consequences to improper sexual practices, the negative value attached to the search for passion was highlighted by contrasting it with the misery that would inevitably result from it. Potentially romantic images were juxtaposed against ones which evoked physical harm or social reprisals, thereby drawing attention to the dangers of indulgence. Passion was associated with the 'abyss' into which those who 'pursued happiness' would fall, and with 'dirt', the only way out of which was to 'crawl' (*Da gong bao* [1951], in Yang 1959, 125). Passion, so Song Tingzhang commented, signified 'dissipated behaviour from which there could be no salvation' (*bu ke jiule de fangdang xingwei*), and, as Deng Yingchao pointed out, could easily lead to the 'betrayal of communist morality' and 'glass of waterism' (*beishuizhuyi*) (Song Tingzhang 1955, 14; Deng Yingchao 1985, 4).[15] Passion, like 'soap bubbles', so a story of the same name suggested, was doomed to burst and disappear (Luo Jia 1955). Brief passionate involvement could not substitute for the more secure understanding built up through work and study. Desire for 'incomparable intimacy' (*titie wu bi*) with their partner made women blind to the 'seeds of misfortune hiding behind [their] happiness ... during moments of passion (*re lian shihou*)' (Liu Lequn 1955).

The danger associated with passion arose from its character as an expression of base physical desire and moral turpitude as much as from its anti-social quality. The idea that sex was merely a 'biological attraction' (*shengwu xiyin*) was a not uncommon mode of indicating its moral inferiority to love of the spirit. When dissociated from the virtues of lofty revolutionary ideals and aspirations, physical love was tarnished, unclean and fundamentally immoral. As one commentator put it,

> thinking and consciousness, feeling, intelligence, cultural accomplishment, interest in life and other such social factors are the determining conditions of lofty love among people; physical attraction between the sexes must be integrated with these social elements . . . before loving conduct [*lian'ai xingwei*] can occur. To reduce sexual relations to the level of biological sexual satisfaction [*shengwu ban de xing manzu*] is the expression of the depraved morals of capitalist society. (Cheng Jinwu 1950)

Sexual desire could have no place within a discursive perspective which customarily treated sex as a mechanical, and somewhat debasing, physiological phenomenon. It was very rarely mentioned in anything but indirect tones. Indeed, the absence of references to love as a sexualized experience implied that mere mention might provoke precisely the kind of behaviour the discourse was at pains to prevent. Amorous inclinations, though, were, by definition, acceptable for young people thinking of marriage. The perceived dangers of active sexual involvement on the part of the pre-marital group were therefore greater than for the younger adolescent group, and the need for preventive measures was more urgent. The view of pre-marital love disseminated by the official discourse promised social approval and even political status to those who conformed to its norms. By contrast, violation of those norms would result in misery, suffering and social disapprobation. The discursive insistence on the social orientation of affective matters before marriage thus offered an indirect but unequivocal means of warning young people away from sexual activity.

A dominant concern behind the representation of passion as divisive and dangerous was to discourage young people from sexual activity before marriage. Indeed, sexual abstinence before marriage was an absolute requirement, to the extent that, even though not strictly illegal, infringement could be treated as a crime.[16] As in advice to adolescents, the unequivocal message to those already considering marriage was that sexual involvement would get in the way of their studies as well as possibly destroy the chances of making a happy marriage. Biological arguments were produced to support advice to young people to abstain from marriage, and therefore sexual activity, as long as possible. An article in *Zhongguo funü* argued that there were strong physiological reasons in favour of women marrying at the 'appropriate' (*shidu*) age, for it was not until they were 25 that the 'internal system' (*neifenmi xitong*) of the female's reproductive organs was fully mature (Lin Qiaozhi 1957). Another argument was that women's pelvic capacity was only fully developed after the age of 25 (Zhang Xijun 1957).

As the 1980s progressed, a rush of surveys about young people's sexual behaviour indicated that sexual attitudes and practices were in the process of significant change. From the mid-1980s, pre-marital cohabitation between couples was reportedly on the increase, and students frequently ignored university regulations prohibiting friends from staying in each other's dormitories.[17] Surveys conducted in the capital between the early and mid-1980s suggested a diminishing number of people who were hostile to the idea of pre-marital sex. A study conducted in twenty higher education institutes between spring 1989 and spring 1990 found that 22 per cent of the male respondents and 11.7 per cent of the female respondents admitted to having experienced sexual intercourse (Geng Wenxiu 1991, 88).[18] Nearly three-quarters of all respondents in the same survey felt that virginity was no longer 'a necessary condition' for marriage. In a random survey of 1550 Beijing residents, about 30.5 per cent of the respondents thought that sex before marriage was acceptable, although only 15.5 per cent acknowledged having had sex before marriage (Li Yinhe 1991, 98). In a third survey conducted in 1991 on the basis of random sampling in Beijing, 36 per cent of the respondents felt that pre-marital sex was permissible, although only 11.3 per cent condoned sexual relations between partners who had not yet decided to marry (Li Yinhe and Wang Xiaobo 1992, 33–4). Liu Dalin's 1992 survey reported that, of 454 male and 168 female students, 52.4 per cent of the former and 48.2 per cent of the latter had experienced sexual intercourse with at least one partner (Liu Dalin 1992b, 191). Despite the variation in these figures, and the common opinion that pre-marital sexual intercourse is morally and socially unacceptable, these reports clearly indicate that young people, and particularly young women, have considerably more sexual experience prior to marriage now than they did in earlier decades (Geng Wenxiu 1991, 86-97).

Significant aspects of the discursive context situating these changes correspond with the challenges to former principles they represent. Media images of young women of the 'ready-to-marry' age group commonly focus on their erotic appeal – bare arms thrown back behind the head, revealing graceful curves from the neck down to the breasts; the provocative and direct gaze of the long-haired girl, head tilted back in semi-abandon, riding pillion on a motorbike behind her male companion; or the coquettish, sweet look of the girl dressed in pale yellow silk, cuddling a fluffy white dog. Such images – which contribute to some of the dominant subject positions available to women in the contemporary media – construct women as an aspect of the male gaze, regardless of whether the viewer is in fact male or female. They tend to exclude areas of women's lives and experiences that seem to be removed from male interests, and instead frame the female in response to male needs and desires. Whether women appear doing caring/domestic things – dressed in pretty clothes, holding a basket of beautifully arranged flowers, or wearing a pink robe standing in a kitchen decked out with all the most modern domestic appliances – they display an awareness of being looked at. They depict the absence of the viewer, and by the same token define the woman as incomplete, waiting to be made a full person by the absent male figure (Edholm 1992, 154–6). Denied autonomy, the women in such images reinforce the representation of female sexuality as dependent on male action, waiting for completion, to be given life, by the active male. The invitation to sexual engagement offered by such images is unmistakable.

The possibilities of romantic experimentation discussed in the last section mark a convergence between the terms of the dominant discourse and changing practice. The major issue no longer concerns simply the permissibility of pre-marital sexual contact, but the limits defining it. Professional opinion to the effect that experience in love may be a good preparation for marriage (Jin Zhu and Bai Yue 1991, 191) is acceptable as long as the appropriate boundaries are not transgressed (Zhi Xin 1992, 137–9). However, while these are clearly more flexibly defined, as has already been suggested, they continue to reveal clear continuities with the moral terms established in the 1950s. Repeated reminders to respect 'culturally and nationally' determined standards of pre-marital virginity, ideally applicable to men as well as women, echo a dominant theme of the earlier discourse. 'Sex before marriage is undesirable because it is not the same as in marriage; it may harm physical development in both women and men, and may leave lasting psychological effects to the detriment of later married life' (Wang Yanming 1988, 67). The limits of 'hot love' (re lian) are repeatedly pointed out in stories which tell of the anguish endured by those who indulge in illicit relations. By contrast with the beneficent effects of sex within marriage, pre-marital sex may leave those involved feeling 'anxious, worried [about being] found out or becoming pregnant [which] may create sexual malfunctioning (xing gongneng zhang'ai) after marriage, in the form of premature ejaculation and frigidity' (Su Fu and Huang Yuxian 1992, 20). 'All in all,' the authors of this approach concluded, 'from a psychological perspective, making love before marriage is not worth encouraging', and, in any case, an exaggerated emphasis on sex diminishes the attention the parties should give to the need for mutual understanding and consideration.

In the absence of any formal legal prohibition of pre-marital sex, a vague invocation of the law is often used to reinforce the general antipathy to it; it is wrong because it is not protected by the law. 'Sexual relationships which are not condoned by the law are invariably conducted in conditions of secrecy and haste', signifying considerable psychological and social pressures on a couple (Li Wenhai and Liu Shuyu 1992, 98–100). Given the stigma attached to pre-marital pregnancy, women are particularly affected by such pressure, and 'worry about work, and about colleagues finding out in the event of an abortion', and so on. Texts in the women's and legal press give sometimes detailed explanations of the consequences, particularly for women, of engaging in a sexual relationship that has no legal backing. Hence, the girl who dies after aborting a fetus conceived outside marriage cannot be shown much sympathy, since the conception was both 'immoral and illegal' (Yang Yong 1985).

Pre-marital sex is also commonly associated with anti-social conduct ranging from offending public morals to criminal activity. In a section entitled 'Why do some young women lose their virginity?', a sex-education booklet argued that pre-marital sex – the result of 'giving in to bodily desires' – indicates the first step in the social and moral descent of many women into crime (Yan Ruizhen and Li Peifang 1989, 93). Biographical stories identify pre-marital sex – 'an impure relationship' (*bu qingbai guanxi*) – as the point of no return, dictating an inevitable fall into promiscuity and criminal behaviour, adversity and suffering. The original mistake of a sixteen-year-old girl whose promiscuous and dissolute behaviour resulted in a stint of 'education through labour' (*lao jiao*) was in giving in to the 'rude' (*feili*) demands of a man almost twice her age. Her punishment appeared as the almost inevitable consequence of pre-marital sexual indulgence (Cheng Xian 1986). As another autobiographical piece revealed, initial indulgence seals a woman's fate of sadness and abandonment (Shao Jun 1993). Another objection arises from the downside of passion – the abandonment, rejection and anguish of 'disappointed love' (*shi lian*). The pain described by the girl recalling her first love (Wen Jianhua et al. 1986, 114–15) or the anguish of the girl whose fiancé decided to call a halt to the marriage when he discovered that she had slept with someone else (Zhang Qingyun et al. 1984, 54–5) push home the message that psychological, social and physical well-being in marriage are closely associated with exercising pre-marital constraints. The inescapable message is that tolerance to pre-marital sex is wasted given that 'problems often occur after one falls ill' (Wang Youqin 1985, 12).

Not all columnists concur with the 'catastrophic model' of pre-marital sex. Some commentators draw a distinction between sex for recreational purposes and sex as a sign of the commitment already made in deciding to get married, delineating new boundaries around an exclusive space where pre-marital sex is permissible. Associated with love leading to marriage, sex loses its implicit association with promiscuity and suffering and becomes a particular aspect of exclusive monogamy. Even after a promise of marriage, however, a woman still needs to be vigilant. When a woman's husband-to-be is her boss at work, and has enough money and charm to 'find a beautiful wife whenever he wants', she still needs to exercise restraint in her own interests, in the event of separation (Su Fu and Huang Yuxian 1992, 19). The need for self-protection, one writer advised, simply means that women should act with caution. 'I am not saying that women should all guard their bodies like jade, not even allowing anyone to touch them. I am saying, rather, that before someone touches you, you should have planned it out' ('Lian'ai fangshi taolun' 1985, 25; quoted in Honig and Hershatter 1988, 119). Or, as another commentator put it, 'women are very romantic, but are also very realistic. Their romanticism creates in them the need for love, but their realism means that, in the end, they can only accept love that comes with the guarantee of a home' (A Che 1995).

## The female standard of pre-marital sexuality

As in many other aspects of contemporary discourses about sexuality, the female emerges as the focus of discussions about pre-marital sexual relations. The woman is the main referent in texts which instruct readers to distinguish between right and wrong. She is the dominant subject of cautionary tales about the perils of 'hot love'. Suggestions that university students are not experienced or mature enough to engage in pre-marital sexual relations are supported by examples of young women beguiled into illicit liaisons or even abducted (Geng Wenxiu 1991, 91). On the one hand, the visual category of the beautiful, erotic woman is the subject and object of romantic long-ings. On the other, through more sober narrative representations, she establishes the standards of acceptable sexual conduct; she is a con-stant reminder of the physical, psychological, familial, social and moral ills which visit those who do not respect normative boundaries.

The gendered focus of these approaches to pre-marital sexuality inherits the discursive practices of the pre-Cultural Revolution period. Then, normative expectations of pre-marital restraint were consistently transmitted through representations of female conduct. Implications of purity were conveyed through images of women's patience and self-sacrificing commitment to public concerns (for example, Gao Guizhen 1953; Tian Liu 1953). Advice to readers that embarking on a second 'love relationship' (*aiqing guanxi*) before marriage 'violates the monogamous requirements of the law' (Lai Gen 1957) was invariably conveyed through invocations of the female. Whether as a deterrent against bourgeois tendencies of 'loving the new and hating the old', or as a paragon of the socialist virtues of self-sacrifice on behalf of the male loved one, women's behaviour was relentlessly presented as the yardstick for normative standards of pre-marital sexual morality.

The use of the female as a metaphor for pre-marital boundaries is particularly prominent in discussions about virginity. Concerns about protecting the female body from damaging actions, and about female virginity in particular, may represent preoccupations with preserving the integrity of the moral and social unit (Goddard 1987, 190; Douglas 1989). A cultural emphasis on pre-marital chastity may identify the need for control of women's sexuality from its destabilizing potential. Since the 1950s, commentators on the moral and social issues raised by requirements of pre-marital virginity have attempted to separate their recommendations from any overt gender bias. Male preoccupations about female virginity, commonly expressed through anxieties about the absence of hymeneal blood on 'the night of the honeymoon', were considered misguided and 'anachronistic' ('Guanyu xing zhishi de jige wenti' 1956; Li Yang 1956). Men who felt humiliated on discovering that their wives did not bleed during sexual intercourse were told that attaching such importance to hymeneal blood indicated 'unreasonable, unscientific and feudal demands for proof of female purity'. In any case, as a medical specialist long ago intoned, 'this matter of the hymen should no longer be treated as a problem, since all it does is make people anxious. Of course, this does not mean that we advocate "sexual chaos" (*xing luan*); it is rather to say that everyone, no matter whether male or female, should adopt a serious approach to resolving problems about love and marriage' (Yan Renying 1955). Similarly, in more recent years, readers have repeatedly been reminded that pre-marital virginity is a 'requirement of both sexes' prior to marriage; as such, it is seen to 'reflect the equality of the

sexes' (Wang Yanming 1988, 78). However, despite attempts to minimize the exclusive emphasis on female virginity as a prerequisite for
marriage, the social desirability of pre-marital chastity – 'the ideal state
for marriage' – continues to be constructed largely through representations of young women (Li Wenhai and Liu Shuyu 1992, 111).
The frequency of texts with titles like 'How correctly to treat the
matter of the hymen'(Wu Zhangming, Zhu Xiaolan and Lang Ying
1990, 106) or 'The mystery of the hymen' (Jin Ma 1987, 151)
indicates the continuing concern, voiced by men and women alike,
with traditional symbols of female sexual purity. Some arguments
further refer to the biologized dichotomy of the impulsive male and
the weak female to explain why pre-marital chastity is not always
protected, and by implication to urge self-restraint of the woman.
'Judging from the differences in physiological and psychological
characteristics, men become aroused earlier on in a relationship than
women, the expression of which is courage and haste. Women, on the
other hand, invariably find themselves lacking in determination,
autonomy and self-control, because of their physical weakness and
emotionality. As a result, women's capacity to resist the pressures of
seduction is pretty weak' (Wang Yanming 1988, 73). In cases where
pre-marital liaisons are considered the cause of psychological and/or
physical damage, women's health provides the main examples (Wang
Yanming 1988, 68). The social and moral arguments against pre-
marital sex are constructed through warnings against the stigma
attached to pre-marital pregnancy, to women's 'loss of honour', and to
the disdain shown young women whose sexual history is subject to
rumour and gossip because they do things like stay out all night (Wei
Biyan 1984), or are known to have had more than one boyfriend (Du
Min 1984).

   The attention these kinds of texts give to the misfortunes that befall
women who lose their virginity before marriage unambiguously indicates a construction of female purity as an asset in establishing a happy
future. The same construction informs the advice widely available to
young women about, on the one hand, how to preserve their 'most
precious gift' in vulnerable situations, and, on the other, what
approach to take in situations where a disclosure about former sexual
experiences may be required. Being honest about their past might
invite public humiliation and violent abuse by their husbands (Honig
and Hershatter 1988, 119–20). Some writers point to the difficulties of
arranging pre-marital abortions in ways that protect a woman's reputation. In response to a letter by a woman abandoned by her lover
because she did not accede to his 'demands', a medical specialist
focused on the 'dangers of pregnancy and pre-marital abortion' as a

result of indulging in pre-marital sex (Wu Yuming 1986). Continuing evidence that doctors often require proof of marital status prior to performing an abortion adds to the implication that a woman should try to avoid pre-marital pregnancy at all costs. Again, young women are advised to keep their emotions under control even though they may be passionately in love. Until marriage, a woman can never know whether a man is totally serious in his intentions, so maintaining a certain distance, by, for example, turning down material temptations of fine clothes and entertainment, is an effective way of ensuring self-protection against the eventuality of abandonment by the partner (Qing Jie 1986).

In more recent years, demographic, eugenic and medical concerns have reinforced official warnings against pre-marital sex.[19] As writers point out time and time again, pre-marital sex inevitably means an increase in pre-marital pregnancies. A report published in 1986 claimed that 27.9 per cent of all abortions were performed on unmarried women, 90 per cent of whom were preparing for marriage (Honig and Hershatter 1988, 114). In a letter warning young women against pre-marital sex, a doctor claimed that, between October 1984 and August 1985, one-third of the 481 abortions he had performed in his hospital were for unmarried women (Wu Yuming 1986). A further figure from Shanghai indicated that one-sixth of all abortions performed in 1985 were for unmarried women (Shi Yubin 1989, 74). Pre-marital births both contravene the guidelines of the fertility-control policy and ignore advice by fertility planners about the measures and precautions to be taken to ensure the birth of 'quality' babies. Women who give birth without the necessary marriage registration certificate cannot be targeted for the obligatory pre-marital check-up required of newly-weds, the key method used to 'ensure (*baozheng*) superior births (*yousheng youyu*) and to safeguard family happiness and social stability' (Ju Ming 1995, 5). The concern to protect women from stigma and abuse also remains a significant factor. Texts repeatedly point out the social pressures on young women whose reputations may be sullied by rumours about pre-marital sexual involvement. Associating pre-marital liaisons with crime, abandonment and suffering, as in the case of a woman who was left pregnant when the man with whom she was having an illicit affair was sent for three years to education through labour (*lao jiao*) for having been involved in black marketeering (Lin Wen 1986), reinforces the discursive disdain of pre-marital involvement.

Sociological and anthropological evidence suggests that such representations correspond widely with actual practice. Indeed, in the countryside, families may protect a daughter's chastity as a means of ensuring a high bride-price.[20] In a 1990 survey on women's status, nearly 70 per cent of all respondents agreed with the statement that 'a woman's virginity is more important than her life'.[21] Liu Dalin's nationwide survey indicated that traditional requirements on women to be chaste before marriage continue to exert a strong influence on the kinds of demands men make of women (Liu Dalin 1992, 425–6). And while evidence suggests that more people are now willing to sympathize with female rape victims (1992, 426–30), the stigma of rape is still so serious that speaking out may jeopardize their chances of making a good marriage. Evidence from women's autobiographical pieces asking for advice about whether they should tell their prospective husbands about previous sexual experiences, including rape, points to similar consequences (Wang Yanming 1988, 59–65). A young woman who, one afternoon in April 1993, phoned in to the Beijing women's hotline the day after having lost her virginity to her boyfriend was distraught about what she had done, and wondered whether it was possible to regain her virginity by having an operation to mend the hymen. Her main anxiety, according to her own explanation, was about the doubtful reputation that she would earn among her friends once it became known that she was no longer 'pure'.[22] Significantly, a women's journal recently published a report on 'hymen repair clinics' that have opened with resounding success in a number of towns 'to give women a second spring' (Gao Yang 1995).

In the years following the first Marriage Law, the dominant gender target of discussion about pre-marital relations corresponded in part, at least, to what was interpreted as women's greater interest in matters of marriage and sexuality. China's historical legacy of gender relations made women potentially more disposed to support change in a system that upheld male prerogative. The introduction of new practices of courtship and free choice of partner was deemed to be of partcular interest to women, given that they stood to gain the most. The gender bias of the 1950s discourse also responded to the particular circumstances of women's sexual vulnerability (Lei Jieqiong 1957). At a time when neither contraception nor abortion were readily available, when women's sexual involvement prior to marriage was treated with extreme severity, and when unmarried mothers had few means of material or social support, requirements of sexual abstinence – often accompanied by warnings to young women to beware the advances of older men – acquired a potentially empowering meaning for women. Advice to refrain from sexual involvement could be interpreted as a means of protecting women from social stigma and sexual abuse.

The significance of the gender imbalance in the construction of pre-marital behaviour may also be understood by referring to the broad dimensions of women's representation as agents of sexual morality. The subtext of the use of women to convey an apparently non-gender-specific message is that the major moral responsibility for upholding the required standards of sexual behaviour, particularly during the potentially vulnerable years between adolescence and marriage, lies with women. Public discussion of sexual propriety defines the limits of acceptable sexual behaviour for both women and men through inscribing different moral values in different images of women – in different kinds of women. However, the persistent use in recent years of female examples to represent acceptable standards of pre-marital sexuality does not simply reiterate the gendered constructions of sexual morality of the pre-Cultural Revolution discourse. The unprecedented presence of romantic and sexual imagery modifies the gendered meanings of contemporary representations. For while many aspects of the contemporary discourse echo important features of its precursor – the same kind of progressive claims might be made for the discourse's cautionary representations of young girls beguiled by the charms of evil men – 'woman' repeatedly emerges as an object of male sexual desire, just as the male appears as the one who is needed and desired by the woman in her search for self-fulfilment. In this sense, the use of women as the dominant exemplar in discussions about pre-marital sexuality suggests the construction of the female as agent of sexual morality in ways which confirm the sexual power of the active, dominant male.

Given the continuing prevalence of traditional ideas about sexual morality, of which female chastity was the standard bearer, it is unsurprising that concerns about pre-marital conduct should converge on women's behaviour. Particularly in the 1950s, fears that granting women freedom of choice was in effect inviting illicit behaviour were consistent with a historical legacy of stringent control of women's sexuality. However, the relentless use of female conduct as the principal agent of sexual morality in dominant discourses of pre-marital sexuality conflicts with official assertions to uphold the principle of sexual equality. A model of sexual morality that both depends on the agency of women and appropriates erotic images of the female body indicates a view of gender difference that reinforces the hierarchy inscribed in the biological definitions of sexuality. Indeed, women's supposed greater interest in 'matters of the heart' is *ipso facto* given inferior value, because it does not have the status accorded commitment to the social, professional and political responsibilities of the masculine world. As Song Tingzhang put it, 'no one can deny that love is of particular importance to young people, but we must in no way think of the question of love as the focus of life and the principal aim of existence' (1955, 1).

Party-state control of pre-marital behaviour has thus been exercised not through control of the ungendered self in relation to the other, as the dominant discourses repeatedly seem to imply, but through the female in relation to herself and the male. The unitary representation of the 'correct' approach to pre-marital love in the 1950s featured a tension between love as a liberator from oppressive 'private' conditions subjecting women's interests to men's needs and desires, and love as a moral and sexual constraint containing and controlling women's behaviour in the name of their own and the general good. However, there has been a shift in the meanings and subject positions inscribed in apparently similar representations, mediated by the changes that have occurred in China's urban society and culture since the early 1980s. The re-evaluation of love and sexuality as categories belonging to the private sphere has expanded the range of subject positions available to women; it has also expanded the social and sexual sites patrolled by woman in her capacity as moral agent. In the process, the use of the female as the standard of sexual morality has acquired meanings that are specific to the socio-economic and cultural context defined by the marketization of the economy and the commercialization of female sexuality. With the reaffirmation of romantic love alongside images of the eroticized female body – the 'privatization' of love and sexuality – the representation of the female as the major signifier and agent of sexual morality has in recent years acquired a complexity absent from the former discourse. The potentially progressive message of protecting unmarried women from stigma and abuse has been superseded, though not eclipsed, by a more generalized interest in maintaining standards of sexual order at a time of increased sexual crime, disease and disorder. The focus on the female as the main agent of sexual morality is thus inscribed with a new tension, between, on the one hand, principles of sexual restraint, and, on the other, suggestions – implicitly or explicitly supported by state agencies – of women's sexual availability to the active, dominant male. The use of the female as the standard of sexual morality is set within a grid of competing representations of female sexuality in which women's self-restraint is imbricated with her sexual desire for, availability to, and dependence on the dominant male. If pre-marital female sexuality has become the focus of a struggle between contending meanings of womanhood – the virtuous, self-sacrificing wife-to-be and the desirable and always available sexual partner – so the discourses through which the party-state constructs and controls women have also expanded.

# 5  The Monogamous Ideal

Official discourses about sexuality and marriage in the People's Republic of China have consistently treated the model of monogamous
marriage set out in the 1950 and 1980 Marriage Laws as the only
legitimate context permitting sexual activity. Marriage or, more specifically, wifehood sexualizes women; it is distinct from other categories
of womanhood in that it acknowledges women as mature rather than
potential sexual identities. Wifehood defines female sexuality principally in two ways, in relation to the husband and to reproduction.
Indeed, the assumption that wifehood rapidly and naturally gives way
to motherhood has until recently limited the discursive attention given
to non-reproductive sexuality. Idealized representations of sexual harmony between wife and husband assume the inevitability of procreation; representations of female sexuality are prevalently situated within
a web of conjugal and reproductive responsibilities. In the past fifteen
years, the imbalance in attention given these dual aspects of wifehood
has been somewhat redressed. Suggestions that women take a more
active part in determining the character of their sexual relationship
with their husbands – whether by indicating pleasure, taking an active
part in expressing sexual desire, or saying 'no' – are frequently found
in popular articles as well as more serious sex education materials.
Incompatibilities produced by the conflict between, on the one hand,
women's perceptions of the male's prioritization of his own sexual
desires and, on the other, their own lack of sexual enjoyment are
reportedly an increasingly important factor in divorce suits. The
representations of women's sexual needs, responses and responsib-

ilities in marriage and the ways in which recent shifts in focus on these demand a reassessment of the gendered meanings of monogamous marriage are the main themes of this chapter.

Dominant discourses since 1949 have insisted that men conform to the same monogamous obligations as women. However, the consistent focus on the latter as the main exemplars of appropriate sexual behaviour within marriage indicates a continuing attachment to female conduct as the principal standard and agent of marital harmony. Official interpretations of monogamy as a principle of sexual and gender relations repeatedly construct wives as faithful and selfless servicers of their husbands. In the earlier discourse, representations of wives suggested a tension between the requirements of commitment to the husband on the one hand and to the state on the other. One mode of resolving this was by minimizing the discursive importance attached to the marital relationship. Another was by indicating that women's duty to the state could be, and at times even should be, mediated by her commitment to her husband and children. Since the early 1980s, the 'privatization' of matters associated with love and marriage has been accompanied by the widespread use of romantic imagery to contextualize descriptions of the ideal marital relationship. As part of this, the wife's self-sacrificing support of her husband has been rein-forced as a gender-specific requirement of the harmonious ideal of conjugality. Thus, despite the media prevalence of positive construc-tions of women as successful achievers in the world of public, male-oriented interests – as the 'strong women' – and as potential initiators of sexual activity, these have not seriously destabilized the hierarchized representation of women's attributes and duties as wives – as sexual-ized women. The use of science to inscribe fixed gender responses in women effectively biologizes the sexual and moral imperatives imposed on women in representations of wifehood.

## Wives and sexual harmony

The dominant construction of monogamous marriage as the only relationship legitimizing sexual relations makes marriage and sexual relations virtually synonymous. The interchangeability of the two is first of all apparent in the use of language; terms such as 'marital relationship' (*fufu guanxi*) and 'married life' (*fufu shenghuo*) are frequently used in preference to the more direct 'sex life' (*xing shenghuo*) or 'sexual relations' (*xing guanxi*) to denote sexual inter-course between a man and a woman, even when the context suggests that a couple are not married. A more formal insistence on conflating the two terms has been apparent in law, where evidence suggests that sexual intercourse before marriage has, on occasions, been treated as a crime, despite the lack of any specific legal item prohibiting pre-marital sexual intercourse.[1] Comments on specific cases sometimes use phrases such as 'sexual relations that are not condoned by law' or 'not given legal protection', thereby conveying a sense of illegality to acts not strictly prohibited by law (e.g., Li Wenhai and Liu Shuyu 1992, 98–100). Writers less concerned with precision, however, show little hesitation in condemning pre- and extra-marital sex as 'immoral and illegal' (Yang Yong 1985, 13). Advice about what are considered appropriate sexual attributes, needs and responses in women is thus bounded by the assumption of a woman's relationship with her husband, her exclusive and life-long sexual partner. Legitimate female sexual conduct is defined with sole reference to her relationship with her husband.

The conflation of sexual relations and marriage is reinforced by the naturalized view of marriage as the inevitable culmination of the developmental processes of adolescence and early adulthood. Of course, there are a few examples of famous women who decide to remain single, and 'there will continue to be some people in the future who, for one reason or another, decide to remain single', but choosing not to marry is not considered an appropriate option, since it signifies 'smothering one's natural desires for future happiness' (Ling Ya 1985). Or, as an earlier commentator put it, 'Marriage is an individual's natural biological need; not to marry is abnormal (bu zhengchang) and does not have any physical benefit' (Zhang Xijun 1957).

The public insistence that women and men are 'on the shelf', and even physically or psychologically 'abnormal', if they have not married by the time they are thirty naturalizes marriage in ways that correspond with dominant practice. As many writers have pointed out, marriage is almost universal in China.[2] However, the assumption that marriage is a natural state has imposed considerable pressure on the lives of many people, as later discussion in Chapter 8 demonstrates. Moreover, personal informants of the Red Guard generation, both women and men, have told me that as they approached their mid-twenties, officially considered the 'appropriate' age for marriage, they quickly identified a partner on the basis of looks and political credentials, and sometimes married within a matter of a few weeks to avoid being stigmatized as unnatural and abnormal.[3] The marriages in many of these cases either terminated in divorce or quickly became shells masking loveless liaisons.[4]

As indicated in Chapter 2, references to the importance of a 'good sex life' in strengthening the relationship between a couple made a fleeting appearance during the brief period of liberalization in early 1957 ('Guanyu xing zhishi de jige wenti' 1956). However, the dominant collectivist ideology between the 1950s and the late 1970s gave little opportunity for public discussion about the affective and sexual aspects of marriage. Cultural constraints added to the difficulties of discussing an area of experience that was subject to moralistic disdain and associated with shame and promiscuity. It might also be argued that the relative infrequency of public references to the issue corresponded to a lack of interest, particularly on the part of women, in the sexual component of married life.[5] The silence about marital sexuality was not a 'reflection' of day-to-day practice, though, any more than it corresponded to prudery on the part of official commentators. Rather, it was ideologically grounded in the depreciation of sexual experience as a factor validating the marital relationship. Despite the construction of sex as an asset to marriage in the period, it was given low priority alongside the other weightier factors considered indispensable to a solid marriage. In any case, as a component of marriage, the notion of 'sexual harmony' (*xing hexie*) did not overtly contradict the collective emphasis of the discourse since it was invoked in the service of conjugal and family happiness – in other words, in the service of the group. The representation of sex as a measure contributing to physical and mental health did not focus on its place in individual experience, but on its function as a means of enabling the individual person to contribute more to the family and society. A 'good sex life' thus appeared more as a bonus to a marital relationship founded on mutual interests in work and political outlook than as an essential component validating the marriage tie. The implication that a good sex life could make the difference between a satisfactory and a merely routine marital relationship gave a significance to the sexual relationship which transcended interests in reproduction alone (Tan Zhen 1956; Wang Wenbin, Zhao Zhiyi and Tan Mingxin 1956, 38).

The desirability of a good sex life to 'deepen the love between a couple' has been a standard component of representations of marriage and marital ideals throughout the 1980s. Alongside the positive gloss put on romantic aspirations in selecting a spouse, acknowledgement that sexual satisfaction is an important component of married life is commonly found in some form or another in contemporary texts about married life and 'domestic morality' (*jiating daode*). Health magazines devote considerable discussion to the benefits of a good sex life. As one publication put it, 'recently, sex has suddenly become a topic everyone talks about with great interest again . . . as if it has again become an important thing in marriage' (Zhang Biao 1991, 30). While considerable efforts are still directed to telling readers not to attach more importance to sex than to other aspects of the marital relationship, the prominent attention paid to 'sexual harmony' in marriage signifies an evident departure from former approaches, consistent with the discursive restoration of the realm of 'private' experience.

Sex education materials published in the last decade suggest that the notion of a good sex life – of sexual satisfaction on the part of both spouses – is premised on the same model of asymmetrical complementarity as the biological explanation of sexual difference.

> The man should do his best to avoid being hurried and rough, and should never satisfy his own desire without thinking about the woman. The woman, for her part, should not force herself to respond because she thinks that sex is an obligation to be fulfilled. The man should caress the woman tenderly, to arouse her excitement, and the woman should make a conscious effort to identify her husband's desire and should spontaneously cooperate with him. (Gao Fang and Zeng Rong 1991, 35–7).

The binary model of male activity and female passivity here invoked differs only marginally from that presented four decades ago. Then, self-restraint of his spontaneous drive was urged of the husband in order to elicit a positive response from his wife. She in turn was asked to be patient and understanding of her husband's needs, and to suppress any feelings of anger or resentment in order to protect her husband from feeling hurt and rejected (Wang Wenbin, Zhao Zhiyi and Tan Mingxin 1956, 42–3). More recent advice to newly-weds reiterates similar suggestions. 'The husband's movements should be light and gentle. He should not think only of himself nor should he be rough during sexual intercourse, because this will make his wife unhappy and may also bring her physical harm, to the point that she will become disgusted with sex' (*Xinhun weisheng bi du* editorial group 1984, 23).

The argument that women's sexual passivity is, in part at least, physiologically determined enjoys wide currency, as I have indicated in previous sections. However, parallel suggestions that women's relative lack of desire is also culturally and socially induced have become more prominent in the relevant texts. Li Wenhai and Liu Shuyu launched an explicit challenge to this approach in arguing that the empirical evidence demonstrating generally low levels of sexual satisfaction among women is invariably based on mistaken ideas about female passivity, shaped by historical and cultural forces (1992, 61–2). They further suggest that the differences between women and men in expressing sexual pleasure are no greater than the similarities; and that the naturalized value given the traditional asymmetry between female and male has been largely responsible for denying and hiding women's potential pleasure.

A significant feature of the concern with the sexual aspect of marriage has been an explicit and unprecedented interest in women's needs and desires as sexual partners. Positive references to women's satisfaction and encouragement to women to take the initiative in expressing sexual desire suggest an approach to sexuality that is no longer associated with the simple binary model of the active male and passive/responsive female. Warnings to women against the negative consequences of treating sex as a conjugal obligation are accompanied by other, no less important suggestions that women begin to view their own bodies and their sexual relationships with their husband as a source of pleasure. Sex-education materials not uncommonly contain references to the bodily and sensual locations of women's sexual pleasure; descriptions of the clitoris and the G spot make explicit references to the sources of female orgasm, signifying a recognition of the autonomous possibility of female pleasure that was with few exceptions absent from the former discourse. Materials for newly-weds – often assumed to be relatively ignorant about the different characteristics of men and women's sexual needs and behaviour – also draw attention to the need for women to assert their desires and dislikes in sexual relationships. Popular newspaper articles urge women to be critical of culturally determined feelings of shame and embarrassment and not to 'hide their orgasm' (*Jiankang wenzhai bao* 14 April 1993).

Evidence linking women's sexual disinterest with the increasing rate of divorce offers one explanation for this apparently new-found interest in women's sexual desire. According to a random sample of divorce cases brought before the court in a particular district of Shanghai, 'sexual incompatibility' was mentioned by one or both partners in 1955 in only 3.5 per cent of the cases, while in 1985 this had risen to 20.9 per cent (Xu Anqi 1990a, 106). Another survey of one hundred divorce cases in the same court in 1985 revealed that, of the 48.4 per cent of partners who noted sexual incompatibility, the majority were women (p. 107). Sociological surveys, presented as scientific evidence of changing sexual practices, reinforce the gender implications of these figures. For example, the 1992 nationwide survey of sexual attitudes and practices found that large numbers of women of different ages, but particularly of the middle-aged and older cohorts, are totally disinterested in sex (Liu Dalin 1992b, 410–25). Various explanations are put forward. In her *Zhongguoren de xing'ai yu hunyin*, Li Yinhe described divorcées' sexual experiences as a series of negative responses, from 'initial lack of interest to total antipathy' (1991, 186). Other analyses link women's low expectations of romantic and sexual gratification to the reportedly 'rough and selfish' sexual behaviour of their husbands (Xu Anqi 1990a, 107), a view which is reinforced by the increasing publicity given to domestic violence against women in recent years. Indeed, according to Xu Anqi, women often attribute the failure of contraceptive methods to their husbands' 'excessive desire and lack of reason' (p. 104). However, Xu Anqi also points out that the greatest barriers to women's sexual enjoyment are the common assumptions that 'a virtuous woman has no sexual desire' (*nüzi wu xing bian shi de*) and that 'the only purpose of sex is reproduction' (*wei shengzhi mudi lun*) (p. 107). Standard publications about love, marriage and the family frequently assume that the wife's sexual desire has to be gently coaxed out of a natural state of reticence and passivity. 'Women have to be educated out of treating sex as a burdensome marital duty' (Gao Fang and Zeng Rong 1991, 35–7). All such representations convey a double message: that women should learn to assert themselves in rejecting unwanted advances, and men should begin to think of sex as an expression of mutual desire rather than as an act driven by unilateral need. A current argument based on such representations suggests a new interpretation of the familiar male/active–female/passive dichotomy. 'Women's power to choose in their sex lives is in fact an extension of their passive role. Since the wife looks on sex as an extra burden, and thinks of it as a duty she has to observe for her husband, she inevitably thinks of sex as something to give and pay out, a kind of sacrifice for the sake of the marriage, all of which gives rise to a psychology of sex premised on notions of bestowal and disadvantage' (Xu Anqi 1990a, 108).

Factors that derive from the implementation of fertility control also explain women's sexual disinterest. Despite the legal requirements on both male and female partners to use contraceptive means to control fertility, evidence demonstrates that the responsibility for doing so invariably falls on women (Liu Dalin 1992b, 552). The very high rate of sterilization of women at 'high tide' periods of implementation of the birth-control policy, and the frequent use of abortion as a follow-up to contraceptive method failure, implicate women's bodies and psychological responses in explaining their resistance to sex in ways that are often associated with pain, brutality and coercion.[6] The fear of becoming pregnant in itself is enough to discourage many women from showing much interest in sex (Xu Anqi 1990a, 104). When penalties are levied for outside-quota conception, and when women are subjected to constant surveillance and pressure to conform to fertility-control regulations, women's sexual subjectivity and experience are necessarily affected – maybe determined – by the concern not to conceive. In conditions already limited by material as well as cultural constraints, the fact that women are the bodily target of the relentless implementation of the birth-control programme may for many destroy altogether the possibility of heeding the experts' encouragement to think positively about sexual desire.

Attention to women's sexual behaviour may be interpreted as an aspect of the increasingly prevalent emphasis on sexual compatibility as an essential component of a satisfactory marriage. By implication, sexual incompatibility is constructed as a potential source of marital conflict in ways that were inapplicable in previous decades. However it is approached, the current interest in women's sexual enjoyment thus concerns the durability of the official model of monogamous marriage, an institution vital to the process and results of economic and social reorganization. Improvements in levels of women's satisfaction are described as a contribution to protecting marital stability, particularly in social contexts in which women potentially enjoy much greater freedom of social, cultural and sexual activity owing to the reduction of their childbearing and childcaring responsibilities. In this light, contemporary discourses construct women's sexual satisfaction as a requirement of and a contribution to demographic and economic policy, with little direct reference to women themselves.

The representation of exclusive monogamy as the only legitimate context for sexual relations has been tempered in recent years by the insertion into public discourses of images and references that are tantamount to condoning sexual activity outside the monogamous boundaries. The case of a woman who, after twelve years of marriage and two children, fell in love with a younger man received an understanding response from some readers when it was published in a magazine debate about the female 'third party' ('Wo ling you xin huan zenmo ban?' 1991). Extensive evidence from urban informants, particularly from the category of unmarried women in their late twenties considered to be 'on the shelf', suggests that extra-marital relationships are not only quite common but acceptable within certain professional and generational circles. A friend in Beijing, a woman academic in her mid-thirties, recently remarked to me that women who were dissatisfied with their marriages sometimes preferred to take lovers rather than divorce because of the social and material difficulties divorce created.

The idealized model of life-long monogamy has been further modified in recent years under the impact of the increasing incidence of divorce, particularly in the larger cities. While the numbers of divorces in 1994 were only 1.2 per cent more than in 1990, and divorces are still uncommon by Western standards, the fact that 12.38 million people ended their marriages in 1994 has attracted widespread public and official concern in China (*People's Daily* (*Overseas Edition*), *CND*, 23 March 1995). Whatever the reasons explaining this increase, the considerable incidence of adultery in divorce cases heard before the courts clearly indicates that attitudes towards sexuality are no longer associated simply with the exclusivity of the marriage contract, even though this may still be the ideal propagated in educational and popular materials. However, as later chapters argue, representations of extra-marital sexual activity are widely associated with a range of negative sanctions that call attention to the dire consequences to body, mind, family and society of nonconformity to the dominant model. The clear contrast between the positive representation of sexual relations within marriage and the harm derived from sexual activity outside marriage constitutes a means of reinforcing the unique legitimacy of sex within marriage.

The unprecedented attention given to the sexual component of marriage in the last decade or so, and the similarly unprecedented emphasis on the desirability of a good sex life, have created new spaces and possibilities for the invocation of sexual difficulties in the dominant discourse. Surveys analysing the various aspects of the married couple's sexual relationship put as great a store on the difficulties and disparities as on the 'good' sexual behaviour constitutive of 'harmony'. Notions of a good sex life are constructed with reference to inverse examples of incompatibility just as much as via affirmative description. Texts analysing the reasons for sexual difficulties – which frequently identify disinterest on the part of the wife and excessive demands of the husband – and their place in cases of marital conflict have made a significant contribution to the message that 'sexual harmony' is the normative objective. Though the immediate concern in such an approach is to identify the sources of sexual incompatibility which are reportedly fuelling the rising divorce rate, it simultaneously reinforces the view that marital harmony depends, among other things, on sexual satisfaction.

As part of this message, the foregrounding of women's sexual experience within marriage has not substantially interfered with the hierarchical representation of the sexual relationship within marriage. Even Li Wenhai and Liu Shuyu's condemnation of the 'myth' of female passivity did not question the fundamentally biological, non-contingent nature of the dominating male urge. Li and Liu's defence of women's right to sexual enjoyment did not, in itself, challenge the dominant view of sexual difference, according to which the leading, confident and biologically driven male facilitates full enjoyment on the part of his female partner. Emphasis on women's sexual enjoyment has not disturbed the assumption that a wife's sexual awakening depends on the assistance and encouragement of her husband. The ideal of mutual orgasm as the ultimate goal of sexual activity – the undisputed aim to be aspired to by all sexually active couples – is thus contained within a paradigm of sexual activity in which the husband is the guide and mentor. Despite specific encouragement for women to discover different aspects of their own sexuality, the relational context for such advice suggests that experimentation should be oriented first and foremost to consolidating the marital relationship. From this perspective, female sexuality continues to be represented as a means of contributing to familial, and thereby to group and social, stability.

## The natural mother

The Marriage Laws of 1950 and 1980 shared a conceptualization of women's role as wives and mothers which centred on a redefinition of the husband–wife relationship. According to this redefinition, the key relationship holding the household network together was, ideally, the monogamous marriage. Indeed, a major interest in the new government's commitment to strengthening the conjugal relationship was to secure a stable source of labour to contribute to the official programme of socio-economic transformation. This emphasis meant a shift in focus from the traditional axis of intergenerational, vertically structured relationships, according to which family authority depended on gender and generation, to one which constructed women and men as equal partners. The legal stipulations concerning the rights and duties of husband and wife represented the wife as the equal partner of her husband, enjoying 'equal status in the home', subject to the same requirements of love, respect and assistance, and with the same 'freedom to engage in production, to work, to study and to participate in social activities' (Article 11, 1980 Marriage Law of the People's Republic of China). The reassessment of the values accorded women as wives and as mothers created the possibility for a new conceptualization of the dominant attributes defining 'woman'. The official discourse no longer recognized motherhood as the major subject position with which women should identify. Motherhood was modified by the new construction of wifehood, a social as well as sexual and gender category, which repositioned women as the equals of their husbands. Women's principal value was no longer to derive from producing male children, and no longer were women obliged to define their gender responsibilities with exclusive reference to husband, sons and mother-in-law.

Such privileging of wifehood did not, of course, exclude motherhood. Since 1949, official discourses have created wifehood not as a substitute for motherhood, but as a site of responsibilities, expectations and new possibilities granting new meaning to the category of woman. Alongside motherhood, wifehood has been given a new status in the hierarchy of roles and positions mediating women's experience. Thus, while discourses about women's natural attributes shifted their emphasis to include subject positions associated with the new image of the working wife – subject positions which were not formerly available to women – they remained, and continue to remain, attached to a notion of motherhood as a desirable state for all women to identify with. From this perspective, motherhood emerges as an inalienable aspect of wifehood. The gender attributes and characteristics associated with women in the conjugal relationship invoke their position as mothers as significantly as that of wives.

The step from constructing wifehood and motherhood as two sides of a coin to naturalizing motherhood as a universal aspect of being a woman is a small one. For a start, it closely corresponds with practice. The vast majority of women in China marry, as noted above, and more than 90 per cent of these have a child within their first year of marriage.[7] The almost universal practice of marriage and motherhood in China, and the common assumption of a biologically grounded correspondence between marriage, sexual intercourse and reproduction, reinforce the image of the 'natural mother'. That women are 'born to be mothers' is variously conveyed in Chinese discourses, from references to women's reproductive functions and physiological structure to the emotional and behavioural responses a young girl develops. In the 1950s, reproduction of the next generation was projected as woman's 'natural duty' (*tianran yiwu*), failure to fulfil which was considered irresponsible (Wei Junyi 1953). More recent representations of womanhood have focused on the psychological loss experienced by childless women. Remaining single, and thereby 'forgoing the joys of motherhood' makes women feel 'incomplete and unfulfilled' (Yu Yan 1993). It may also be the expression of sexual needs and desires not condoned by the exclusively heterosexual bias of the dominant discourse. In exceptional cases of 'mental or contagious disease' it is considered legitimate – indeed, given the full backing of a eugenics law – for women 'to defer marriage' and not to have a child.[8] In recent years, occasional articles have also appeared which question the universal equation between wifehood and motherhood. A 1992 article entitled 'Do good men marry and good women stay single?' ended on a note of encouragement to those 'who waver in front of the gates of marriage': 'Go on, in front of you is a heaven!' (Si Wuliu 1992). Notwithstanding the disruption of the link between sexuality and reproduction signified by the prevalent use of contraceptive methods, as well as the frustrations of having to obtain bureaucratic permission from the work unit and street committee in order to conceive, the common assumption is that marriage means children, and that as soon as people marry they begin trying to have a child. Indeed, those who delay having a child are frequently subject to gossip and ridicule; women who show no signs of pregnancy within a year or so of marriage may be rumoured to be sick or too old, or their husband 'too weak', or, as in the 1950s, reneging on their duty (Honig and Hershatter 1988, 188).

The natural positioning of women as mothers in dominant discourses since 1949 has clearly emerged in advice and information about contraception. Coinciding with the formation of a rudimentary birth-control policy in the mid-1950s, much of the early discussion about contraception set out to persuade a cautious audience of the benefits of the different methods available. Details of contraceptive techniques which made use of Chinese medicine as well as more standard Western methods were explained to allay popular worries that, for example, the use of condoms would impair male potency, or would cause tuberculosis – a disease commonly associated in the 1950s with female sexuality – in women by preventing the 'yin and yang from joining together' (Tan Zhen 1956; Liang Zhao 1957).[9] Through the 1970s, as the 'later, more spaced, fewer' birth-control policy gathered steam, discussion about contraception emphasized its more general benefits to 'the health of mothers and the next generation' by reducing the average number of babies to which women gave birth (e.g., Shanghai diyi yixue yuan fushu Zhongshan yiyuan fuchan ke 1974, 10). Since then, discussion about contraception has been situated firmly within the context of the single-child family policy, and has also assumed a much greater familiarity on the part of its audience. Official statistics from the State Statistics Bureau in 1991 indicated an increase in the national use of contraceptive methods among married women, from 13.47 per cent in 1970 to 73.24 per cent in 1988 (Zheng Xiaoying 1995, 247). Even though family-planning methods were still less popular in the rural areas than in the towns and cities – by 1988, 64.45 per cent of rural married women were using contraceptives – these figures clearly demonstrated that persuading a reluctant constituency of potential users was no longer the major problem.[10] However, detailed information about and access to contraception remains firmly controlled by the family-planning agencies, and is not generally available to unmarried couples. Although contraceptives are available for sale over the counter in pharmacies, and unmarried couples often obtain them through married friends, sex education courses, even at university level, do not formally include information about contraceptive methods. To include such would be inconsistent with the administrative attempts – such as obliging visitors to register their name and work unit, or not permitting friends to stay overnight in the same room – to prohibit students from sexual activity and marriage. While, as earlier chapters have shown, sex education is considered vital to the health and happiness of the married couple, and pre-marital pregnancies are often attributed to sexual ignorance, contraception is still formally excluded from discussion in materials for young people on the grounds that its inclusion would be an invitation to pre-marital promiscuity. Public discussion about contraception is bound by the assumption that sex can be referred to legitimately only within the context of marriage.

Advice about the benefits of contraception draws a direct link between fertility control and the quality of a couple's sex life. Ever since it appeared as an item on the official agenda, the use of contraception has been represented as an aid to 'marital feeling', and to 'resolving the difficulties of early marriage' imposed by the burdens of childcare (e.g., 'Bu yao guo zao jiehun' 1957). However, contraception is useful because it limits the number of children, not because it challenges the requirement to reproduce. While, in theoretical terms, contraception severs the link between sexuality and reproduction, in the terms of the dominant discourse it is treated as a means of controlling that link. The representation of reproduction as a natural biological need and a social duty denies women any alternative. In this light, contraception grants women no more than the possibility of determining the length and timing of their childbearing career. Though the government's insistence on controlling the birth rate would logically be served by encouraging women not to have children – by positively constructing childless women as an aid to social and economic development – the dominant discourse offers women no real alternative to their naturalized role as mother.

Despite the legal requirements on both partners to use contraceptive methods, texts about contraception commonly – though not exclusively – assume that birth control is principally a woman's responsibility.[11] Evidence from surveys indicates that the intra-uterine device (IUD) and tubal ligation are the preferred methods of contraception, with the pill, condoms and the cap ranking some way behind.[12] Female responsibility for practising birth control, however, does not simply refer to women's instrumentality in deciding when contraception should be used and what form it should take. Policy and official discourse construct women as the responsible agents of birth control; it is their bodies that are targeted as the means of restricting the numbers of pregnancies at any particular time, whether through the use of the IUD or abortion. A survey carried out between 1991 and 1992 among women of the 30- to 39-year-old age group in two counties in Sichuan and Jiangsu provinces showed that, between 1980 and 1990, most abortions were performed to terminate pregnancies after the first birth, and that in all cases these pregnancies occurred without official permission.[13] Some accounts, including those of personal informants, document the coercive methods used to force women to undergo an abortion, sometimes as late as the seventh or eighth month of pregnancy (Mosher 1994). Indeed, evidence of use of coercion – from summarily obliging village women to report to a makeshift clinic where a visiting family-planning agent checks that methods of contraception are being used, to making surprise visits to women to 'persuade' them to undergo an abortion, to rounding up village women in the middle of the night to pack them off to 'clinics' where their unreported pregnancies are terminated, to forcibly holding down women struggling to prevent the operation – has been widely publicized by human rights activists and organizations.[14] Moreover, as if women's 'responsibility' for implementing the fertility limitation programme were not enough, the eugenic concerns of the state's family-planning personnel, recently expressed in the Law on Maternal and Infantile Health Care, also construct women as the key agents guaranteeing the wholesome birth, physical health, intelligence and psychological development of the next generation. Contemporary discourses on sexuality thus concur with empirical evidence in showing that women bear the major responsibility for supporting the state's demographic policy. While theoretically removed from reproductive considerations, female sexuality continues to be underpinned by a series of expectations, naturalized assumptions, responsibilities and burdens inextricably identified with women's reproductive functions.

The assumption that being a woman means being a mother is also foregrounded in medical and educational advice about sexual behaviour during menstruation and pregnancy.[15] As Chapter 2 demonstrated, expert opinion of the 1950s was consistent in its warnings against sexual intercourse during menstruation and during the first three and last three months of pregnancy, on the grounds that the introduction of bacteria into the uterus would cause uterine inflammation, potentially impairing fertility. Texts of the 1970s reiterated the same message in almost identical terms (Xie Bozhang 1975, 81;

Shanghai diyi yixue yuan fushu Zhongshan yiyuan fuchan ke 1974, 4).
Nor have these been substantially modified in more recent texts. Sex
during pregnancy is still regarded as a possible cause of miscarriage
and premature labour (e.g., Guangdong sheng funü lianhehui 1986,
26). And whether in advice booklets distributed to newly-weds, or in
more general texts about female physiology and psychology, sex
during menstruation continues to be seen as a potential danger to the
female reproductive capacity because of the vagina's vulnerability to
bacterial infection and because of its effect of prolonging the menstrual
period (*Xinhun weisheng bi du* editorial group 1984, 24; Fang Fang
1987, 117). Even though women's desire for sex sometimes increases
around the menstrual period, both women and men are urged to
exercise self-restraint in order to prevent any reproductive complications (Fang Fang 1987, 117).

The greater diversity of contemporary discourses of sexuality has
created spaces in which women may be constituted as sexual beings
without any necessarily reproductive content. One effect of the single-
child family policy, moreover, has been to extend the non-reproductive
sexually active life of enormous numbers of women. However, when
combined with persistent references to the damage to fertility and fetal
development caused by having sexual intercourse at specific moments
of the female cycle, and with the explicit association between contraceptive use and marital status, reproduction remains a key organizing
principle of the discourse about female sexuality.

## Sex and the older woman

The overriding focus on the twenty- to thirty-year-old age group in
public representations of female sexuality does not entirely preclude
references to older women. Though limited and muted by comparison
with the attention given to the dominant category, texts about sexual
desire and activity during middle and old age contribute a theme to the
public discourses of sexuality which was ignored in the texts of the
pre-Cultural Revolution period. Medical and educational works
devote entire sections to 'sexual responses of older women', and books
are now published on the menopause (e.g., Li Wenhai and Liu Shuyu
1992, 144–6; Zhang Yiwen and Wu Yiyong 1990). The inclusion in
one such text of a preface originally written in 1964 by Deng
Yingchao, former chairwoman of the All China Women's Federation
and widow of China's famous former premier Zhou Enlai, adds to the
discursive acceptability of a delicate topic (Deng Yingchao, in Xu Chen

and Zhang Kongqian 1987). The bodily and psychological changes that women experience during the menopause invariably have a considerable effect on their work and family life. They can also have a determining influence on a woman's relationship with her husband. Indeed, Xu and Zhang suggest that divorce among middle-aged couples is often provoked by the 'psychological abnormalities' (*jingshen xinli biantai*) which menopausal women experience (Xu Chen and Zhang Kongqian 1987, 11). Introducing the menopause into public discussion thus signifies acknowledgement of an issue considered to have a potentially vital bearing on marital relations as well as on women's health.

Some writers attribute the habitual silence about old people's sexuality to the dominating influence of cultural bias, which has made it 'difficult to imagine that men and women in their later years still have sexual feelings, needs, and relations' (Wu Jieping et al. 1983, 30, 80). 'There is one point that we must clarify,' one commentator noted, 'namely that the menopause does not mean the end of one's sex life, but rather its development to a higher stage – to even greater emotional exchange' (Zheng Lunian 1987, 45). However, the assumption that women cease to be sexually active once their fertile years are over is widespread. While medical experts urge menopausal women to 'maintain a normal sex life', and ask husbands to be 'understanding about the unfortunate influence the menopause has on the structure of the vagina' (Zhang Yiwen and Wu Yiyong 1990, 52), they also refer to biological changes to explain the reduction in frequency and intensity of intercourse for women during this period. The terms used represent the menopause as a process of sexual decline. It is a period when the 'ovaries' function deteriorates and the reproductive organs begin to wither' (Xu Chen and Zhang Kongqian 1987, 27), when the uterus 'shrivels', the 'folds of the labia slacken' and the vagina 'shrinks' (Zhang Yiwen and Wu Yiyong 1990, 10).[16] The decrease in the amount of estrogen in the body, the cessation of fertility and the reduction of secretions lubricating the vagina provoke sexual changes which increase women's tension and physical discomfort (Xu Chen and Zhang Kongqian 1987, 11). Women may also want to stop having sex because of sickness or weakness during their 'transition to old age', or they may feel that sex is no longer an appropriate activity for persons of middle age (Xu Chen and Zhang Kongqian 1987, 11).

Approaches to women's sexuality during and after the menopause are no mere repetition of the taboos against sexual activity during menstruation and pregnancy. Some texts argue that, far from disappearing, women's sexual desire may 'flourish' (*bijiao wangsheng*) in their forties or fifties, considerably later than the height of sexual desire in men. They quote the findings of Western surveys to argue that older women often experience an increase in sexual desire – 'more beautiful, easier, and more leisurely' – during the menopause (Li Wenhai and Liu Shuyu 1992, 144–5). Advice to women about how to maintain strength and vitality as they approach old age includes suggestions that 'frequent use of the muscles of the reproductive organs, just like muscles in other parts of the body, helps maintain the body's vigour and strength' (Lu Shumin and Tang Jianhua 1991, 189). While such texts mention that the menopause may produce mood fluctuations and physical complaints that exacerbate marital problems and increase women's disinterest in sex, they also suggest that this is by no means necessarily the case, and may often occur among women who did not have a particularly satisfactory sexual relationship during their fertile years (Li Wenhai and Liu Shuyu 1992, 146).

There is thus a clear contrast between the relative diversity of discursive representations of female sexuality during and after the menopause and the uniformity of the views about sex during menstruation and pregnancy. One possible explanation of this is that post-menopausal sexuality does not constitute a threat either to the successful implementation of the fertility limitation programme or to social and familial stability. The menopausal woman does not challenge the naturalized attributes associated with female gender in wifehood and motherhood. The menopausal woman remains a wife and mother, at a different stage of her life. With the cessation of her fertility, a woman's sexuality no longer appears as a major target of control, either by herself or by the state. Nor are older women constructed as a potential danger to marital and familial stability; the infamous 'third party' invariably refers to younger, beautiful women whose fertile sexuality is not in doubt. Freed from the real and discursive constraints of having to exercise auto-surveillance for the sake of demographic and social stability, many women may indeed experience an unaccustomed sexual desire, a 'second spring', during their later years. From this perspective, just as older women are given social licence to behave in ways which are still considered somewhat risqué for younger women of childbearing age – for example, drinking alcohol and smoking in public – so they may be allowed the unique possibility of discovering hidden sources of sexual enjoyment once their potential threat to the social and moral order has disappeared.

Representations of female sexuality during the menopause thus contain a dual and contradictory message. On the one hand, they challenge the assumption that women's sexuality is concurrent with female fertility, that the duration as well as the mode of expression of female sexual activity is determined by women's reproductive capacity.

They challenge the definition of female sexuality in terms of its reproductive aspect. On the other hand, acknowledgement of female desire in later life may correspond more to the assumption that, because fertility has declined, control of sexuality through the attachment of informal sanctions is no longer important, either for demographic or for health reasons. In this sense, it would be an inverse mode of affirming the power associated with reproductive sexuality. Chapter 8 shows how Li Yinhe uses a similar argument to explain what, in her view, seems to be the stronger popular antipathy to 'inappropriate heterosexual acts' than to homosexuality (Li Yinhe 1991, 232–3).

## Monogamy and marital fidelity

By 1953, when a series of intensive month-long campaigns to publicize the Marriage Law came to an end, the state recognized that the initial stages of the law's implementation had fallen far short of universal success. A government report of 1953 estimated that, each year since 1950, 70,000 to 80,000 women had been killed or had committed suicide as a result of hostility to the new model of free-choice marriage (*Guanche hunyin fa yundong de zhongyao wenjian* 1953, 12; Evans 1992, 150–1). The law's exponents had failed to convince the rural population of the need or desirability of replacing traditional arrangements; rather, the antagonism it provoked was a response to its threat to the 'patrilineal family structure on which the rural communities were based' (Johnson 1983, 147). In response, the government shifted its emphasis away from the radical implications of the law towards protecting marital stability, now considered vital to the success of its programme of rural collectivization. This strategic shift in approach to the law was amply reflected in the publicity accompanying it. Divorce was no longer discussed as a progressive challenge to the feudal constraints on women, but as an unnecessary disruption of family life that could be avoided by mediation.

The implications for representations of women as wives were striking. If monogamy signified a unique opportunity to achieve sexual harmony, it now was a synonym for normative sexual relations according to which, as sexual partners, a woman and a man were bound together for life. Women's interests were no longer to be served by prioritizing their new rights in asking for divorce, but by making concessions to conservative opinion in order to preserve family stability. Women were now encouraged to be caring and supportive wives and efficient domestic managers. Coinciding with the increase in urban unemployment in 1955, they were told that being a housewife was a sensible alternative to social employment. They were also told that dressing up in nice clothes and curling their hair to look pretty for their husbands was no longer to to be disdained as a bourgeois activity.[17]

As part of this new emphasis, the discussion about monogamy shifted ground. Cases where the monogamous principle had been violated by adulterous actions were presented no longer simply as examples of the need to eradicate the injustices of the feudal past, but much more as instances of the individualism and degeneracy of 'bourgeois behaviour'. This change in orientation also granted an ideological justification for expanding the targets of criticism. The male focus of the feudal label did not easily permit criticism of female behaviour, given that women were seen as victims of an oppressive system. Discarding the notion that the feudal system was responsible for sexual misdemeanours, therefore, permitted identification of women's behaviour, alongside men's, as examples of sexual immorality. It also gave space for discussion of practices and attitudes which could not simply be dismissed as remnants of China's feudal past. The meaning of monogamy as a discursive practice was extended to identify what it was not. It marked positive forms of behaviour and simultaneously isolated 'deviant' modes of conduct which could not be assimilated into the standards of the official discourse. Monogamy acquired the status of a moralizing as well as an ideological principle of order.

As in many other aspects of the official discourse of sexuality, the evident focus on female behaviour suggested a positioning of women as the key agents responsible for patrolling the boundaries of monogamy. Just as the norm of pre-marital chastity almost exclusively invoked the female standard, so marital fidelity was discussed principally with reference to women. Disruption of marriages because of the intrusion of a 'third party' was described as 'invariably the fault of women' (Evans 1992, 153). Women's violation of the monogamous principle by committing adultery or interfering in a stable relationship could lead to dire consequences, and even to petty crime. Even when violation of the monogamous principle was the man's responsibility just as much as the woman's, she was frequently censured in more severe tones.[18]

Most allusions to female fidelity in the pre-Cultural Revolution discourse did not explicitly refer to requirements of sexual purity. Rather, they projected ideals of commitment, loyalty, support and selflessness which served to convey messages about desirable political attitudes for everyone, men as well as women, as much as about marital harmony. Nevertheless, the gendered characteristics of descriptions of model wives were distinct from the active decisiveness, the creative strength and initiative associated with model husbands. Whether in descriptions of the peasant woman who after seven years of separation from her husband was commended for her loyalty and encouragement to him to continue fighting in Korea, or of the wife whose gratification lay in caring for her husband so that he could become a member of the party, images of marital harmony invariably included that of the woman serving the husband in the name of the public good. By contrast, the husband's support of his wife was described through references to his encouragement to her to learn to read or participate in political meetings or to enable her to gain closer access to the serious and authoritative world of masculine events and activities (e.g., Liu Dezhen 1952). The husband's contribution was creative, whereas the wife's tended to be servicing.

The gendered dichotomy between creativity and service was echoed in 1950s representations of male and female infidelity. Requirements of male fidelity were commonly associated with concerns to protect the wives of arranged marriages, particularly in the rural sector, whose security was threatened by the new Marriage Law. Relevant examples suggested that the husband's infidelity was often the consequence of being caught between traditional parental authority and the new modern values of 'free love'. Instances of young men who left their peasant wives to go to the city to study or work, or who sought release from the constraints imposed by their first, arranged marriage in favour of a more fulfilling relationship, were commonly constructed as undesirable consequences of the feudal marriage system. After 1953, male infidelity was increasingly identified as a bourgeois tendency engendered by aspirations to higher social and political status. In the terms of the official discourse of sexuality, the implication was that male infidelity was first and foremost associated with a failure to exercise self-control within the context of new social pressures and possibilities. From this perspective, infidelity was almost a metaphor for aspirations to creativity and status. Requirements of female fidelity, by contrast, were directly linked to a woman's sexual and gender responsibilities to her husband.

Representations of women as wives in the public discourses of the post-Mao period have clearly presented them with a range of new subject positions. The 1980s essentialist vindication of women's natural femininity against the collective-spirited, selfless and androgynous images of the former discourse gave new meanings to the notion of wifehood. The wife could now be variously represented as the busy professional mother, the comfortable manager of a happy home, the pretty and endlessly available companion to a busy husband, the diligent educator of a growing child. She could now withdraw from social production to identify entirely with domestic concerns. Personal and individual gratification in matters such as appearance, fashion, social and cultural activities were no longer equated with bourgeois indulgence. Sex acquired new status in marriage as a source of shared enjoyment. The increasing rate of divorce also suggested that the meaning of monogamy was shifting away from the exclusive, life-long bond to multiple or serial relationships. Stories about '*dingke*' (dinky) couples – double income no kids – further made it clear that wifehood no longer always automatically invoked motherhood. The requirement on couples to have only one child in accordance with the government's birth limitation policy expanded the potential time and financial resources available to the wife-mother to devote to non-domestic and non-child-centred interests. The contradictory combination of increasing unemployment, greater consumer capacity and more opportunities to engage in a wide range of leisure activities, from disco-dancing to watching beauty contests, all indicated that the category of woman inscribed in the image of the wife–mother was no longer defined by a unitary set of characteristics and aspirations. The fact that, as Li Xiaojiang and others have pointed out, many of these new subject positions derive from fundamentally economic considerations does not necessarily diminish their significance for women.[19]

However, another look at representations of wives and happy marriages in the last fifteen years indicates that the monogamous relationship, defined in terms that bear striking similarities to some of those of the 1950s, continues to be constructed as the dominant site for the realization of women's proper responsibilities to society. Since the 1980s, women's magazines have published numerous debates about the ideal wife, surveys about the criteria men and women use in selecting a spouse, and advice about how a wife should behave in order to patch up domestic quarrels and liven up a dull marriage. Surveys conducted among students and professionals have repeatedly indicated that men want a wife who will put her interests after their own (e.g., Li Jiangtao 1986). They also show that men rank 'gentleness and softness' (*wenrou*) high up on their list of priorities in selecting a wife (Jiang Wenyu 1986). The dominant image foregrounded in a series of articles on 'Do you want to be a good wife?', published in a popular women's compendium in May 1991, was that of the supportive, caring and servicing wife ('Ni xiang zuo ge hao qizi ma?' 1991). Even *Nüxing yanjiu*, the women's studies journal published by the research branch of the Beijing Women's Federation, used the argument

that men 'really do have more responsibilities than women' to legitimize expectations of a wife's support for her husband (Shu Huaimeng
1993).

The extent of the appeal of the gentle and caring wife was apparent
in the popular reception given 'Yearning' (*Kewang*), a soap shown on
national television in 1991, and widely referred to in magazine debates
and articles for some time after.[20] The story centred on Liu Huifang, a
factory worker and a modern 'virtuous wife and good mother' (*xianqi
liangmu*). Liu Huifang married a university student called Wang
Husheng, but her marriage fell apart as it became apparent that Wang
was a selfish and weak coward, and completely insensitive to her
needs. After failing her university entrance exam, other disasters befell
Liu. Her marriage broke up, she had a car accident, and, in the end,
the child she had struggled to bring up walked away from her. Public
response to the film not only indicated sympathy for the plight of Liu
Huifang, but also suggested that the image of the self-effacing, gentle
and unassertive wife was incredibly popular, among both the young
and the middle-aged. For the younger group, Liu Huifang represented
the gentle femininity currently associated with the ideal wife, whereas,
for the older group, she represented the selfless commitment and hard
work reminiscent of the gendered images of the 1950s.

Advising women about how to keep hold of their husbands' affection, particularly during the vulnerable years of middle age when
husbands are led astray by younger, more beautiful women, signifies
another aspect of the dominant representation of the self-sacrificing,
considerate and nurturing wife. Women have access to various ploys
and techniques to liven up a dull marriage and thereby divert their
husbands' attention from potential attractions elsewhere (Gao Fang
and Zeng Rong 1991, 18–22). They might decide to 'go away for a
brief trip on their own', or 'pay attention to their appearance', or even
'behave coquettishly' in order to maintain their husbands' interest. In
the event of a husband paying attention to other women, a wife should
refrain from taking him to task (pp. 37–9). Nor should she speak
critically of his mother. Above all, a wife should take care not to
criticize her husband too much, and she should 'not treat him as a
child' by reminding him to do things that he has forgotten (p. 23).
Again, women whose husbands were having an affair with a 'third
party' were encouraged to be understanding rather than critical. Being
supportive of the husband by doing all the housework, for example, or
by protecting him from children's demands, might persuade him of the
benefits of maintaining his marriage rather than pursuing a new
relationship ('Wo shi zenmo yang bangzhu airen baituo disanzhe de?'
1991).

Whether in discussions about domestic duties or about wives' responsibilities in the face of their husbands' infidelities, texts published over the last ten years or so reveal an evident asymmetry in the assignment of gender attributes that echoes the biological construction of sexual and gender difference. Editorial comments about such representations are by no means always uncritical. Men's desire for a self-sacrificing wife was attacked in an editorial of *Zhongguo funü* for showing that the 'progressive attitudes of men about women are totally superficial; expecting self-sacrifice of a wife signifies nothing less than the husband's desire to build his career and ambitions on her shoulders . . . If self-sacrifice is to be demanded, then it should be on both sides' (Li Jiangtao 1986, 6). However, while representations of wives in current public discourses in China no longer conform to a unitary set of principles and objectives, the familiar dichotomy between male creativity and female care and support is writ large in the prevalent image of the gentle, selfless and nurturing wife. The view that women's reproductive role provides a natural biological explanation for their gender characteristics continues to exercise considerable appeal.

## Clothing the female body

The 'socialist androgyny' of the Maoist years fixed the sartorial style of the true revolutionary for more than three decades.[21] Between the Yan'an period in the early 1940s and the late 1970s, communist apparel was more or less the same for women and men. Overt signs of femininity in dress were considered the reflection of individualistic and bourgeois interests, incompatible with the frugal, selfless commitment to the collective good required by party ideology. Simple trousers, in grey, green or blue, accompanied by the high-collared Sun Yatsen jacket – often renamed the Mao jacket – were the dominant themes, varying only in texture and cut. Long sleeves, long trousers, high necklines and buttons ensured that little flesh was exposed. Short sleeves and skirts were risqué, and seen in any numbers only in the hot summer months in the big southern cities. Urban hairstyles were mainly short, either bobbed or in tight plaits and pig-tails. Long hair – often associated with the less modern outlook of young rural women – was kept in plaits, and never let loose in public. Occasional glimpses of a trouser suit, or of brightly coloured socks – more often than not in Shanghai, away from the sober restrictions of the capital – indicated desires for variation. Some daring young women even wore colourful and patterned blouses under the standard jackets. In general, however, bright reds, greens and yellows and shiny, tinselly adornments were reserved for infants and small children. 'Socialist androgyny' homogenized women and men as the uniformed cohorts of the faithful.

The images of women which appeared on the front covers of *Zhongguo funü* in these years conformed to the same homogenizing standards. Invariably set in contexts where social production was the dominant theme, images of women steelworkers, farmers, parachutists and cotton-pickers rarely differed in their dominant meaning. With shining eyes gazing into the distance, they signified passionate commitment to a revolutionary ideal. Ruddy-cheeked, robust and healthy, they also symbolized energy, hard work and determination. The outlines of their bodies celebrated a physical strength and vigour that rejected all implication of soft feminine curves. Far from serving or waiting for men, as many of the contemporary narrative constructions of wifehood anticipated, they acted on their environment, they did and created things, through inventing, manufacturing or tilling the land. The only significant exceptions were the images of women as teachers or creche workers, as doctors and mothers. To all intents and purposes, the image of the woman mirrored that of the man. Seen in this light, gender equality meant the destruction of difference in a new ideal of 'sameness'. If the proper modes of response required of everyone, men as well as women, to the party and collective were service and self-sacrifice, then for women this also meant denial of the female body.

Conversely, the slightest suggestion that (particularly female) appearance might convey some sexual or erotic meaning was enough to invite suspicions of shamelessness and immorality. Fancy clothes were a metaphor for moral degeneration and ideological impurity. A story entitled 'The twisted path I once went along', which described a woman's rejection of her rural husband in favour of a Japanese lover, suggested that the first sign of her descent into depravity was her love of dressing up in pretty urban clothes (Zheng Hao 1957). Women who 'wasted their time' on attending to their appearance, or who spent money on fashionable clothes, were represented as self-seeking temptresses (Yu Feng 1955). Physical beauty and fashionable clothes could disguise evil intentions, and even criminal behaviour. Feminine pleasures and feminine beauty were thus used as a metaphor for moral degeneration or ideological impurity. Stories about the pitfalls of 'love at first sight' often included descriptions of the female party's appearance, as if to emphasize the dangers of attaching importance to looks. An article criticizing a young woman who had had an extra-marital affair after seven years of marriage began with a description of how she became interested in fine clothes (Liu Dezeng and Hao Shimin 1950). Women described as the 'third party' or whose sexual conduct was somewhat suspect often appeared in contexts where detailed attention was drawn to symbols of bourgeois pleasure, like shiny, high-heeled shoes, tight dresses and sleek hair (Geng Xi 1958; Chen Yanping 1957). Images of the female body suggestive of sexual interest and removed from associations with utilitarian practicality became a metaphor for subject positions with which women could identify only at their peril.

On the other hand, a simple and unexceptional appearance might cover truly wonderful 'internal' qualities. The true revolutionary paid no attention to appearance either for herself or in selecting a marriage partner, since it was 'internal beauty', not external appeal, that contributed to a felicitous union. Just as 'external beauty' in a woman had often been represented as a sign of danger in China's imperial history, so clothing the female body in loose-fitting and frugal clothes thus contained the further implication that bodily concealment was a condition of ideological and sexual purity, in terms reminiscent of traditional values in female appearance. The contrast between the voluptuous looks of a wife and the sober appearance of Ning Lao T'ai-t'ai's 'good woman' was reworked in communist discourse as the difference between bourgeois degeneracy and revolutionary virtue.[22] The insistence on seemingly androgynous values in women's appearance, and the suspicion levelled against any overt signs of feminine taste, was a mode of suggesting that women should patrol their own desires and impulses for the sake of general standards of sexual propriety. Gender-neutral clothing covering the female body functioned – among other purposes – to reinforce a representation of sexual order that depended on the woman's denial of potential interests of her own in favour of those defined by external agencies.

The official attack on conventional signs of feminine beauty was explained as a means of freeing women from the medical harm and degradation associated with the 'exploiting class's notion of beauty'. Young women were explicitly told that breast-binding – often practised to produce the slim elegance associated with the image of the beautiful woman – would harm their natural development (Huang Shuze 1953). In a context of material deprivation and moralistic antipathy to individual self-expression, the official critique also signified an attempt to revise the gender constructs associated with female appearance so as to correspond with the ideological shift towards the public sphere in matters associated with sexual and bodily management. Women's dress should be comfortable, simple and functional, and should indicate the nature of an individual's political commitment rather than provide a statement about gender or sexuality. The robust demeanour of a guerrilla fighter of peasant background whose 'man-like' large feet caught the attention of the interviewer represented the supposedly gender-neutral ideal of determination and revolutionary commitment (Zhu Keyu 1951).

The apparently sudden halt to the emphasis on defeminizing appearance in the mid-1950s was, therefore, surprising. Sartorial politics took a new turn when, after the long war years of frugal sameness, a clothes reform campaign which aimed at boosting the self-image of the housewife explicitly encouraged gender distinctions in dress. Symbolic suggestions of femininity such as dress patterns and instructions about how to refashion old clothes started appearing in the media alongside articles encouraging women to discard the 'mistaken notion' that being interested in fashion was bourgeois. An unfamiliar note of approval was given the new femininity in suggestions that, for example, 'long trousers were not an aesthetic accompaniment to the narrow shoulders of women' (Yu Feng 1955).

Coinciding with the government's attempt to persuade women to withdraw from the labour force in the mid-1950s, in order to relieve levels of urban unemployment, the refeminization of female appearance depended on the deployment of hierarchical gender constructs for reasons that had nothing to do with women's interests *per se*. Media discussion clearly identified interest in appearance as a feminine characteristic associated with women's 'natural tendency' to occupy themselves with private and domestic concerns. Inasmuch as references to dress and external appearance, particularly in their unacceptable forms, almost invariably invoked women, the conceptualization of the body was therefore also gendered. Assumptions about the links between women, the body and the private sphere were used to subordinate the interests of women, however these might have been defined at the time, to the needs of economic organization. Female gender thus emerged as a dual category, despite its grounding in biological structures. On the one hand – subject to the requirements of the party-state and integrated into the public world of social labour, study and politics – it was identified with the progressive constructs of work and public commitment, defined according to the male standard. On the other hand, when social and economic need demanded the withdrawal of women from the public sites that offered equal status with men, representations of female gender invoked either the petty-minded and materialistic interests of the feminine, domestic sphere or women's association with the body – by definition inferior to the serious male world of intellectual and political matters. The identification of women's interests and private affairs – including appearance –

was a useful mechanism legitimizing the party-state's decision to reduce expenditure on women's employment.

Coinciding with the launch of the economic reform programme in the late 1970s, the reorganization of the Women's Federation was followed by the relaunch of its organ, *Zhongguo funü*, and the appearance of numerous popular women's magazines about marriage, the family and related matters.[23] While, in the early 1980s, key ideological principles – for example, concerning expectations of commitment to the collective, and the relationship between private and collective responsibilities – which informed the narrative discourse about women continued to overlap with those of the earlier period, the quantity and diversity of images of feminine beauty signified a radical departure from the social and gender values formerly inscribed in representations of women. The first women's fashion magazine, *Xiandai fuzhuang*, started publication in 1980. Articles about feminine beauty began to appear in publications about feminine physiology and psychology, making it clear that concern with good looks was no longer an ideological error. Chinese and Western fashions quickly made their way into women's magazines and television advertising. Magazines about feminine hairstyles and make-up techniques were published in seemingly endless quantities, often with detailed instructions about how to apply eye make-up or how to keep breasts in good shape. Moreover, the range of women's bodies featured in such materials was increasingly diverse. Photographs of Chinese women were placed alongside others of white, Western women, in apparently random combinations. Some are fully clothed, while others are more scantily clad in daring poses; some are sporty and athletic, while others suggest fragility and the need for protection. However, while the diversity of these images suggests a range of possibilities not available to women in the 1950s and 1970s, a quick glance at the cover pictures of standard women's magazines conveys some idea of the dominant values currently associated with female gender. Beautiful, slender, young, urban women have replaced the representations of the robust cotton-picker and the healthy sportswoman of the previous decades. Dressed in a variety of fashion clothes, from Chinese haute-couture to the designer labels of Europe's big fashion houses, and from tight blouses emphasizing feminine curves to diaphanous negligées in pastel pink, the young women of these images invariably possess or point to some symbol of the consumerist values of recent economic policies in China, such as a motorbike, expensive domestic appliances or luxurious household furniture. The convergence of apparent variety in the figure of the young, urban beauty rehomogenizes the subject positions available to women, albeit along very different lines than in the previous decades. While the inside pages of some of these magazines occasionally feature photographs of unfashionable, middle-aged pro-fessionals or of elderly revolutionaries unconcerned with physical appearance, readers are left in no doubt about the dominant gender values in dress to which they should aspire.

The representational authority exercised by the beautiful young urbanite may be the predictable consequence of the permeation of patriarchal structures by commercial values widely associated with the material culture of the West, in an economic context that has encour-aged the growth of the fashion industry both for export and domestic consumption. It is also the result of a comprehensive re-evaluation of the meanings associated with dress and appearance. Coinciding with the reassertion of the essentialist *nüxing* (female), the visual vindica-tion of femininity as an essential aspect of female gender, the dominant themes in women's fashions since the early 1980s overtly challenge the category of woman associated with the previous three decades. Cloth-ing has long since ceased to be purely functional and frugal, nor is it a cover obscuring gender and sexual difference. Availability of almost any type of clothing from high fashion to plain T-shirts now offers the possibility of experimenting with meanings of femininity effectively denied to two generations of women. After decades of enforced monotony, fashion has opened up an avenue for women – particularly urban women with financial means – to explore the meaning of difference in understanding and articulating their own gendered iden-tities.

Indicating some of the new possibilities associated with women's dress, a writer commented in 1991 that 'clothing nowadays is no longer simply to cover the body and to keep warm. It also expresses an individual's unique style and attainments. Through clothes, one can invariably tell a person's identity and profession. Women's dress in particular attracts other people's attention' (Gao Fang and Zeng Rong 1991, 219). Within the context of the present discussion, the sugges-tion that women may approach fashion as a means of self-expression grants the individual a legitimacy to experiment with forms and styles which is completely divorced from all notions of collective responsibil-ity. The individual is free to assemble and disassemble clothing in ways that are constrained by the market, by individual consumer-capacity, and by social norms and personal tastes that have nothing to do with ideological fiat. Approval is also implicitly given to the possibility of using clothes as a form of sexual signalling. The suggestion that feminine beauty is 'for the other, for the other of the opposite sex, as well as for self-improvement' (Ma Li, 1991, 16) by implication subordinates pleasure in sartorial experimentation to the final approval of the male other.

As if indicative of their distance from the era of collective responsibility, the visual representations of women in contemporary magazines often suggest a self-containment and a self-absorption that denotes oblivion to anything and everything of social significance. As they appear on the pages of women's magazines, beautiful women are often removed from significant social contexts to enter into a direct relationship with the viewer. Their spatial domination of the page gives them extraordinary power to beckon, to invite attention, to provoke and even to seduce. Aware of their appeal to the other, these figures are simultaneously dependent on the other. They wait for the other's approval or arrival in images which clearly suggest what Laura Mulvey called the 'to-be-looked-at-ness quality' (Mulvey, 1989, 19).

In conversation with me, many women, particularly of the professional middle-aged generation who were brought up to regard gender-neutrality in dress as a signifier of emancipation, have indicated their antipathy to images which, in their eyes, reduce women to the objectified status they have devoted their lives to combating. The idea that clothing the female body may offer women, and men, the possibility of experimenting with a variety of gendered and sexual meanings is explicitly contested by women who identify with the collective-spirited *funü* subject position of the pre-reform period. The Women's Federation, for example, opposes beauty contests, by whomever they are organized, on the grounds that they 'misguide' young people, especially young women, by fostering an unbalanced focus on external beauty at the cost of 'internal beauty' (*Qingnian shibao*, 30 July 1993). An exaggerated interest in physical beauty undermines the more serious values associated with commitment to studies and work. In repeating the dichotomy between external and internal beauty found in the materials of the 1950s, this argument attempts to rescue women from dependence on and objectification by the male gaze. Simultaneously, however, it maintains its links with the hierarchical construction of sexuality which defines bodily expressions of desire as the impure manifestations of a sullied soul.

The public focus on female appearance in the past fifteen years has inscribed the female body with metaphors of self-control and surveillance which are quite different from those of the former period. Practices of bodily management, long and obsessively publicized in Western societies, are now prominent in the Chinese media. How to cultivate beautiful, pale skin, exercise to keep the body slim and supple, and massage to keep breasts in shape are all familiar topics in women's magazines. Alongside the seemingly omnipresent images of blonde, wide-eyed beauties of Western fashion magazines, advice about how to use make-up to make the eyes seem larger, or even about the kind of operation available to make the eyes rounder, takes on complex meanings. In so far as these interests are associated with Western standards of female beauty and desirability, and in turn are associated – at least indirectly – with the goals of the reform programme, managing the female body along such lines has become a new symbol of social and economic attainment. The rewards for bodily management are the material and emotional emblems of commercial success: romantic engagement with wealthy young entrepreneurs, fashionable clothes and exciting social and travel opportunities. By implication, the West is simultaneously constructed as an object of desire and, as Chapter 7 argues, a source of danger, contamination and disease. Desirability and erotic interest are inscribed in the female body together with prescriptions for scrupulous self-control. As Susan Bordo argued in her analysis of the meanings written into the slender female body, the female body simultaneously emerges as the potentially harmful provocatrice of male desire as well as the patrolling agent of her own and thereby others' sexual appetites (Bordo 1995, 185–212).

The recuperation of an essential femininity and the sexualized female body that has taken place in official and popular discourses over the last fifteen years has diversified the meanings associated with wifehood. A range of possibilities, including the happy housewife and the desiring sexual partner, have superseded the uniform image of the collective-spirited spouse of the past. These shifts have been paralleled by a redefinition of the features thought to contribute to a felicitous marriage. While the 1950s discussions about marriage subjugated individual interests to the requirements of social and moral order, those of more recent years have emphasized a range of individuated emotional and sexual experiences which are explicitly sited within the sphere of private considerations. The foregrounding of *nüxing* and *nüren* since the mid-1980s has given women's sexual needs and desires an unprecedented discursive status. Differences between women have also come into focus, not simply as a contrastive means of reinforcing the legitimacy of the dominant view, but as testimony to the diversity – potential and real – of gendered and sexual subject positions now available in urban Chinese society. Difference is no longer necessarily resisted as divisive and potentially damaging. Nor, in association with the individual subject, is it automatically considered the expression of an ideologically unsound mind. Hence, texts which reveal specific experiences of individual women no longer insist on subordinating these to the more important issues of collective and group concern. Recognition of difference has permitted the reconstruction of the relationship between individual person and collective.

The legitimation of individual interests in sexual and erotic pleasures signifies an apparently total rejection of the ideological and gender concerns of the past. The new respectability accorded the image of woman as housewife and beautiful sexual partner similarly seems to share little with the emphases of earlier discourses. However, the narrative descriptions of ideal marital relationships and wifely conduct I have examined in this chapter suggest other readings. Their modes of representation may have changed – indeed, almost beyond recognition – but the Maoist and the reformist discourses converge in identifying woman as wife with woman as marital and domestic support. While the 1950s protagonists of the 'new socialist woman' vilified the old image of the 'virtuous wife and good mother', the naturalized gender assumptions shaping official representations of a wife's loyalty, service and commitment to her husband continued to subscribe to the primary identification between women and the domestic sphere. Images of wifely support, consideration and care constructed women as the main agents responsible for ensuring the appropriate moral orientation and stability of the marital relationship. Wifehood signified expectations of female self-denial in favour of the dominant male. The identification of women as the main custodians of sexual fidelity complemented their function as servicers of their husbands' interests. From this perspective, the discursive 'reprivatization' of affective and sexual matters in recent years has simply given a legitimacy to assumptions about women's 'nature' which had been partially obscured by the universal message of collective service. As the state transfers its former responsibilities for the provision of childcare and welfare facilities to often unwilling enterprise managers, many women find themselves being pressurized to withdraw from the labour force and to reidentify with their domestic role. In this context, the publicity given to images of the gentle, dependent and supportive wife has not brought new meanings to the construction of female gender, but has reinforced the gender asymmetry inherited from the former discourse.

Advice about 'sexual harmony' in marriage demonstrates that this asymmetry is grounded in a naturalized view of the marital relationship, according to which sexual difference is constructed as a felicitous meeting of complementary qualities. The ideal wife combines sexual responsiveness to her husband with attention to hygiene to protect her reproductive capacity. A wife's sexual activity is mainly represented either as a boost to conjugal harmony or as a series of measures taken for reproductive purposes. Sexual incompatibility and conflict are explained as consequences of the failure to understand and meet the needs of complementarity; the husband is unable to control his natural excitability, or the woman refuses to respond in a way which gives confidence to her husband. From these perspectives, women's sexuality is acknowledged in the name of the same goals of marital and familial harmony as is her wifely service and support. Representations of women's sexuality in marriage establishes standards of behaviour which subordinate her own potentially different needs and interests to those of the naturally driven, dominant male.

# 6 Healthy Bodies

Dominant discourses of sexuality in China give a privileged place to matters of 'sexual hygiene' (*xing shenghuo weisheng*). Articles written by medical experts offer detailed advice about how to maintain standards of hygiene at different stages of sexual development and experience. Discussion about 'biological hygiene' is prominent in sex education classes and publications for adolescents. Pictures of diseased genitalia, the gruesome message of which is often reinforced by the addition of lurid colour, are included in books about reproductive health and sexually transmitted diseases. Photographs of people with terrible skin diseases and physical deformities are displayed on notice-boards in front of office buildings to warn the public of the ghastly consequences of 'unhygienic sex', promiscuity and incest. Accompanying lists of '10 do's and don'ts' inform their readers of the proper techniques of healthy sex. In a social and political context in which concerns about reproductive and fetal health are prominent, and as public consciousness about the spread of sexually transmitted disease and AIDS increases, the abundance of such materials now available in China identifies the preservation of 'sexual hygiene' as a significant objective in disseminating information about sexual matters.

In its most general interpretation, sexual hygiene refers to all matters deemed to have a bearing on sexual and reproductive health. A manual called *Adolescent Hygiene* (*Qingchunqi weisheng*) gives an idea of the understanding of sexual hygiene that prevailed between the 1950s and the early 1980s (Xie Bozhang 1975). After a brief introduction defining the term 'adolescence', a longer section on adolescent development sets out the bodily and hormonal changes that occur at puberty and sexual differences in reproductive development. Sections 3 and 4 explain the benefits of physical exercise and manual labour, and section 5 surveys those aspects of daily life that are essential to ensure healthy development: diet and nutrition, clothing and bodily comfort, washing, rest and sleep, and vigilance against bad habits such as smoking and drinking. The largest section of the book then reviews some of the specific problems that may surface during adolescence. In boys, these are associated principally with nocturnal emissions and masturbation, while in girls they are mainly the menstrual difficulties, infections and reproductive disorders associated with lack of adequate attention to menstrual hygiene. By the mid-1980s, while approaches to sexual and 'physiological hygiene' (shengli weisheng) continued to borrow many terms from earlier publications, the formulation of the new category of 'psychological hygiene' introduced the possibility of broadening the definition of health in ways which had been barred by biological and ideological bias. This new consideration effectively expanded the possible interpretations of 'sexual hygiene' by acknowledging that psychological difficulties were a significant aspect of the changes and experiences accompanying sexual development (for example, Shen Wenjiang et al. 1987; Fang Fang 1987).

The specific target of attempts to protect and improve levels of sexual hygiene and health has varied since 1949. In the early years of the People's Republic, the government put considerable energy into eradicating syphilis and other venereal diseases. Hu Chuankui, a famous dermatologist and later president of the Peking Medical College, estimated that, in the rural areas of northwestern China, instances of syphilis and gonorrhea ran at between 40 and 70 per cent and even higher in some areas (Lampton 1977, 25). After the official abolition of prostitution, announced shortly after the Communist Party took control of Beijing on 3 February 1949, the new government offered free medical treatment to prostitutes in order to eliminate venereal disease. According to the Beijing Public Security Bureau, a survey of 1303 prostitutes in 1950 found that 96.5 per cent had nonspecific venereal infections, 84.9 per cent had syphilis and 53.8 per cent had active gonorrhea (Ruan 1991, 75–6). An intensive approach to treatment by a special corps of doctors and nurses resulted in the cure of some 40 per cent of syphilis patients and the vast majority of those afflicted with gonorrhea. By the time an international conference on sexology was held in 1964, the government claimed that sexually transmitted diseases had disappeared from China.

The reappearance of sexually transmitted diseases (STDs) in China nearly two decades after its officially proclaimed eradication sounded the alarm among medical specialists, population workers and health officials. Between 1977 – when only three cases of STDs were reported – and June 1992, numbers had risen to 700,000, and this only included figures for those admitted to hospital (Zhang Ping 1993). Sex-education publications began to include sections on sexually transmitted diseases to explain their development and offer some basic preventive techniques. Family-planning agencies attached increasing importance to the requirement that couples have a medical examination prior to registering their marriage, and by the late 1980s proof of having had the pre-marital check-up was generally necessary in order to obtain a marriage certificate. By the late 1980s, professional and official concern about the spread of sexually transmitted diseases had extended to AIDS, the presence of which in China the government reluctantly admitted after it was diagnosed in Yunnan Province. However, public information about AIDS and other diseases is still very limited, and constrained by moralistic prejudice and ignorance. Doctors and other concerned professionals acknowledge extremely low levels of public awareness about sexually transmitted diseases, and, despite some specialists' commitment to providing the public with basic preventive information, government funds to finance such ventures remain limited.

The clinical orientation of much of the discussion about sexual hygiene obscures the moralism that pervades professional advice about how to preserve sexual health. If the injunctions against practices deemed to impair sexual health – masturbation, for example – are no longer as rigid or as uniform as they once were, the idea that the body needs to be protected against contaminating influences is more prominent a theme than ever before in the People's Republic of China. Moreover, alongside the encouragement to young women to take measures to ensure the reproduction of offspring of 'superior quality' (*youzhi*), the defence of bodily boundaries against external invasion becomes even more important. The thrust of advice about sexual health and hygiene has thus shifted away from vigilance of the self to vigilance against invasion of the self by external forces. Protection of the clean and pure against the contaminating influence of foreign physical and moral forces establishes the means to preserve bodily and spiritual health.

## Reproductive health

The conceptualization of women's physical and mental well-being foregrounded in popular medical literature since the early 1950s has centred on reproductive health, whether in advice about the use of hygienic techniques during the menstrual period, about the dangers to fertility and reproduction of physical over-exertion and severe emotional fluctuations, or about the optimum conditions for conception, pregnancy and childbirth. Concerns about the maintenance of reproductive health are also apparent in the provision of a range of self-help techniques enabling ordinary people, particularly women, to observe minimum standards of hygiene in conditions of sometimes extreme poverty. Advice about the appropriate moments during the female cycle for sexual intercourse, about how and when to wash during the menstrual period, or about the potential dangers to fertility of female masturbation is commonly given in the name of maintaining standards of sexual and reproductive hygiene.

With minimal access to education in basic hygiene in the 1950s, young women often did not take any notice of menstrual blood, or used rags which they never washed and which 'they threw away into a dark corner when they had finished with [them]' (Wang Wenbin, Zhao Zhiyi and Tan Mingxin 1956, 45). The consequences of this were disastrous, in particular in spreading what were popularly known as 'the three many's' (san duo): 'a lot of menstrual sickness and disease, a high maternal and child mortality rate, and many women who could not work in the fields' (Ya Ping 1958). As a survey conducted among middle-school students indicated, failure to give proper attention to menstrual hygiene could lead to irregular menstruation and to nervous complaints ('Xiang xie shenmo banfa lai zengjia xuesheng de jiankang?' 1950). According to this survey, more than four-fifths of girls menstruated irregularly, and a considerable number manifested nervous complaints. A key feature of articles about women's 'sexual hygiene' in the 1950s was therefore the provision of basic self-help techniques to help them contain the possible effects of the poverty and deprivation in which most of them lived. They were advised to wash each day in warm boiled water, and twice a day during menstruation and the morning after intercourse (Yan Renying 1958; Wang Wenbin, Zhao Zhiyi and Tan Mingxin 1956, 50). During menstruation, women were told to take care not to let water enter the vagina because of vulnerability to bacterial infection. In order to avoid transmitting infection, the towel and basin used had to be kept separate and never shared with other people (Wang Wenbin, Zhao Zhiyi and Tan Mingxin 1956, 50). Menstrual pads were to be washed and hung out at specific moments of the day. Sitting on cold ground, getting wet and washing in cold water were also to be avoided, as were swimming and strenuous physical work (Yan Renying 1958).[1] Much of this advice was repeated almost verbatim in later texts. For example, 1980s instructions for washing 'menstrual belts' (*yuejing dai*) include similar detail to the texts of the earlier period, together with advice about the appropriate water temperature to use and warnings against using fabric of deep colours because of possible irritation to the skin (Wu Zhangming, Zhu Xiaolan and Lang Ying 1990, 17). Information about the dangers of vaginal infections, about the negative effects on the organism of physical over-exertion, and about the appropriate foods to eat during menstruation and pregnancy similarly reiterates the principles of the earlier discourse.

Much of this advice clearly echoes traditional medical beliefs that the introduction of particular substances or the creation of particular emotional states during negative or 'cold' bodily conditions has deleterious effects. Warnings to women against stimulants such as alcohol and spicy foods during menstruation are set within a context of dietary rules for 'nourishing life' which articulate the dangers to women of *yang* or hot foods during *yin* moments of the cycle (Yan Renying 1958). Women are warned not to get angry during menstruation, to avoid provoking changes in the body that would impair fertility. The implication is that women who control their emotions and appetites are awarded good health and the birth of healthy offspring. On the other hand, failure to adhere to medical advice about sexual hygiene may create a series of physical difficulties: infection, impaired fertility or miscarriage. These views dovetail with classical reproductive theory that the physical and psychological characteristics of the fetus were determined both at conception and by the mother's psychological and medical condition during pregnancy (Furth 1987). As in traditional medical views about the moral and physical value of 'fetal education' (*tai jiao*), medicine identifies women through their sexuality as the key figures in preserving their own and their unborn child's health – and, by extension, marital and family harmony.[2]

The protection of women's fertility and reproductive capacity has been central to another distinct aspect of discussion about sexual hygiene concerning the effects of sexual intercourse at specific moments of the female cycle. Medical advice since the 1950s has consistently maintained that sexual intercourse during menstruation can have potentially disastrous effects on women's fertility. During the menstrual period, vigorous movement may cause engorgement of the uterus, and penetration exposes the vagina to bacterial infection and thus severely threatens fertility ('Guanyu xing zhishi de jige wenti' 1956, 28; Wang Shancheng; *Funü zhi you* (xia) 1991, 98). Furthermore, as one doctor advised, the physical harm that may result from sexual activity during menstruation makes it 'totally wrong' (*jiduan cuowude*) to have sex during the menstrual period as a means of avoiding pregnancy (Zhou Efen 1955). In the name of 'family happiness and conjugal sexual harmony', couples are urged to 'control themselves' and 'strictly abstain from sex' during the menstrual period (Lu Shumin and Tang Jianhua 1991, 61; Wang Shancheng 1956; Wang Wenbin, Zhao Zhiyi and Tan Mingxin 1956, 47). Even in a context in which the government seems willing to use all available means to control women's fertility, medical views about the physical harm and possible infertility caused by sexual contact during menstruation proscribe using the 'safe period' as a birth-control measure.

Pregnancy is another condition in which sexual intercourse is widely thought to be medically inadvisable. Abstention is recommended for the first three and last two or three months of pregnancy on the grounds that intercourse during these periods, as in menstruation, disturbs the developing fetus and engorges the uterus (Zeng Zhaoyi 1952; Wang Shancheng 1956). If intercourse takes place in the intervening months, special care should be taken to minimize movement. Wang Wenmin, Zhao Zhiyi and Tan Mingxin argued that women 'prone to miscarriage or premature childbirth' should refrain from sex altogether during pregnancy (1956, 48). Some texts further argue that intercourse should be avoided throughout pregnancy, on the grounds that miscarriages, premature births, premature rupture of the membranes and infections may 'all be produced by sexual intercourse' (Lu Shumin and Tang Jianhua 1991, 86). During the post-partum period of confinement advised by the experts, still widely recommended in China in the interests of women's health, total abstention is also generally required. As Wang, Zhao and Tan put it, the 'man is not allowed to stay in the woman's room' (Wang Wenmin, Zhao Zhiyi and Tan Mingxin 1956, 72). Combined with women's retreat from all physical exertion – doing housework, working in the fields, cooking, or looking after older children – 'sitting the month out' (*zuo yuezi*) is thought to enable the 'womb to return to normal' without running the risk of uterine hemorrhaging (Ye Tong 1954).[3] However, traditional assumptions about the negative effects of excitement, shock and physical movement on a weak organism during pregnancy and after childbirth are no longer always uncritically accepted. A 1991 text suggested that women who want to have sex right up to a month or two before giving birth should have no anxieties about doing so, and that fears about harmful effects on the unborn child are completely unfounded (Gao Fang and Zeng Rong 1991, 178). Similarly, though 'sitting the month out' has long been considered one of the few popular traditions of childbirth worthy of medical support, the legitimacy of this is also now being questioned. If the womb has recovered enough to make sexual intercourse comfortable before the end of the six weeks normally recommended for the period of confinement, then sexual intercourse is permissible (Gao Fang and Zeng Rong 1991, 181).

Constructing sexual intercourse as a potential danger during menstruation and pregnancy undoubtedly coincided with the common assumption that women were not likely to have sexual intercourse during menstruation and pregnancy because it was deemed unclean or unhealthy. Chinese women with whom I have spoken about such issues – friends of many years' standing, and colleagues and students with whom I have worked over the last ten years, nearly all of them from intellectual and professional backgrounds – have reinforced their agreement with this view by pointing to medical arguments current in China about hygiene and reproduction. Indeed, a number of them have explicitly stated that sexual intercourse during menstruation is both harmful and unpleasant. Many of them have also indicated their agreement with traditional medical theories about the effects of cold on women's health during vulnerable moments of the cycle. During a stint of 'open-door schooling' in spring 1976 in the paddy fields of a farm belonging to Beijing University, a fellow student told me that the reason she was wearing rubber boots to plant the seedlings while her peers were barefoot was that she was menstruating, and should not touch water. As with the texts of the 1950s, the implication of her comment was not that, as Margery Wolf wrote, 'menstruating women who stepped into a rice paddy would cause the roots to shrivel' (Wolf 1985, 81–2) but that cold substances would bring harm to the menstruating woman.[4]

The hygienic and health-strengthening objectives of these views undoubtedly reflected and continue to reflect the daily needs of enormous numbers of Chinese women. In conditions in which knowledge about basic hygiene was extremely limited, when many rural areas experienced epidemics, and when the elimination of sexually transmitted disease was a priority of medical authorities, preventive measures against infection clearly served a practical function. At the same time, however, advice about sexual hygiene has reinforced the view that women are particularly vulnerable to disease because of their reproductive function. In her analysis of views about menstruation and pregnancy in the Qing period, Charlotte Furth wrote that 'menstruation, gestation, and childbirth subjected women to more or less serious depletions of blood', an essential part of women's vital essence, which according to traditional medical theory made women 'chronically susceptible to the disorders accompanying such bodily loss' (Furth 1987, 13). Despite the assertion that menstruation is a 'normal physiological function', medical opinion continues to represent women in the category of what Charlotte Furth called the 'not-quite-well' (Furth 1987, 17). Relevant materials of the last four decades have with few exceptions maintained a similar argument. The loss of menstrual blood diminishes women's defences against sickness; women's vulnerability at certain moments of the cycle by nature subjects them to the dangers of disease. Moreover, if considered to have produced hemorrhaging and infertility, sexual intercourse became discursively associated not simply with vulnerability to disease, but with disease itself. To use Furth's words again, 'women exposed to this model of female health and disease would recognise female gender as implying a choice between negative sexual power and socially acceptable weakness' (Furth 1987, 9). Warnings against sexual intercourse during menstruation and pregnancy and after childbirth serve to remind women that their sexuality is still fundamentally defined by their reproductive function.

## Superior births

Since the early days of the single-child family programme, the language of eugenics has occupied a prominent place in the articulation of the government's aims. The explicit intention of 'improving the quality of the population' has been consistently put forward as a parallel goal to that of limiting its size (Croll 1993–4, 32). Recent Chinese texts define 'eugenics' (*youshengxue*) in ways that combine a number of possible interpretations. 'Popularly defined, eugenics refers to giving birth to healthy, intelligent children' (Wu Zhangming, Zhu Xiaolan and Lang Ying 1990, 114), an objective which 'has become the common desire of all of humanity' (p. 88). Eugenics refers to 'passing on good health' (*yichuan jiankang*) through the 'positive means of promoting the multiplication of superior individuals in both body and mind'; it also refers to the deployment of measures to 'prevent the birth of individuals with serious hereditary diseases or congenital defects' (p. 89). Explained in these ways, the eugenic thrust of China's population policy could be interpreted benignly to refer to the various social and educational measures taken to reduce disabilities. However, it also clearly resonates with the notion of controlled breeding through the selection and elimination of inherited characteristics.[5] Indeed, the Chinese authorities' belated recognition that such language evoked comparisons with the sterilization campaign launched by Hitler in 1933 was seen first of all in the modification of the title of the Draft Law on Eugenics to the Law for Maternal and Infantile Health Care, and in the substitution of the term 'better birth and health care' for 'eugenics' in the English translation of the text.

However, these modifications do not in themselves signify the disappearance of the potentially brutal implications of current policy. The objective of 'superior births' lies behind many official pronouncements about preventing the reproduction of mental defectives, schizophrenics, manic depressives, those with severe deformities and the hereditarily blind. The law itself makes no mention about the nature of a mother's rights in decisions about the future of her fetus, any more than it refers to parental participation in the decision to terminate a pregnancy. Prime Minister Li Peng's famous statement that 'mentally retarded people will give birth to idiotic children', and official opinion that 'the births of more than 10 million disabled people could have been prevented had a law permitting the abortion of fetuses with hereditary diseases and restricting marriages among people with mental problems or contagious diseases been in operation', offer little assurance to those concerned about the dangers of coercion in implementing policy.[6] The Law on Maternal and Infantile Health Care, formally ratified on 1 June 1995, specifies the desirability of sterilization and abortion 'in certain conditions' without any reference to the protection of women's bodies from coercive operations. In the absence of any explicit mechanisms granting safeguards against the coercive implications of the population planners' eugenic concerns, women's bodies remain vulnerable to decisions by agencies over which they have no control. As John Aird has argued, the authority invested in agencies removed from women's interests but empowered to make decisions about reproductive possibilities is tantamount to an invitation to a potentially gross violation of women's human rights (Aird 1990).

The eugenic considerations of population policy have considerable implications for women and their sexual choices and identities, highlighted by the fact that most texts about 'superior births' and related topics seem to be written about and for women. On the one hand, the concern for births of 'superior quality' may function to limit women's – and men's – choices of marriage partner. As explicitly pointed out when the 1980 Marriage Law was passed, the 'physical health of the partner should be given priority in deciding on marriage' (Xiang Hua 1980). Individuals who are deemed not to meet certain basic requirements of bodily and mental health may be legally prohibited from marrying and reproducing. Indeed, the agencies responsible for the obligatory pre-marital check-up can withhold permission to obtain a marriage certificate, thus making reproduction a difficult if not an impossible option. Though the 1980 Marriage Law omits specific reference to venereal disease and mental disorder, current approaches do not differ substanitally from those of the 1950s, when marriage could be prohibited 'where one party [was] suffering from venereal disease, mental disorder, leprosy or any other disease which is regarded by medical science as rendering a person unfit for marriage' (Article 5, Marriage Law of the PRC, 1950).

However, within a demographic context dominated by concerns to control both size and 'quality' (*suzhi*) of population, in which advanced ultrasound technology is widely used to ascertain the health as well as sex of the fetus, the specificity of women's construction as the major target of such advice has changed. In a very important sense it has expanded, to cover possibilities and eventualities neither considered nor applicable in the former period. Decisions concerning choice of marriage partner, for example, acquire an added dimension, implicitly oriented to concerns about the health and 'quality' of the nation's future, as the following story reveals (Su Fu and Huang Yuxian 1992, 15–16). A woman who was schizophrenic and a man suffering from hepatitis fell in love, but they decided not to marry since they were cousins. After three months of misery, they finally slept together, and, despite the fact that the woman thought that she should not have children because of her schizophrenia, and that his hepatitis meant that it was unwise to make love too much, they went on to marry. Some time after this, the woman had an abortion, and the man returned to hospital with hepatitis. Such tribulations were too great for their childless marriage to withstand, and their affection for each other waned. 'Love needs feeling and wisdom', so the final editorial comment put it. Other stories published to warn women of the dangers of not having a pre-marital examination carry similar implications. A letter printed in *Zhongguo funü* told the autobiographical story of a 34-year-old woman whose husband did not tell her before their marriage that he had had a history of mental illness (Lei Jing 1986). The letter revealed how he often beat her during their marriage, sometimes so severely that on one occasion he beat her head against the ground until she began to bleed. The man's elder brother dissuaded the woman from asking for a divorce on the grounds that her husband was sick, but eventually she took the case to court, where it was turned down for the same reason. The editorial response to the woman's request for advice supported her case for divorce on the grounds of protecting women's interests. The editors' dominant concern, though, was not to sympathize with the woman but to reiterate the message that, had the woman had a check-up before marriage and had her husband's illness been ascertained, she would probably not have been allowed to marry, and would thus have protected herself from unnecessary suffering. Quoting the relevant articles of the 1980 Marriage Law, the editorial comment further stated that, in the case of hereditary mental illness, like schizophrenia, 'marriage is clearly disadvantageous both to later generations and to society'.[7] It was reported not long ago that, in Shanghai and Liaoning, 99 per cent and 72 per cent of marrying couples respectively underwent the pre-marital check-up (*China Daily*, 4 January 1994). While, in the absence of comprehensive figures, it is unclear how widely the examination is used to prevent couples from marrying or from having children, its explicit purpose to check against hereditary disorders and sexual diseases does little to assuage anxieties that it may be used more in the interests of abstract notions of 'quality' than in the interests of the parties involved.

The overt presence of eugenic concerns in recent discussions about women's reproductive health gives a prominence and persistence to advice about the optimum conditions for sexual intercourse and conception that depart from the milder preoccupations with reproductive hygiene of the 1950s. Questions such as 'What is the optimum age for marrying?', 'How should we rationally choose the best moment for marrying?' or 'Which month is best for getting pregnant?' mobilize young people's decisions, hopes, anxieties and fears in the direct service of eugenic concerns to ensure the health and intelligence of the new-born baby (Wu Zhangming, Zhu Xiaolan and Lang Ying 1990, 93). The responses to such questions invariably assume that procreation will take place very soon after marrying; advice concerning the age of marriage can be read as advice about the optimum conditions for childbearing. Unsurprisingly, most such advice coincides with the policy recommendations for the appropriate (*shidu*) age of marriage – 25 for women and 27 for men.[8] A handbook of 'youth hygiene' suggested that a woman's body is best suited for childbirth around the mid-twenties; too close to twenty was too young, since 'the development of women's reproductive organs and pelvic capacity is not complete until about twenty-three or four years old' (Shen Wenjiang et al. 1987, 157). On the other hand, postponing childbirth until after the age of thirty is also unwise, since the uterus loses its capacity to contract and the danger of perinatal difficulties and fetal deformities increases (pp. 90–1). As one writer pointed out in a book originally entitled *Zenyang sheng yige jiankang congming de haizi* (How to give birth to a healthy and intelligent child), 'of course, some people go on postponing childbirth until the age of thirty or even thirty-five, but this does not satisfy eugenic requirements' (Fu Caiying 1991, 18). The timing of sexual experience is also a significant factor to take into consideration. Before the age of 25 in men and 24 in women, the fact that the 'brain has not reached full maturity [means that a person] is often in a state of excitement, with weakened resistance, and so their sex life may be too active, making the central nervous system over excited, which in time may produce an imbalance and debilitation of sexual function' (Shen Wenjiang et al. 1987, 157). Furthermore, the 'month of conception' is also decisive in preserving the health of the new-born baby. 'It is generally accepted that the third month of pregnancy is when the cerebral cortex of the fetus is formed and it is at this point that the normal development of the fetus requires appropriate external temperature and rational nutritional conditions. Thus from the perspective of the optimum conditions for growth of the fetus, it is best to conceive between June and August' (Wu Zhangming, Zhu Xiaolan and Lang Ying 1990, 93).

While the present context does not allow for full discussion about fetal education – the expectant mother's educational and emotional responsibility for fetal development – expert advice about the optimum timing, age and conditions for conception projects a message of overriding female responsibility for the health of future offspring. These texts pay little attention to the specific effects of male physiology on fetal development. Apart from the advice to men to refrain from ejaculating under the effects of alcohol on the grounds that conception under such conditions might produce an unhealthy fetus, advice about 'superior births' – both direct and indirect – clearly targets women. In itself, of course, this is unsurprising, given that in China, as elsewhere, women invariably – though not universally – identify themselves as the primary carers of their children at all stages of their development. However, in a context in which many women – both in China and internationally – are concerned about the Chinese government's neglect of women's human rights in reproductive issues, the gendered focus of the advice literature simply adds to the immense burdens women already bear for the fertility control programme. Women have long been required to patrol their own sexual desires and conduct in order to conform to normative standards of conjugal morality. Now, in addition, they are enjoined to make decisions about a range of sex-related matters, from choice of marriage partner through to timing of sexual intercourse, in the service of the health and intelligence of the nation's future.

Current birth-control policy foregrounds the issue of gender – and by implication the government's brutal neglect of it – in Chinese society in many, sometimes devastating, ways. Some of these, most notably the effects of demographic and economic policy on rates of abortion and female sterilization, female infanticide, abandonment of baby girls and the sale of girls into prostitution and marriage, clearly construct girls and women as targets and instruments to be used and controlled as the authorities see fit. In her analysis of gender as a key organizational principle of social and economic life in rural north China, Ellen Judd wrote that 'the culture of rural China is marked by a pervasive devaluation of women that is constantly denied in the practice of everyday life' (Judd 1994, 254). The same contradiction is evident in the representation of women's responsibilities in the implementation of the state's birth-control policy. While the official discourse clearly – if often implicitly – projects women as the key to success of the policy in almost every respect – as protectors of healthy sexuality and reproductive strength, as custodians of reproductive knowledge, as self-sacrificing educators of the unborn fetus – women are accorded little – if any – positive value as autonomous persons. In this particular context, being a woman means little more than having a particular sex and a gender fixed by it, qualified by different degrees of physical and mental health, to be deployed in the service of state policy.

## Abortion

Ever since September 1980, when the Central Committee's Open Letter announced a crash programme to restrict population size to 1.2 billion by the year 2000, the control of women's bodies has been crucial to the government's strategy of economic development.[9] As far as state policy towards women is concerned, women's health, education, employment, marriage and social status have all been subordinated to the goal of controlling fertility. Abortion has been a crucial aspect of the methods and mechanisms adopted to achieve this goal, provoking extensive debate among human rights activists and feminists. Considerable evidence suggests that birth-control policy has been implemented with often scant regard for women or women's rights. Indeed, as far as state policy towards women in concerned, the recent formulation by a family-planning specialist in Beijing of a set of 'ethical guidelines' justifying abortion after the twenty-seventh week of pregnancy, not only in cases of rape and incest but also for 'outside the plan' fetuses, confirms what some observers argue is already the practice in many areas (Lawrence 1994). Individual women have testified to their unwilling 'agreement' to have an abortion, to the cavalier approach of the medical practitioners involved, and to the unhygienic and alienating conditions in which abortions are frequently performed.[10] The kind of advice and information given to women about contraceptive choices and their side-effects is often very inadequate (Kaufman et al. 1991). Large numbers of women have IUD insertions and sterilizations – the two commonest methods of contraception – without any understanding of their possible side-effects.

In numerical terms alone, the figures for abortion give some idea of the broad parameters of their effects on women. A household survey of married women under fifty years of age in Xi'an found that the average number of abortions among women of between 25 and 39 years old was 74 per cent higher in 1981 than in 1977, and that, of the women who had had an abortion, 71 per cent did so after the birth of the first child (Kane 1987, 141). Coinciding with the increasingly stringent and often coercive implementation in 1983 of the campaign to limit fertility, the number of abortions performed annually shot up to more than 14 million from about 12.5 million the previous year. In 1984, total numbers of sterilizations dropped to about one-third of the 1983 level, and abortions dropped to about 62 per cent of the 1983 level (Aird 1990, 39). In 1987 and 1990, 45.6 per cent of married women had had at least one abortion. More than a third of these had had at least two abortions (*US News and World Report*, 19 September 1994). Reports further suggest that an enormous number of abortions are performed on young unmarried women. According to a publication of early 1993, one of the medical professors in Shanghai's Tongji Hospital claimed that every month about 100 girls under the age of twenty, including children of thirteen, were having abortions in this hospital alone (*Jiankang wenzhai bao*, 14 April 1993).

Although precise abortion figures are unavailable, these and other reports suggest that, while abortion may often be used primarily as a back-up for failed contraception (Kaufman et al. 1989, 725–7), this is by no means always the case, nor is it always the result of voluntary decisions on the part of the women involved. Increased reliance on abortion as a means of contraception indicates that, as Penny Kane put it, 'many women are being pressured into terminating a second pregnancy which they really want' (Kane 1987, 141). Pressure from husbands and family to produce sons has resulted in numerous abortions of female fetuses, the sex of which has been ascertained through ultrasound scanning methods and amniocentesis.[11] Official insistence on 'prohibiting unplanned births' in recent years has also given local cadres considerable leverage to experiment with different methods in order to fulfil birth-control targets. Although field work suggests relatively low levels of abortion in many areas (Greenhalgh 1993, 236; Kaufman et al. 1989, 725), public statements about 'resolutely forbidding multiple births' are a constant reminder of the possibility of coercion.

If, in the 1950s and early 1960s, relatively few articles were published about contraceptive methods and abortion, this was in large part owing to the fact that birth control was neither perceived to be a necessity, nor – with a brief exception in the mid-1950s – an important policy objective of the central government. Limited though it was, however, discussion about contraception was positive, in that it was oriented primarily to concerns about women's health and to persuading a reluctant audience of the benefits to marital and family life of spacing and limiting births. Articles related the experience of women who decided to use contraceptive methods after having had children, or sought to convince readers that the use of contraceptives would not impair sexual capacity (Liang Zhao 1957; 'Bu yao guo zao jiehun' 1957). Since the early 1980s, public discussion about contraception and abortion has been dominated by the view that, as instruments of demographic control, they benefit social order and economic progress. Media discussion about contraception has vastly increased in quantity, and, as an inevitable aspect of the fertility-control programme, assumes acceptance on the part of its audience. And though Joan Kaufman's evidence suggests that knowledge about the possible side-effects of different contraceptive methods may be limited, popular publications about marriage and family life devote considerable space to explaining the disadvantages and advantages of different methods of contraception, including warnings to women about uterine inflammation as a result of the use of intra-uterine devices (IUD), and about reactions to the varying estrogen levels in different brands of the contraceptive pill.[12]

However, discussion about 'what you need to pay attention to when having an abortion' tends not to be so informative. The suggestion, for example, that abortion 'has some effect on the body, but with due attention to rest and diet, it soon recovers its usual state' is a standard approach (Shen Wenjiang et al. 1987, 169). Lay information about the conditions making induced abortion necessary or desirable is limited, and the hormonal and psychological effects of abortion are almost entirely omitted from discussion. The focus on abortion as an 'important measure in making superior births a reality' (shishi renlei yousheng) precludes making the pregnant woman the subject of concerns, except when her condition might rebound negatively on the health of the future generation (Lu Shumin and Tang Jianhua 1991, 85).

Women's experiences that challenge the dominant approach to abortion are not easily available to popular readers. A number of eyewitness accounts describe women's attempts to conceal their pregnancies, even though they risk having to have an abortion when the fetus is nearly fully developed.[13] Research also suggests that, given the choice, many women – urban as well as rural – would prefer to have two children (Greenhalgh 1993; Mu Aiping 1995). Despite evidence that Chinese women tend to express a very much more matter-of-fact attitude towards abortion than is often the case in the West, where the issue has become inextricably enmeshed with the 'right to life' debate, the absence of references to women's different experiences of abortion and of sterilization – except where these are positive – does not mean that abortions are performed on a passive and accepting constituency of women.

Abortion identifies an aspect of contemporary discourses of sexuality that is probably more constrained by official policy than any other. The combined interests in utilizing abortion as an effective means of birth control and minimizing publicity about its more coercive implications foreclose the possibility of any open-ended, critical evaluation of its social and psychological effects. Many Chinese women who have experienced abortion may indeed find little reason to disagree with the government's assessment of it as an unproblematic means towards an identified end. However, such agreement does not necessarily extend to support for the insensitively applied insistence on notions of quantity and quality in discussions about birth control. The absence of women as living and bodily subjects in discussion about abortion cancels out the possibility of hearing the views of those whose experience contests dominant approaches. The official emphasis on the long-term benefits to be derived from what to many is a brutal neglect of their rights effectively silences the voices of the millions of women affected. Descriptions of individual cases where pre-marital abortion has led to personal tragedy focus on the young women involved as objects of pity, scorn or sympathy, depending on the merits of the case. Instances of pre-marital abortion are described either to warn readers against immoral conduct, or to castigate specific actions as a kind of sanction against potential waywardness. For example, a sixteen-year-old girl, already engaged to be married, was impregnated by a married soldier, and had an abortion when their affair was discovered. When news of her actions got around she acquired the reputation of a 'bad element', since she had already had affairs with two men and was thought to have 'destroyed a soldier's marriage' (*pohuai junhun*). The editorial comment argued that, if the girl was simply innocent and had been seduced by the second soldier, she could be forgiven, but her behaviour indicated otherwise. Only the law could give her the 'help' she needed, and she was sent to reform through education (*lao jiao*) for three years (Cheng Xian 1986, 18–20).

Abortion thus acquires a symbolic as well as a physical significance – as the act of a woman committed to the economic and social development of her country, and as the miserable consequence of moral depravity. Abortion appears as a sign of collective loyalty or as the just retribution for a woman's wrongdoing. In any event, whether it is to limit the size of the population, eliminate unwanted or unhealthy fetuses, or punish women for actions that marginalize them from the dominant discourse, it is represented as a means to preserve order. In no instance does abortion appear as an act principally effected on women's bodies – and therefore on their health, their sexual choices and their gender identities. Women appear not as persons in such contexts, but as the vessels and self-sacrificing agents of demographic control, bound by patriarchal structures of power.

## Sexually transmitted diseases

Public discussion about sexually transmitted disease in China since 1949 has been shaped by social and moral as much as by medical concerns. Inheriting arguments already prominent in the literature on 'sex diseases' (*xing bing*) since the 1920s, the twin themes of prostitution and foreign contagion have dominated the articulation of political and professional opinion about how to halt the spread of sexually transmitted disease.[14] In the early 1950s, the government's efforts to eradicate what was considered an epidemic of venereal disease targeted urban prostitution and ethnic minorities. Government teams organized under the auspices of the Ministry of Health set out to educate the public in the rudiments of sexual health and hygiene, and mass campaigns against syphilis resulted in the closure of brothels in Beijing and other cities in 1950, and the subsequent arrests of thousands of prostitutes, brothel owners, procurers and pimps. Prostitutes were routinely screened and given medical treatment, and were subject to a series of rehabilitation programmes in urban detention centres often specifically set up for the purpose. In October 1957, as the anti-rightist movement got under way, the Standing Committee of the First National People's Congress adopted a law on the Control of and Punishment concerning Public Security, which banned prostitution and subjected clients to detentions and fines (Ruan 1991, 76). By 1964, the central government claimed that venereal disease had been completely eradicated.

The officially acclaimed suppression of prostitution and the eradication of venereal disease before the Cultural Revolution did nothing to prevent their re-emergence in Chinese society two decades later, encouraged by the new commercial opportunities offered by market reform.[15] The total number of VD cases reported between 1980 and 1988 was 140,648, probably a small proportion of the total incidence (Dikötter 1993, 345). Figures from the Ministry of Health claimed that 204,077 cases of STDs were reported in June 1989, among which men accounted for 134,691 and women for 69,386. According to figures issued by specialist clinics, the rate of STDs in the first half of 1989 was 105.16 per cent higher than in the same period of the previous year (*Jiankang bao*, 21 November 1989, quoted in Wang Xingjuan 1992, 421). By 1990, 70 per cent of prostitutes reportedly suffered from STDs, and the extent of infection had increased 44 times since 1985 (Office for Criminal Law of the Standing Committee of the People's Republic of China 1991, 13). The Criminal Law of the People's Republic of China, which took effect on 1 January 1980, stipulated terms of imprisonment for pimps of between three to ten years, and nationwide crackdowns were carried out in June 1981 and June 1982. Such measures were of little effect, however, and the numbers involved in prostitution have increased astronomically. Between January 1986 and July 1987 alone, eighteen new prison camps for prostitutes were set up, and by December 1987 the number of camps had tripled (Du, Yi and Xiong 1988, in Ruan 1991, 79). In the first seven months of 1987, there were 87 per cent more arrests of prostitutes than in the same period of 1986. Ten thousand were arrested during a two-month crackdown in south China in 1992, more than 4600 of whom were sent to labour camps for six months to two years (*AP*, 13 June 1992). According to Chinese statistics, the numbers of those arrested rose from 25,000 in 1986 to 200,000 in 1990 (*AP*, 11 September 1993). With hotels, bars and hairdressing salons involved in the trade, as well as underground brothels and racketeers, prostitution is once again a common feature of urban life. Indeed, some reports have suggested that the trade is more active now than it was before 1949 (Ruan 1991, 79).

The moralism that characterized general approaches to venereal disease in the 1950s was clear in the limited popular information that was published about prostitution and public health. Despite the CCP's analysis of prostitution as the product of economic deprivation and exploitation, official approaches emphasized its character as the expression of salacious interests. Articles in the national press tended to focus on the linked themes of 'sexual disease' and social and moral degeneration. Prostitution was the product of a corrupt and bourgeois mind as well as a bodily evil. Relevant stories thus tended to celebrate the achievements of the anti-syphilis campaigns by publicizing the gratitude of former prostitutes cured and reformed in specially established vocational training programmes.

Since the revival of public fears about the spread of sexually transmitted disease in the late 1980s, the moralistic prejudice of former decades has resurfaced, with only recent – and minimal – modifications. Its basis is explicit in the state council's Directive on Banning Prostitution and Curbing the Spread of Sexual Diseases. Few newspaper articles appear about 'sexual disease' without invoking images of social degeneration and national decay. Though occasional specialist commentators and campaigners for greater tolerance clearly distance themselves from such bias (e.g., Chen Chunming 1995), the standard view is that sexually transmitted diseases 'are the product of a bourgeois life style . . . and are seriously damaging to the body; they penetrate the internal organs and other structures, leading to disabilities and threatening the life of the infected, and they affect the physical quality of future generations, the growth and the prosperity of the nation' (Luo Hanchao and Lou Youyi 1989, 1). Advice about how to prevent the spread of such diseases reiterates a similar message: 'to stop the spread of sexual diseases, we should reinforce education in spiritual civilization. We should launch education in ideals, morals, the legal system and hygiene to enable people, particularly the young, to consciously resist the penetration of corrupt bourgeois ideology and life styles' (Xue Fagui and Deng Zongxiu 1988, 2).

Official acknowledgement of the presence of AIDS in China in 1989 revived concerns about the 'health of the nation', another theme favoured between the 1920s and the 1940s. Rampant venereal disease once again became the morbid metaphor for racial decline and national humiliation. Until large numbers of HIV carriers were identified in Yunnan in the early 1990s, official reports claimed that AIDS was a foreign import. 'Following the open door policy, sexual disease seized the opportunity to penetrate China from abroad, and then gradually spread to a number of areas' (Luo Hanchao and Lou Youyi 1989, 1). By late 1994, a total of 1774 people had tested HIV positive, of whom 65 had developed AIDS and 45 had died (CND 17 April 1995). According to Qi Xiaoqu, deputy director of the Department of Epidemic Prevention, the real figures of HIV carriers were probably between 5000 and 10,000 (Philadelphia Inquirer, 23 September 1994). A National Blood Products Management Committee dedicated to handling blood products throughout the country was set up in response to Beijing's warning that the numbers of AIDS cases could quadruple in ten years unless China's blood products are properly controlled (Guangming ribao, reported by Reuter, CND, 17 April 1995). Despite recognition that intravenous drug use is responsible for a sizeable proportion of this increase, the idea that the threat to public health comes from beyond China's borders continues to be a prominent theme, fuelled by popular prejudice as well as medical opinion. Foreign residents and Chinese citizens who travel abroad or who have regular contact with foreigners, such as employees of joint-venture firms and hotels, are obliged to undergo testing for the HIV virus. Further barriers against the contaminating influence of foreigners were erected in Shanghai's Hongqiao airport, which reportedly developed techniques for testing those entering and leaving China's border within two minutes, by taking a drop of blood from the fingertips. According to a report in a local Shanghai newspaper in April 1993, some 14,000 people were tested in this manner in 1990 and 50,000 in 1993 (*Shanghai dazhong weisheng bao*, 14 April 1993). This policy continued until the suspension in February 1993 of random testing of travellers crossing the border from Hong Kong. With implicit recognition that such testing fell short of requirements of scientificity, programmes to monitor the disease shifted from targeting the foreigner and traveller to the domestic sources of the disease. Two national surveillance centres were set up in Guangdong and Yunnan – the two most affected provinces – to do blood tests and provide technical assistance to health departments. Special clinics for sexually transmitted diseases were established in some towns. An AIDS telephone hotline was set up in Beijing to provide information and support to concerned callers. However, voluntarily operated by students from the Beijing Medical College, the hotline continues to serve as a critical reminder of the government's sluggishness in responding to the growing concern about AIDS. Despite government plans for campaigns to popularize information through the television network, newspapers and exhibitions, there is an 'alarming lack of knowledge' about the disease among the general public (*Liaowang*, reported in *CND*, 20 September 1994). Even those who present themselves as experts on the topic subscribe to fears that STDs may be propagated by clothes and sitting on places where infected people have been (Xue Fagui and Deng Zongxiu, 1988, 2–4). With limited resources to fund educa-tional programmes, widespread prejudice about AIDS and sexually transmitted disease as the expression of contaminating influences associated with degenerate and criminal behaviour has scarcely been dented.

The language used in media references to AIDS and sexually transmitted diseases suggests key distinctions between the 'them' and the 'us', between the dreaded enemy beyond and the essentialized body of Chinese society. Discussion about sexually transmitted diseases serves to reinforce a range of basic binary assumptions about differences between good and evil, Chinese and foreign, and arguably between male and female. The enemy appears as both the foreigner and the female prostitute. As Chapter 8 maintains, the male homosexual – another facet of the sexually perverse – is also making an appearance as one of the sources of contamination. The foreigner, the female and the sexual misfit thus appear as the multiple form of the contemporary threat to public health introduced into post-reform China via the open market. Maintaining a distance from the suspect foreigner represents a barrier against contamination. Criminalizing the prostitute and the homosexual offers another means of isolating the source of pollution. A law introduced in September 1991 made it an additional criminal offence for persons who know that they are infected with some sexually transmitted disease to engage in prostitution (AP, 23 November 1992). The consciousness of the prostitute who 'plies her trade despite knowing that she has the disease' merely adds to her capacity as an evil-doer. The representation of the prostitute as the potential polluter also extends to those with whom she comes into contact (Sontag 1989, 48). Li Peng recently signed regulations requiring that prostitutes and their customers be held in custody for between six months and two years if they refuse legal and moral education (AP, 11 September 1993). That the victim is implicated with guilt, and thus becomes a polluter by association, was made clear by an example of popular treatment of HIV carriers in the southern province of Yunnan. A group of men who were positively tested for HIV were physically isolated and imprisoned in a house on the outskirts of the village by their fellow villagers, including members of their families, and left there without food or water. Another example involved a man in Hebei province who was sacked from his job on the grounds that his son was HIV positive; the brother found it impossible to find employment for the same reason.[16] In these cases, the attribution of guilt extended from the polluted to the polluters' kin. Contaminating powers were ascribed not simply to the individual polluter, but by association to others related to him by blood. The victim thus becomes the evil-doer at the very moment of victimization by another; the hidden truth of the innocent victim is revealed as he becomes an agent of the polluting enemy.

The model of sexual health that emerges from analysis of these issues encompasses fertility and reproductive fitness and the physical and psychological conditions needed to produce offspring of 'superior quality'. By definition, it is also associated with freedom from sexually transmitted disease. The meanings associated with sexual health are bound by notions of the individual's capacity to fulfil her duty to protect social and national health as much as by the autonomous requirements of the single person. As a category referring to the single body, sexual health identifies both the strengths of the individual and her capacity to use these, on the one hand for reproductive purposes, and on the other to resist the damaging influence of polluting contacts. Negative as well as positive forces, associated with external as well as internal conditions, thus shape the meaning of sexual health.

Alongside professional advice about menstruation and mastur-bation, the materials examined in the above analysis inscribe clear gender meanings in the category of sexual health. Concerns with male sexual health refer only minimally to reproductive issues; the dominant issues of male sexuality revolve around requirements of self-control of instinctual urges in order to preserve bodily vitality. By contrast with representations of female health, those of male health proclaim the man's relationship mainly with himself, not with the other. For women, sexual health and hygiene acquires a different dimension; the concerns with fertility, fertility control and reproductive health transform female health into a metaphor for the well-being of the nation's future. Yet, a notable feature of such representations is the absence of women's bodies. The gender ascription of many of the elements associated with reproductive health does not, in itself, give living, corporal substance to women's bodies. The fact that women's bodies are frequently subject to appalling brutality is obscured by the symbolic emphasis on the female as the guardian of the nation's future.

The positioning of female gender in discursive concerns that are inseparable from service to others invites the use of the female – and, in the present discussion, of female health – as a symbol in ways already noted by scholars in other contexts. Tien Ju-k'ang argued that female chastity and filiality, including the extreme expression of female suicide, became symbols of national dignity at a time of extreme vulnerability to external threat in the late Ming and early Qing dynasties (Tien Ju-k'ang 1988). More recently Meng Yue has shown how the female image has been used in modern Chinese literature to denote political and ideological values espoused by the Communist Party (Meng Yue 1993). In the present context, female sexuality is the key to the articulation of both eugenic concerns and public health. Whether in its desirable form as the guarantor of superior births, or in its unwanted aspect as the disease of the depraved prostitute, women's sexual health and the lack of it similarly become metaphors for national purity and strength or national humiliation. Representations of the sources of sexually transmitted disease are arguably just as significantly gendered. Sexually transmitted disease, and AIDS in particular, is pervasively represented as the threat from outside or from the depraved other within; the contaminating and corrupting agent is by definition the other, foreign or female.[17] Linking the foreigner with the prostitute, and associating male homosexuality with a perverse rejection of masculinity, feminizes the polluter.

# 7 Sex and the Open Market

The 1980s market reforms put into acute relief a fundamental paradox in the relationship between the state and women. As the state intensified its intervention in women's lives – their choices, their bodies, their identities – through its fertility limitation programme, its disengagement from total control over labour, land and markets created new spaces for the construction of women as commodities for sale – and often violent abuse – on the open market. The commercialization of women for their sexual value has many different facets, from the banal use of pretty women to advertise fashions and domestic appliances to the violation of women's basic rights to bodily integrity. In particular, the violent abduction and sale of young women and girls into marriage, concubinage and prostitution have caught the headlines of the national and international press in recent years. Such 'feudal practices', as they are often described, have been reported in every province of China. National newspapers publish horrifying accounts of brutality against young women sold into marriage thousands of miles away from their natal home. Numerous accounts are presented as attempts to warn young women against the perils of being taken in by strangers. Other publications carry reports about police round-ups and punishment of traffickers operating nationwide networks for the abduction and sale of women. They also relate young women's experiences of escape from captivity. If these abuses of women's rights seem to mirror pre-revolutionary practices in a changed socio-economic context, other forms of commercial appropriation of women's bodies are more immediately associated with China's new market environment. The production and trafficking of pornographic materials is a thriving business in many parts of China, aided, according to many accounts, by the international trading opportunities offered by the open-door policy. Prostitution also flourishes throughout China, in as wide a variety of forms as is suggested by the market disparities between wealth and poverty. The increasing incidence of rape and other sexual crimes against women is also widely associated with the impact on social and sexual behaviour of the commercialization of sex. As in other instances of the violation of women's rights, extensive media coverage is given both to the sufferings of the victims and to the punishment of the offenders.

The different constitutions of female sexuality implicit in the uses and abuses of women's bodies encouraged by commercial opportunity converge in a number of important aspects. They all represent women's sexuality in some way or other as being available for male consumption, whether as an item to be purchased on the market or as a body to be brutalized. The women in such representations appear either as vulnerable victims or as wilful examples of moral turpitude – on the one hand, whose condition has arisen out of ignorance, and, on the other, whose victimization is the consequence of deliberate non-conformity to the dominant sexual order. Whether in media references to the innocent young girl or to the depraved prostitute, the meanings associated with female gender do not substantially depart from subject positions well established by patriarchal interests. Many writers are deeply concerned about the climate of sexual violence in which so many women live; nearly as many, so it seems, describe the manifestations of this as a 'social disease' (*shehui bingtai*) and apply a fundamentally Marxist analysis to explaining its appearance as a function of private ownership. The lack of an adequate gender critique which goes much beyond condemnation of China's 'feudal legacy' or 'bourgeois degeneracy' effectively perpetuates the naturalized construction of women as dependent subjects or as dangerous perpetrators of social chaos.

## Women for sale

'Marriage by sale' (*maimai hunyin*) – the term used by the communist authorities to denote a marriage that was 'arranged or coerced by a third party for the purpose of obtaining property' (Ocko 1991, 321) – and other venal practices involved in the negotations of marriage were outlawed by the 1950 Marriage Law.[1] In particular, the law targeted those who demanded a bride-price or gifts as a condition for agreeing to the marriage of their daughter (Meijer 1971, 172). However, despite claims to have eradicated such 'feudal' anachronisms, and assertions that the collective structures of production and distribution in the countryside had destroyed the economic rationale sustaining the exaction of goods in relation to marriage, the 'buying and selling of wives continued' (Ocko 1991, 320–1); the multiple interests sustaining marriage as an economic transaction between households and families were temporarily obscured, rather than eliminated, by the collective structures of the previous two decades.[2] Since the late 1970s, stimulated by the restoration of the household as the basic economic unit in the countryside, and with it the consolidation of economic interests linking household/family members, the costs of marriage have risen substantially as dowries have increased (Siu 1993, 165–88) and as 'the brides' households demand more compensation from the grooms' (Croll 1994, 168–9).[3] In conditions of extreme poverty and geographical isolation, where surname exogamy and virilocal marriage are standard practices, the procedures of marriage can be demanding and economically crippling. Some physical or mental disability might further impair a person's marriageability. The 'sale' of daughters may represent a means for poor parents to finance a son's marriage as well as a last-resort response to economic deprivation.[4]

Analysis of the renewed increase of venal marriage practices in recent years also has to consider the near universality of marriage in China, both as aspiration and practice. Failure to marry is still widely seen as evidence of impoverishment, or of some physical or mental irregularity. In a cultural context profoundly mediated by patriarchal interests, in which formal provision for old-age pensions is minimal, a significant rationale for marriage still lies in the view of offspring, particularly sons, as security for old age. The naturalization of women's role as mothers and wives discussed in earlier chapters is but one response to this. Even in socio-economic contexts in which women's economic power is considerable and in which women actively seek to limit their childbearing, many still fear sonlessness (Gates 1993, 262).[5] Where economic opportunities and demographic factors have resulted in a scarcity of women of marriageable age, the poor and marginalized may have few options but to seek a wife through the channels available on the market. Furthermore, as the cases written up by Guo Yuhua reveal, women may also accept sale into marriage as an economic necessity (Guo Yuhua 1993). The story of one Lan is revealing. She was originally from a village in the poor mountainous region of northern Sichuan Province, where she had a son at school and a sick husband. She decided to move to the 'central plain' (*zhongyuan*) to find work to support her family. A handicapped peasant bought her for 1500 yuan, but a complaint was brought against her at the local police station, and her ID was destroyed. However, she eventually became the wife of another man, whose previous wife, for whom he had paid 1000 yuan, had run away after six months. As her new husband, he bought her clothes and took care of her, even though he refused to send money back to her family in Sichuan. Illiterate, and with no money, Lan decided to stay. As a common saying at the end of Guo Yuhua's article suggested, 'marry a man, and you have clothes to wear and food to eat' (*jia han, jia han, chuan yi chi fan*).

A survey of venal marriage practices commonly found in rural areas put forward a number of generalizations about the abduction and sale of women in recent years (Zhang Ping 1993). First, contrary to the widely held assumption that 'feudal' customs victimize mainly the uneducated and the underprivileged from the countryside, increasing numbers of the women and children affected come from the urban sector, and include students and foreigners as well as unemployed workers.[6] As the practice spreads, women are sold into towns as well as villages, and even abroad. In the coastal areas they are often sold to provide pimps with prostitutes. Violent gangs – a recurring feature of newspaper reports – form inter-regional networks facilitating the different tasks involved, from the initial meeting and abduction to transportation and reception at the point of destination.

Extensive media publicity has been given to the abduction and sale of women in recent years. Articles in the national press publish details of the numbers of women released from captivity, and of gangsters executed for their crimes, often specifying the age and education of those involved. Though there are major loopholes in legislation against the kidnapping of women, figures are often produced to testify to the government's commitment to eradicating this brutal abuse of women's rights.[7] In 1991 and 1992 alone, according to police statistics, 50,000 cases of abduction of women and children were reportedly solved, and 75,000 people connected with the traffic were arrested (*Survey of China Mainland Press*, 5 November 1993). Official statistics for the province of Shandong showed that more than 30,000 women were abducted into Shandong in the late 1980s (Zhang Ping 1993, 4). According to China's legal press, some 33,000 women were 'abducted and sold' between mid-1993, when a major crackdown against trafficking was launched, and early 1995.[8] According to the Public Security Ministry, nearly 25,000 women and nearly 3000 children were freed from their abductors between 1993 and 1995 (*CND*, 22 April 1995). Another source states that, between 1991 and 1994, nearly 70,000 cases of abduction of women and children were uncovered, leading to the arrests of more than 100,000 criminals and the release from captivity of more than 60,000 children and women (*Zhongguo falü nianjian* bianji bu 1995, 128). Some reports tell of groups of women rounded up by 'traders in human flesh' to be peddled at auction in the 'human market' (*renkou shichang*) for anything between two and five thousand yuan. An article published in the *Wenhui Monthly* in early 1989 described one such scene in a busy rural market on the borders of Shandong and Henan provinces (Xie Zhihong and Jia Lusheng 1989, 3). Seven young girls were lined up against a wall wearing nothing but underpants and vests, their prices, between 2000 and 3000 yuan, written with brush and ink on their vests. Other accounts focus on the difficulties local officials face in freeing the women concerned. They describe the attempts to obstruct rescue efforts by local villagers who see little wrong in the sale of women, or who feel that the husband should not be penalized if he has already paid for a wife (Wong 1992). Descriptions of the conditions in which women are kept, and the violent abuse to which they are subjected by their husbands and husbands' relatives are also common. Horrifying accounts of individual women's experiences are published as warnings to unsuspecting young women whose innocence may lead them to make fatal decisions. Alternatively, disguised as legal case histories for the education of the readers, they are specifically designed for their sensationalist value.[9]

Standard descriptions of the women subjected to abduction and sale are clearly constructed by external observers at a safe distance from the brutal realities of such practices. Few accounts approach the voices and experiences of the women involved, even when they purport to be autobiographical. Most of the media reports used for this analysis are also considerably more homogeneous in their descriptions of the women involved than Zhang Ping's survey, for example, would suggest. The pervasive image is of the young, uneducated and unworldly girl from the rural backwater, attracted by the lure of unskilled urban employment, naively unaware of the potential dangers of trusting strangers, and totally ignorant about legal procedures. A fourteen-year-old's autobiographical account, published in a popular women's journal, is a typical example (*Funü zhi you* 1991, vol. 1, 5–6, 10). It begins with a description of how the girl, a schoolgirl from the countryside, was duped into being sold to a peasant from Hebei Province by the mother of a friend of hers and her nephew. The mother told the girl that her nephew worked in the Ministry of Trade in Beijing and knew of some factory jobs going for female workers in the city. Despite her anxieties about leaving her mother, the girl decided to take up the offer, and once she reached Beijing, where the nephew showed her the sights and took her to the department store, she began to feel that her decision had been the right one. However, almost immediately, she was told that she had to go to Baoding, to meet the factory boss. The nephew handed her over to two strangers to accompany her to Baoding. Once on the train, the girl was raped by one of these before before being dumped back in Beijing with another man whom the rapist claimed was the younger brother of the boss of the factory where she was going to work. She eventually discovered that she had been sold to the second man for 800 yuan. She was kept like a prisoner, repeatedly beaten and raped by different men. She was finally discovered by the local police, and returned to her home village.

The rural–urban opposition invoked in contemporary Chinese discourses about social and cultural matters is a frequent metaphor for backwardness and feudal tradition on the one hand, and modernity, progress and development on the other. The inscription of this opposition in the figure of the abducted women functions as a clear marker distinguishing the wiser, better-educated and urban women from their innocent and ignorant rural cousins. In these contexts, woman becomes a signifier for all that is categorized as 'backward' by the exponents of market reform. The abducted girl also appears as a passive and guileless victim; as such, she rarely challenges the gender hierarchy which condemns her to her fate. Her ignorance and poverty – often used to explain the gendered tendency of women to be more drawn than men to material attractions – make her easy prey to the ruses of traffickers masquerading as intermediaries for official agencies. The implied message is unmistakable; with education and better economic circumstances, young women will develop the capacity to resolve the conditions currently subjecting them to the potential and real dangers of servitude.

For every meaning inscribed in the standard representation of the abducted woman, there are probably just as many that remain hidden. The increasing victimization of college students as targets for kidnapping and sale is a direct challenge to the representational focus on ignorant, rural women. Furthermore, how many of the figures published about the numbers of women abducted and released refer to those women duped, kidnapped and sold against their will, and how many to women who feel obliged to go along with their parents' arrangements? In conditions in which parental participation or control of marriage arrangements is still normative practice, how many women see marriage to a stranger in another part of the country, arranged through a third party, as an opportunity for a better life?

How many young women in such situations are fully aware of the nature of the monetary transactions involved? The recruitment of a daughter-in-law usually requires considerable family savings and often explains parents' early arrangement for their sons' marriage.[10] Among the rich the bride-price may often be returned to the groom's family in the form of furnishings and other household accoutrements. But in poor families one common means of meeting the costs of a son's marriage is to marry out a daughter first. With such arrangements, a daughter's opinion may or may not be ignored; in either event, the sale of a daughter may be seen as a convenient method of realizing the principal objective.[11]

Media reports about the re-emergence of the abduction and sale of women give a privileged place to the socio-economic factors involved. Rural poverty, lack of education, urban employment opportunities, and marketization of the economy are the conditions generally emphasized in explaining this particular form of gender exploitation. Little space is given to the argument that the continued abuse of women's basic rights in this particular form is grounded in hierarchical gender structures and ideologies. The suggestion that the abduction of women is associated with the ways in which men – and women – construct female gender in historically and culturally overdetermined contexts is rarely put forward. When represented as a gender issue, the abduction and sale of women is described as a particularly venal example of the 'feudal' subordination of women – 'men are respected, women are disdained' (*nanzun nübei*) – in backward rural conditions. The attribution of the practice to the pernicious influence of history effectively invalidates the view that, as an aspect of gendered power relations, it is also produced and sustained by structures and discourses situated in the current, radically different socio-economic context. The significance of gender in analysing this particular form of gender subjugation is obscured by a discursive emphasis on the primacy of socio-economic factors.

The dominant representations of abducted women in recent Chinese reports correspond with a range of assumptions and stereotypes that place the discursive agent in a position of superiority *vis-à-vis* the subject. The categorization of female victims as ignorant rural girls defines them as the 'other' to the urban – developed, educated, worldly and self-confident – subject of the dominant discourse of sexuality. The abduction of women thus also appears as a metaphor for the need for urban-oriented development of the countryside. From this perspective, the agents responsible for the public representations of female abduction – editors, journalists, lawyers, official personnel – would seem more committed to extolling the links between urban modernization and social and cultural development than to condemning the abuse suffered. However implausible such an argument sounds, it might help explain the neglect of the fundamental gender issues at stake in the violent enslavement of women for economic and sexual ends.

## Prostitution[12]

'China is a country that once proclaimed that it had eradicated prostitution and venereal disease . . . Thirty years passed and to their astonishment people discover that prostitution has revived and that sexual diseases are once again spreading, at an alarming speed' (Wang Xingjuan 1992, 420). The assumptions embedded in this comment, made by one of China's pioneer researchers in prostitution and female crime, are common to many contemporary views about the history and recent resurgence of prostitution in China. According to these, the early years of the People's Republic, the period when prostitution was largely eliminated, was a time when purity of spirit was reflected in unimpeachable morals, and when ordinary women and men shared at least some of the collective ideals extolled in official rhetoric. By contrast, the reappearance of prostitution in the past fifteen years is identified with policies and practices legitimizing individual desire over collective commitment within a context of flourishing commercial opportunity. The lack of available data about prostitution during the Cultural Revolution inscribes in this view a simple opposition, between the healthy idealism of a China contained from contact with the West and the degenerate effects on Chinese society of individual enterprise and foreign trade.[13] The discursive construction of the (female) prostitute symbolizes the social chaos introduced by the commercial opportunity.

Within little more than two months of the founding of the PRC, a series of measures outlawing prostitution adopted by the central communist authorities resulted in the closure of some 220 brothels in the capital, the 'salvation' (*jiejiu*) of 1200 prostitutes and the sentencing of more than three hundred brothel owners and pimps (Wang Xingjuan 1992, 420). By 1951, similar actions had been taken in Shanghai, the thriving centre of China's sex industry, resulting in the 'salvation' of more than 7000 prostitutes. A series of local campaigns organized under 'Committees for Dealing with Prostitutes' (*chuli jinü weiyuanhui*) in 1954 focused on eradicating prostitution in smaller towns. Throughout the country, prostitutes were rounded up and sent to special detention centres, where they were subjected to a joint strategy of medical attention to cure them of venereal disease and educate them in basic hygiene, occupational rehabilitation to give them employable skills, and attempts to reunite them with their families. Central to this project was 'teaching the women to think – and to speak – as recently liberated subalterns' (Hershatter 1994, 170). Prostitutes were organized in study sessions and encouraged to recognize their former oppression and their own inglorious role in it in terms established by the official discourse.[14] The view of prostitutes as a threat to the social and moral order was apparent in the suggestion – immediately criticized by those in Shanghai responsible for staging the imminent closure of the city's brothels – that women who had been working as prostitutes for more than three years should be categorized as 'vagrants' (*youmin*), the déclassé elements at the bottom of the urban hierarchy (Yang Jiezeng and He Wannan 1988, 33).[15] By 1958, when the eradication of prostitution in Shanghai was announced, prostitution was already presented to the public as a practice of the feudal past. The culminating act indicating the success of the official onslaught on the 'system of prostitution' was the declaration in 1964 that, with the closure of the country's last hospital for venereal diseases in Shanghai, venereal diseases no longer existed in China (Quanguo renda changweihui fazhi gongzuo weiyuanhui xingfa shi 1991, 1).

Since the early years of the post-Mao reform programme, prostitution has once again caught the authorities' attention. According to official figures, between 1986 and 1990 the numbers engaged in prostitution increased fourfold over the previous five years, despite repeated crackdowns and police raids (Quanguo renda changweihui fazhi gongzuo weiyuanhui xingfa shi 1991, 12). According to Ruan, 62 prison camps were set up for prostitutes between January 1986 and the end of 1987 (Ruan 1991, 79). Formal acknowledgement of official concern was made in March 1988 when the deputy minister of the Public Security Ministry announced at a session of the Chinese People's Political Consultative Committee that China had set up 68 detention and re-education centres for prostitutes (Wang Xingjuan 1992, 420). However, despite considerable media attention to such developments, official commitment to eradicating the sex trade seems to have borne little fruit. Not only has prostitution continued to flourish, particularly in the commercial zones of the south and southeast, but its social composition has expanded. A publication explaining the clauses of the 1991 Decision on the Prohibition of Prostitution contained the following view: 'In the past, [prostitutes] came principally from the unemployed and the poorly educated; a few were foreign. But now, in addition to these, employees from state, collective and private enterprises, party and state cadres, intellectuals, science and technology personnel, and even university students and researchers, are becoming prostitutes' (Quanguo renda changweihui fazhi gongzuo weiyuanhui xingfa shi 1991, 12). A high-ranking politician from Canton was further reported in 1990 as stating that some prostitutes were the daughters of high officials (Ruan 1991, 80). No longer is prostitution represented as the response of impoverished and uneducated young women at the bottom of the urban and rural social hierarchy to the difficulties of making a livelihood. Recent evidence suggests that increasing numbers of educated and upwardly mobile young women are joining the sex trade since prostitution offers more lucrative prospects than the relatively meagre incomes afforded by other professions. The big joint-venture hotels and expensive restaurants of the large cities are now major work locations for the high-class prostitutes whose clients include foreigners and wealthy Chinese businessmen. Massage parlours are a common venue for prostitutes slightly lower down the hierarchy, while women sold into prostitution may find themselves working to the orders of their husband-owner.

The changing social composition of sex work in recent years has introduced new elements into public discussion. Dominant representations now clearly situate prostitution as an aspect of the aspirations and practices encouraged by the commercial possibilities of the market economy. Prostitution is a symbol of both the possibilities and the dangers of modernity. Young women who become prostitutes are thus commonly described as well educated, with aspirations for a university education and travel abroad.[16] They are also invariably urban-based, and enjoy easy access to the economic opportunities offered by the private sector. Indeed, their introduction into sex work is frequently associated with their access to private entrepreneurs (geti hu). However, the prostitute also emerges as a sign for the moral dangers associated with commercialization. The language used in writing about prostitutes alone suggests as much, even in articles which offer sympathy rather than condemnation. Prostitutes are described as 'that kind of person', as 'fallen' (zhuiluo) women (Liu Xiaocong 1991, 12–15). They are considered 'shameful' and 'immoral', and are criticized for using 'improper methods (bu zhengdang fangfa) of sustaining a living' (Yang Jiezeng and He Wannan 1988, 33). A distinct attribute also associated with prostitutes' susceptibility to depravity is greed for material luxuries. Repeated descriptions emphasize how girls' fall from grace began with their desire for money – to travel abroad, to dress well, to spend on entertainment (Liu Xiaocong 1991). Some commentators have argued that, since the women who become prostitutes are 'not without employment, nor are they poor, and even less are they the target of social disdain and oppression', the main reasons explaining their position is 'first and foremost [the fact that they are] morally degenerate (*daode zhuiluozhe*), and secondly that they are individualistic pleasure seekers' (Kang Shuhua, Liu Lanpu and Zhao Ke 1988, 55). The appropriation of the prostitute for the purposes of moral control is also apparent in the view that the recent increase in prostitution is an aspect of the corrupting influence of 'sexual liberation' from abroad (Kang Shuhua, Liu Lanpu and Zhao Ke 1988, 155–7; *Gongren ribao sixiang jiaoyu bu* 1983, 38–9).[17] Indeed, the entire programme of moral and ideological education which prostitutes are obliged to undergo as part of their rehabilitation is premised on the supposition that, as prostitutes, their outlook has been tainted by undesirable tendencies. The idea that 'sex work' might be a legitimate form of employment that should enjoy the same legal and social status as any other is, by definition, excluded from this construction.

The representation of the prostitute as a threat to social order is a predictable extension of the above views. Wang Xingjuan wrote that prostitution is a 'sign of a sick society that poisons the social atmosphere and harms the social order' (Wang Xingjuan 1992, 421, 436). Or, in the words of another commentator, 'prostitution poisons the social environment, harms human rights, destroys the family, affects productive work, and leads to all sorts of crime ...' (Zhang Ping 1993, 2). An explanatory text on the law against prostitution put it very clearly: 'the flourishing growth of prostitution and the existence of criminal activities such as ... coercing women into prostitution seriously harm the social environment and social order by encouraging crimes such as robbery, extortion, murder, bodily harm and rape' (Quanguo renda changweihui fazhi gongzuo weiyuanhui xingfa shi 1991, 13). From this perspective, criminalizing prostitution functions as more than a means of targeting a specific practice and its practitioners. It confirms the representation of prostitution as a source of disorder through its links with the world beyond the law; it also reaffirms what Mary Douglas called the 'internal lines of the social system' against the dangers of contamination from within (1989, 138–9, 140). The criminalization of prostitution thus signifies not first and foremost the 'salvation' of the women involved, but the attempt to halt the destructive spread of its baleful effects.

The visibility of prostitution in Chinese society has brought with it fears about physical as well as moral contamination. References to prostitution rarely fail to include some warning note about sexually transmitted diseases, often by pointing out the percentage of prostitutes affected. The link made between disease and prostitution underlies the control of prostitution as one of the key features of government policies to monitor and reduce the spread of STDs and AIDS. Legal regulations introduced in 1991 permit specific penalties for women for working as prostitutes if they have a sexually transmitted disease.[18] Prostitutes known to work with foreign clients have been singled out for particularly harsh treatment, with prison sentences of up to two years, and longer for their pimps (Ruan 1991, 80–1). The dangers of prostitution are, by extension, also linked to eugenic considerations. Much in the terms used by the social reformers of the 1930s, who linked venereal disease with gruesome consequences for the individual, family and 'race' (Dikötter 1995, 126–37), the evil of prostitution is thought to derive from its capacity to attack the health of the nation – 'the health of our sons' and grandsons' generations' – as much as from its threat to the social and moral order (Wang Xingjuan 1992, 421).[19] As in discussions about eugenics and reproductive health, the fact that prostitution is inseparable from women's lives and women's bodies is glossed over; whether as gendered persons or as sexed bodies, women become marginal to the processes of the trade. The weight of its association with the grander themes of national health and dignity precludes a critical approach to prostitution as a complex gender issue.

Gail Hershatter has pointed out that, although the spatial and social organization of the sex trade bears little resemblance to the brothels of the republican era, current 'regulatory discourse' shares many of the features of former campaigns (Hershatter 1994, 170). As before, state policy towards prostitutes centres on offering women the chance to rebuild a stable work and family situation. Reform and rehabilitation are the key principles in persuading prostitutes to review their own experiences in the terms established by official discourse. The invitation to 'bourgeois liberalization' that prostitution is widely thought to represent can as a result be intercepted. However, the prominence of the prostitute as a signifier of depravity and vulgarity in changing economic conditions also suggests an important departure from the themes of the 1950s. Contained – criminalized or reformed – the prostitute stands for the success of state attempts to thwart the spread of 'bourgeois liberalization'; set loose on society, she represents the dangers of Western decadence that economic commercialization has not been able to resist. In this light, the prostitute embodies some of the major contrasts and contradictions inscribed in the reform programme. At stake, as Gail Hershatter suggested, is 'what modernity looks like and means, as well as what "women" are and should be' (Hershatter 1994, 171).

## Yellow materials

Immediately after its violent suppression of the 1989 democracy movement, the government launched a nationwide campaign against the 'six evils', one objective of which was to 'sweep away the yellow' (*sao huang*) and rid society of pornographic materials.[20] The timing of the campaign was not coincidental; as the state tried to convince the public of the legitimacy of its actions, it sought to vilify the political arguments of its opponents by linking them with the erosion of moral standards. The proliferation of 'social ills' in China was in large part the result of the 'open-door policy' and the invitation it gave to unmonitored influences from beyond China's borders. The circulation of pornographic materials was thus explicitly linked with the bourgeois potential within Chinese society – represented particularly by the young supporters of the democracy movement – and the commercial infiltration of salacious influences from abroad. Since late 1989, there have been frequent newspaper reports about the seizure of pornographic materials, often in the commercial conurbations of south China. Considerable publicity has also been given to the legal penalties faced by producers and distributors of pornographic materials. In an article about the effects of 'sexual publications' on their audience, Pan Suiming noted that at least twenty persons were put to death in 1989 for selling pornographic materials (Pan Suiming 1993, 59). A Beijing court recently sentenced to death Gu Jieshu, the head of the capital's largest pornographic network, which was reportedly responsible for printing 833,000 illegal books and magazines (China News Service, *The Guardian*, 19 September 1994). And, dubbed the 'vanguard' against pornographic material coming from outside the borders, the Chinese customs has vowed to intensify its efforts to halt the influx of 'moral toxin' being smuggled into China (*CND*, 8 January 1996).

Discussion about pornography in China is complicated by problems of definition. Official texts commonly apply the term 'yellow' to all visual, written and audio materials that explicitly describe sexual behaviour. Hence 'yellow' materials can include the erotic images of women found in the fashion advertisements of women's magazines as well as the pornographic videos sold on the black market. *China Youth News* reported some teachers as telling their students that pictures of people 'not wearing clothes, with bare bellies' were 'yellow' (*AP*, 13 December 1989). Works of art that contain sexually explicit images may also be condemned as pornographic; as far as the censors are concerned, aesthetic distinctions do not apply to representations of the human body. Zhang Yimou's films *Red Sorghum*, *Judou* and *Raise the Red Lantern* were all reportedly banned because of the erotic scenes they contained.[21] Zhang Xianliang's *Half of Man is Woman* was criticized for the corrupting influence of its 'incorrect' view of sex. China's first art exhibition of nudes, held by the Central Art College in Beijing and Shanghai between late 1988 and early 1989, was also banned on the grounds that images of naked bodies contaminated the mind. 'Romantic novels and romantic films' are similarly deemed to exert an unfortunate influence on the minds, and bodies, of the young. Such is the zeal of the official censors to protect the public from moral contamination that their concerns about sensitive political matters may seem pale by comparison.

State control of representations of the sexualized body has been a consistent aspect of official discourses on sexuality since 1949. Between the 1950s and the late 1970s, any reference, whether narrative or visual, to explicitly erotic interests was subject to stringent censorship. As we have seen, photographs and illustrations of women during this period acknowledged their bodily existences only as labourers and revolutionary fighters. The tightly closed buttons of the Mao jacket hid all female shape and texture from view, transforming the woman into a metaphor for revolutionary commitment and hard work. The absence of erotic and pornographic materials from public circulation was, in official terms at least, total.

Since the early 1980s, the marketization of the economy has given a new public prominence to sex, and pornographic publications flourish on the black market. Thus, although during the Cultural Revolution pornographic materials circulated clandestinely, particularly among young people in the towns and cities, it has only been since the introduction of the post-Mao reforms that pornography has become an issue of explicit official concern. The government's response to the prevalence of erotically suggestive images has veered between bans on the importation of 'yellow' materials and crackdowns on those involved in the domestic pornographic industry. A circular issued jointly by the General Offices of the Central Committee of the Communist Party and the State Council announced that 'the publication of sexually explicit literature, pornographic pictures, violent and superstitious videos . . . must be banned', in order to 'ensure healthy culture' (*Beijing Review*, Vol. 37 No. 51, 1994). Motivated by a moralistic commitment to protect the public from depravity, the official argument is that corrupting images lead directly to illicit actions. Erotic images must therefore be prohibited on the grounds that those who absorb such materials become sexual offenders (Pan Suiming 1993, 59). Official support for expanding the provision of sex education in schools is similarly substantiated as a means to divert young people's attention away from erotic materials (Pan Suiming 1993, 65). Reports about sexual crime repeat the same theme in constructing a continuum between absorption of romantic materials, sexual promiscuity, moral turpitude and criminal behaviour. A legal text published in 1990, for example, claimed that some 80 per cent of the defendants in rape cases heard in the court of some small town became rapists after seeing or reading pornographic materials (Wang Ranji et al. 1990, 119).

The official objection to representations of the sexualized body depends on a simple categorization of the images of the naked, invariably female, body as a source of moral corruption and shame, regardless of the place or narrative context within which it appears, and regardless of the different meanings that the viewer might read into it. Without clothes, the female body must be banned, despite the sexualized meanings that might be inscribed in fashion photographs of the clothed female body; it is the perpetrator of depravity and danger. Such a position makes no distinction between hard pornography, in which women's bodies are subjects of physical brutality as well as sexual titillation, and images of the female body which are constructed for aesthetic purposes. Nor is it accompanied by any critical discussion about the gender and social issues involved in the production and consumption of pornographic materials. Indeed, the official ban on pornographic materials seems only incidentally to have anything to do with women and hierarchical gender relations. In an article about child sex abuse, the explanation given for the rapes of two girls aged seven and thirteen, in the latter case by her brother, was that visual images of sex exercise a powerful influence on young people who are ignorant about sex (Liu Dalin 1992a). No comment was made about the unequal power relations between men and women that are inscribed in 'visual images of sex'. The fact that the production of 'yellow' materials depends predominantly on appropriating the female body for male absorption, perusal and use, and on the female's sexual and physical subjugation to male and commercial exploitation, seems to escape the attention of official commentators. The 'yellow female' thus emerges as a generic signifier of degeneration, vulgarity and criminality. The failure to approach pornography as a gender issue, rather than as an issue of social morality and control, reinforces the negative attributes, already widely represented in public images, associated with female gender and sexuality.

## Rape and sexual violence

After years of very scant media coverage, sexual violence against women has recently become a prominent issue of public debate, in large part inspired by the debates that took place in the run-up to the Fourth UN Conference on Women held in Beijing in September 1995. Unofficial women's groups have pointed out that the international focus on women in 1995 gave them their first opportunity to bring the issue into the public arena. Discussions have begun to focus on women's experiences and difficulties in reporting rape that signify a qualitative difference from the more distanced, 'factual' reporting of the mid-1980s. However, government publications indicate that the issue of sexual violence against women has been a significant – though maybe not prime – concern for the past decade or so. In August 1983, as alarm about the rate of sexual crimes began to penetrate official bodies, the government took the decision to identify rape as one of the most serious. Accordingly, the criminal law identified different categories of rape which carried sentences of varying severity. Rape 'by violence, coercion, or other means' carried three to ten years' imprisonment. Sexual relations with children under the age of fourteen was categorized as rape, 'and is to be given a heavier punishment'. 'Especially serious circumstances', when rape involves a 'person's injury or death', and cases of multiple and gang rapes carried life imprisonment or even the death sentence (Article 139). Liu Dalin estimated that the incidence of rape showed an increase of 345 per cent between 1979 and 1983, a significant proportion of which was committed by juveniles (Liu Dalin 1987). Official statistics of the late 1980s showed that, in terms of numbers of cases reported according to categories of crime, rape was second only to robbery, with reported instances rising in the spring and summer months (Wang Ranji et al. 1990, 3). Figures for domestic violence, including wife battering and sexual abuse, also indicate an increase, leading to public discussion of questions like 'Is the family a special zone of violence?' (Chen Huilin 1984, 26).

Media coverage of rape cases in recent years suggests varying analyses of its causes and effects.[22] Condemnation of rape and other forms of sexual violence frequently accompanies reports about the 'feudal' maltreatment of women, alongside their abduction and sale into marriage and prostitution. Alternatively, it is explained as a result of the social dislocation engendered by reform policies, and as a significant factor in a large proportion of murder and assault cases (Amnesty International 1995, 2). Considerable attention also focuses on cases in which powerful, well-placed and wealthy men – factory managers, middle-ranking officials and older colleagues – abuse their authority to take advantage of young women and intimidate them into silence. One such case was of a young girl whose fear of the consequences to her own reputation prevented her from bringing a complaint against a fellow worker for some time (Si Ren 1986). When she eventually did, her bosses were clearly not enthusiastic about investigating the case, and only cautioned the man. Finally the case went to court, and the man was executed. In another case, a doctor in a Shanghai hospital was given a fifteen-year sentence after it was discovered that he was using his medical authority and prestige as a doctor to rape a young peasant woman during treatment (*Shanghai qingnian bao*, 6 January 1984, 5, quoted in Honig and Hershatter 1988, 280). Yet more reports target the sons of high party cadres, the infamous *gaogan zidi* whose corrupt life styles and abuse of power fuelled popular hostility to the government in the events leading up to the protests of spring 1989.

The interests informing the publicization of such cases also vary. In some instances, they serve the political function of exposing corruption and abuse of power in high places, while in others they encourage the sensationalization of sexual violence for commercial purposes. While the popular press doubtless derives considerable financial gain from publishing detailed accounts, often semi-fictionalized, of rape cases, other publications have a more didactic and moralistic purpose. A main objective of many such reports, for example, often noted in an introductory paragraph, is to warn young women of the perils of mixing with certain types of people, of indulging in certain fashions and leisure activities, or of entertaining upwardly mobile social aspirations. Many accounts seek to expose the inefficiency and unwillingness of local authorities to investigate rape cases, and to criticize the pressures and interests which effectively prevent young women from reporting rape to the authorities.[23] The press has from time to time been extremely critical of the failure of legal organs to offer adequate protection to women who report rape. Articles in *Fazhi ribao*, for example, have argued that the procedures involved in questioning women are often excessively prolonged and repetitive, and that interviews with the victim are often conducted in the presence of persons who have nothing to do with the case. They have also denounced the negligence of legal personnel in allowing rapists access to information about the personal details of the victim, and in permitting all sorts of people, including representatives from the rapist's work unit, into the court room (e.g. Zhu Fengwen 1987; Li Shuhuai and Gai Xing 1988). Such articles shared the opinion that women's right to confidentiality needed to be guaranteed in order to encourage victims to report assault.

Many reports, however, leave the reader with a somewhat ambivalent understanding of the principles on which accusations are made. Indeed, even when a commentator's ostensible purpose is to expose discriminatory attitudes, the narrative techniques used in describing the details of a particular case may suggest otherwise. A typical mode of this is the narrative use of personal characteristics – appearance, marital status, sexual history – of the victimized woman to contextualize the description of a case. Descriptions of 'a dark slippery road' along which an unsuspecting young woman walks 'in high heels' give a particular framework to accounts of resistance against an assailant, which implicates the woman in responsibility for her own misfortune (Jia Zheng 1987). A young woman's experience in confronting the reluctance of her employers to act on her behalf after being raped by a colleague may begin with descriptions of her youth and innocence and her fondness for fashionable clothes, again as if to suggest that she is in some way responsible for having attracted her assailant's attention (Si Ren 1986). Autobiographical accounts often include references to the victim's 'natural timidity' (*tiansheng qienuo*) and unworldliness, with the implication that more courage and *savoir faire* would have saved them from a nasty fate ('San ge shouru nü qingnian de huyu' 1984). The appearance of words like 'error' or 'mistake' (*cuo*) to describe women's role in being raped further suggests the lingering influence of notions of female guilt. Explicit sympathy may be given a woman who is tormented by her husband for having told him that she was raped before marriage (Wang Yanming 1988, 59). But the suggestion that 'women should hold their heads up and objectively face life' after being raped takes on a different meaning when accompanied by the comment that 'losing your purity is a mistake, not a crime' (p. 66).

One unmistakable implication of these approaches is that women should learn to be brave in order to resist attack. Women are told, in one form or another, that it is up to them to protect themselves. They are told to rely on their 'intelligence and bravery' when forced to face a powerful attacker (Jia Zheng 1987). Alongside standard advice to women to be alert for men who may be following them and to avoid deserted places at night, the praise given to those who successfully thwart attacks may be read to imply that failure to resist invites assault (Honig and Hershatter 1988, 282).

There is a prominent contrast in these articles between the attention given to describing the personal attributes and responsibilities of the victim and the lack of interest in formulating a gender analysis of rape.

Explanations of the causes of rape sometimes fail to mention gender at all. A book on the recognition and prevention of rape, for example, listed a 'corrupt outlook on life', a 'selfish value system', 'degenerate morality' and a 'psychology of sexual pursuit and enjoyment' as possible causes of sexual assault against women without once mentioning the gender-specific nature of rape (Wang Ranji et al. 1990, 99–101). References to the patriarchal structures within which sexual violence occurs are infrequent, and generally associated with the re-emergence of feudal practices. Few articles approach sexual violence against women in terms which challenge the gender hierarchy represented in the dominant discourse of sexuality. Simple comments to the effect that a rapist enjoyed reading pornographic materials, or that he had no knowledge of sex education, or that his parents had not brought him up properly, hardly compensate for this lack. Nor do general comments that seek explanations for rape in, for example, the social disruption caused by the Cultural Revolution, or the pressures of living in a rapidly changing social environment in the late 1980s.

One explanation for this lack lies in the reluctance of party-state institutions to undertake any serious gender analysis except in contexts that are deemed to have a significant bearing on economic and political developments. Considerable official attention has been devoted to women's education, employment and migration, health and childcare, and so on. However, analyses of women's disadvantaged position in all these areas have tended to focus on factors such as the lack of resources, inequalities in development and population pressure rather than on gender – even though, in both its construction and effects, gender necessarily intersects with other discourses. Discussion about gender issues considered to have only a tenuous relationship to the broader, more pressing matters of economic and social development – sexual violence, abduction of women, the increase in venal marriage practices, and female infanticide, to name but a few – is often subsumed under general categories such as 'social ills'. Even in cases such as female infanticide, where the issue of sexual discrimination is at its most basic, substantive analysis of the gender issues involved continues to be secondary to the imperatives of population control. In line with these general approaches, discussion about rape is oriented either to the elucidation of general problems of social order or to the inadequacies of the legal system and the public's legal understanding. Suggestions that rape might be avoided if women were less ingenuous and ignorant do not really contribute much to a gender analysis.

Recent debate about non-consensual sex within marriage represents a contestation of this position. In the early 1980s, the definition of rape set out in the legal press included coercive sex between betrothed and divorced couples, but it did not include rape within marriage. Legal opinion was that, if a couple registered marriage before sleeping together, and the man forced the woman to have sexual intercourse, this could not be classified as rape, since registering the marriage legalized the sexual relationship between husband and wife.[24] One response to this definition argued that, if the registration of a marriage was forced on a woman and she did not want to have sex with her husband, then this should be treated as rape ('Dui "lüe lun qiangjian zui" de bu tong yijian' 1981). A more recent example, published in *Zhongguo funü*, argued that the premise for defining rape should be whether sexual intercourse occurs against the woman's will (Song Meiya 1991). This article argued that there was no reason to alter this principle simply because of a woman's change in status on marriage. Indeed, evidence was that marital rape was not infrequent. A survey carried out among 1079 rural women included thirty who said that they had experienced marital rape (*Jiating yisheng* 5, 1992, 4–7). Liu Dalin also pointed out that rape and sexual abuse in marriage is quite widespread, and commonly coincides with the husband's assumption that his wife is his sexual property.[25] Liu Dalin further cited evidence from divorce cases brought before the courts to argue that, while women commonly assume that sexual intercourse is a wifely duty, whether they want it or not, increasing numbers of women are expressing their dissatisfaction with an abusive relationship (Liu Dalin 1992b, 425, 599–600). In defence of the category of marital rape, one commentator wrote that 'sexual autonomy [means] the right to voluntarily participate in and refuse sexual relations. Today's imbalance in sexual relations is principally manifested in a depreciation and lack of respect for a woman's sexual rights' (Song Meiya 1991). That the demands – both explicit and implicit – for recognition of marital rape as a legal category have seen some results has been demonstrated in the decisions of several provincial courts to give prison terms to men who raped wives who were engaged in divorce proceedings or who attempted to leave arranged marriages (Amnesty International 1995, 2). In one of the first such reported cases, a man was sentenced to six years in prison in Heilongjiang for raping his wife during a court recess of their divorce trial. In another similar case, in Gansu Province, a man was charged with sexually assaulting his wife, with the help of his relatives, 'to prevent her leaving a loveless marriage' (Reuter, 3 January 1995). However, legal opinion continues to uphold the dominant view of women's sexual duties in marriage. A legal textbook stated the position very clearly. 'If a husband forces a woman to have sex against her will only in order to satisfy the requirements of sex, rape is not a suitable definition. If the husband's intentions are obscene, or designed to humiliate ... where the circumstances are serious, this may be defined as the offence of humiliation or hooliganism' (Zui gao renmin jiancha yuan 1991, 159). In a climate in which a woman's decision to report rape may result in further abuse, humiliation and suffering, the implication of such an opinion is that not much short of murder would be considered adequate evidence.

The brutal lives that countless numbers of women and men live in every part of the world defy representation. That girls and women are killed, abandoned, abducted, sold, raped, violently abused, commodified and objectified for their sex alone reinforces the difficulties of representation. Many of the issues examined in this chapter constitute a terrible violation of women's basic rights to physical and sexual integrity. However, little of the publicity given to the crimes against women affords any indication of the extent and the depth of the brutality suffered. The figures the government produces for numbers of criminals executed or sentenced for rape or abduction provide little indication of an attempt to analyse the gender issues at stake in the abuse of women's rights. Although the government repeatedly declares its commitment to eradicating crimes enacted against women on the grounds of their sex, this cannot compensate for the horrific wounds women suffer for the simple fact that they are female.

The above analysis – brief though it is – shows that there is a very limited field of meanings associated with being female in recent discussions about gender and sexual violence against women. Women are represented as guileless victims, taken in by good looks and power, or motivated by social and material aspirations. Representing women as either the victims of patriarchal structures of power or as malicious perpetrators of disease and degeneration caricatures the realities of women's lives. The subject positions constructed for women here neither coincide with those identified by real live women nor grant any space for women's own voices. These dominant representations, moreover, are nurtured by the contexts within which reports about women's abuse are located. Commitment to reform policy is not destabilized by its association, via the open door, with pornography, prostitution and sexually transmitted disease. The commercial abuse of women's sexualized bodies is not constructed as a critique of reform policy, but rather as an unfortunate distortion of it. Representing the women subjected to violence and abuse as guileless, powerless victims of criminals leaves the view of reform as a collective good undisturbed. Identifying the prostitute as the wanton woman, the carrier of disease and the agent of crime ultimately has the same effect, for punishment of individuals who are seen to attack the system from within performs the symbolic function of reaffirming its legitimacy (Douglas 1989, 140–1).

The most disturbing aspect of such representations is the disjuncture between the repeated brutality against women and the government's failure to extend any real gender analysis of the realities involved. The government has consistently ignored the gender issues present in the commercial and violent abuse of women, defining them instead as social, economic or moral issues. The condemnation of prostitution, pornography and sexual crime is part of an official discourse that is moulded more by moralistic assumptions about sexual propriety, women's in particular, than by an understanding of gender hierarchy. Official statements situate the policy of suppressing prostitution within an ideological framework which views the feudal past and the bourgeois present as a dual repository of depravity and corruption. While a rhetoric of gender equality continues to establish the parameters within which discussion about women takes place, standard analyses of commercial practices which exploit women neglect the crucial function of gender hierarchies of power in favour of generally articulated ideological injustices.

# 8 Sexualities under Suspicion

'Sexual perversion refers to a distorted approach to the selection of sexual partners, and to inhibitions of sexual excitement, commonly found in adolescents, and expressed in homosexuality, transvestism, promiscuity and so on' (Wu Zhangming, Zhu Xiaolan and Lang Ying 1990, 77). Expressions of sexual love in contexts and relationships dissociated from marriage – 'the ultimate sign of heterosexual love' – are commonly considered 'abnormal' or 'perverse' (*biantai*) in contemporary Chinese society (Li Wenhai and Liu Shuyu 1992, 88–100). Attention to sexual practices and identities that disturb the boundaries of socially acceptable sexuality is a powerful mode of reinforcing the principles of dominant discourses (Foucault 1984). Identification of a range of 'abnormal' or 'deviant' behaviours in the considerable quantity of writings about 'improper sexual behaviour' (*bu zhengchang xing xingwei*) that have been produced since the early days of the People's Republic has served to legitimize the values and practices subscribed to by official medical and professional agencies. When contained by a state discourse, as in China, public discussion about 'peripheral' sexualities functions to support an agenda that corresponds with official interests in social control.

Challenges to the dominant model of monogamous marriage have been represented in various forms and discourses – medical, legal, popular and official – over the past four decades. The emphasis given to identifying particular dangers, or to condemning particular relationships and modes of conduct, has shifted constantly, following the contours of the changing economic and social practices within which these discourses are situated. Thus, before the political turmoil of the Cultural Revolution, concerns about sexual practices which were seen to threaten the success of the monogamous model of marriage corresponded primarily with the official project of stabilizing the new structure of marriage and family relationships in order to maximize energies for economic construction. The sexual issues associated with these concerns were most notably female virginity and adultery, both of which were represented as having a direct bearing on marital stability. Since the Cultural Revolution, and in particular since the late 1980s, as the new social environment has widened the debate about sex-related issues, so the range of sexual activities and choices considered inconsistent with the norms of the dominant discourse has expanded. The identification of pre-marital sexuality, homosexuality, promiscuity, celibacy and spinsterhood as 'abnormal' and 'improper' behaviours is located within a context of official attempts to impose order at a time of social chaos. Order, in this context, is defined with reference to the social and economic objectives informing state policies on population, the family, crime and health.

Between the mid-1950s and the Cultural Revolution, the protection of the moral and social foundations of 'socialist monogamy' dominated discussion about threatening sexual behaviour. Coinciding with a period of 'lower standards of sexual morality' after 1953 (Meijer 1971, 143), attention to the requirements of marital harmony was accompanied by a redefinition of the ideological character of sexual misdemeanours. Biographical sketches and cautionary tales extended their focus from the need to eliminate the pernicious practices of the feudal past to the need for vigilance against 'individualistic' and 'bourgeois' attitudes towards love and marriage; official interest shifted from condemning feudal abuse of women to identifying bourgeois errors in sexual conduct. Representations of sexual morality simultaneously moved away from safeguarding women's rights of free choice and divorce, towards implicating the dangers to marital stability that would result from a failure to understand the requirements of the new model of monogamy. The main emphasis was on the consolidation of felicitous marital relations; warnings against extra-marital affairs on the grounds that 'freedom of marriage does not mean the freedom to have affairs with a person who is already married and has children' were issued in the name of preserving 'communist morality' (Xu Mingjiang 1955).

This ideological shift permitted another transition, away from targeting men as the main culprits of feudal abuse of women, towards representing female behaviour as an agent of improper conduct. It allowed for a switch in the subject positions identified with women, from powerless victims to agents of harm. The representation of women as autonomous sexual agents outside the proper boundaries of responsive wifehood interfered with the biologically based model of sexual complementarity and, therefore, to the requirements of marital harmony. Identification of female conduct that did not conform to the discursive categories of wife and mother functioned as a means of reaffirming the control of female sexuality as an instrument of conjugal stability. Sexual order was thus proscriptively defined through representations of female 'deviance'. Discussion about women's sexual conduct functioned to demarcate the boundaries between acceptable and illicit sexual practice. The concept of female deviance was a construct designed to protect the majority from moral contamination. Discursive control of women's sexual behaviour emerged as the key to preserving the social and moral order.

The radical changes in Chinese society in the past decade have not substantially altered the focus on women's sexuality as the fulcrum of sexual and moral order. Indeed, the greater diversity of sexual 'abnormalities' identified in the dominant discourse in recent years means that the construction of female sexuality as a regulator of sexual standards in general has acquired unprecedented dimensions. Whether in discussions about adultery and the responsibilities of the iniquitous 'third party', about the desirability of virginity on marriage, or about the unnaturalness of remaining single, female behaviour remains the standard for distinguishing between acceptable and unacceptable behaviour. Through representations of female deviance, female sexuality establishes the boundaries safeguarding monogamous marriage as the only legitimate context for sexual activity. The only noticeable exception is in discussion about homosexuality, almost exclusively represented as a male phenomenon. Here too, however, female sexuality persists as the ultimate reference for acceptable practice; dominant public objections to homosexuality lie in the essentialist heterosexist values inscribed in the model of monogamous marriage.

## Virgins and victims

I have argued in earlier chapters that representations of women as sexualized persons have been consistently shaped by discursive contexts that foreground the autonomy and power of the active male urge. Within these contexts – whether they refer to ideals of marriage or the 'scientific' explanations of sexual difference – female sexuality is identified as passive, reluctant and responsive, dependent on the male partner for awakening. Repeated references to the male – male desires and shortcomings, the need for male sensitivity and understanding – create female sexuality as anything but an independent site of experience. Positive representations of female sexuality rarely contradict normative expectations of reproduction and motherhood. Female sexuality is generally represented as a source of pleasure and benefit only in so far as it contributes to marital and family harmony. Indeed, the idea that sexuality might be a site of individual enjoyment and expression removed from responsibilities to maintaining conjugal stability does not really feature in dominant discussions. Views about female sexuality are centrally mediated by concerns about marriage and reproduction.

It almost goes without saying that such representations are probably a far cry from the subjective experience of sexuality and sexual identity of living, individual women. In earlier decades, when very few contributors to magazine debates openly confessed to having had extra-marital liaisons, such suggestions were invariably veiled by the use of euphemism; comments like 'they had gone beyond ordinary friendship' (*chaoguole pengyou guanxi*) or she had 'liked him' (*gen ta haoguo*) were often circumlocutions for sexual intercourse. Alternatively, they were published as examples of 'illegal and mistaken' behaviour (Chen Ying 1982). Since the mid-1980s, more explicit references have accompanied the greater diversity of sexual relationships surveyed – though not encouraged – in public discourses. Letters and autobiographical accounts published in women's magazines often suggest that women not infrequently engage in pre-marital and extra-marital relationships. And though the absence of explicit references to sexual behaviour is sometimes striking, for example in sex education publications targeted at adolescents, it is no longer uncommon to come across descriptions of sexual behaviour that do not conform to dominant moral and cultural values. Whether explicit or not, such references challenge the standards of sexual fidelity upheld as 'socialist morality' since the early days of the People's Republic. Moreover, in so far as evidence of women's sexual interests – potential or real – outside the framework of marriage points to desires that contest the responsive and dependent attributes of the biological model of sexuality, these have to be explained by means which minimize their potential for destabilizing the terms of the dominant discourse. If women are by nature passive respondents to the dominant male drive, then indications of a more active and autonomous female sexuality, associated neither with marriage nor with reproduction, can be explained only by resorting to concepts of abnormality and/or deviance, or by removing from women responsibility for their own actions.

The tensions between these polarized constructions of women have been particularly apparent in representing women who transgress the boundaries of respectable sexual behaviour as innocent victims of corrupt and evil men. Cautionary tales have repeatedly warned young girls against being led astray by the empty charms of older, worldly men. The following example, entitled 'My lesson' (*Wode jiaoxun*), is typical of many (Su Fan 1956). The story described how a twenty-year-old girl was pursued by her boss, but refused to respond because she knew that he was married. He persisted, and played on her innocence to persuade her that he was trustworthy. She eventually gave in and agreed to have sex with him, only to find herself being sent to another workplace when the liaison was discovered. However, it was not until some time later, when she heard that her former boss was up to the same game with another young woman, that she realized the truth about his intentions. Full of remorse, she acknowledged her errors, which she then publicized to warn other young women against falling victim to similar deception. More recent examples invoke women's vulnerability to the temptations offered by the commercial and social opportunities of the reform era. Some describe women's interest in material gain and the seductive appeal of film and fashion; others warn against entertaining exaggerated hopes of travelling abroad. An example from a 1985 magazine narrated the experience of a young woman whose eagerness to become a fashion model was the cause of her seduction (Wang Qiuliang and Zhu Wenjie, *XDJT* 7 1985, 13, quoted in Honig and Hershatter 1988, 65). The girl was an expert at dancing the tango, and, having caught the attention of a man who was posing as an employee of a model agency, she agreed to strip for him so that he could obtain her vital statistics. She also agreed to pose in the nude for him, and only became suspicious when he demanded that she dance naked with him, ostensibly to see how well she moved her legs. So common were such cautionary tales that *Time* magazine reported the official publication of a book entitled *Girls, Be Vigilant!*, issued by the government in 1985 (John Leo and Richard Hornik, *Time*, 10 February 1986, 46).[1]

Focusing on the figure of the ingenuous victim also makes it possible to explain pre-marital sexual experience in ways that are acceptable to conservative concerns. Plenty of evidence demonstrates that female purity continues to be a major preoccupation for many people, women and men. As indicated in Chapter 4, husbands continue to write of their anger and anxiety on discovering that their wives were not virgins 'on the night of the honeymoon'. Women who are known to have been the object of a man's attentions, or who are known to have had a boyfriend before marriage, are commonly represented as being free with their sexual favours (e.g., Su Yuan 1956; Jin Ruiying and Shang Shaohua 1980). An innocent nineteen-year-old could become the object of scorn and ridicule, and even arouse the concern of the police, if she stayed out too late at night, as a letter from a reader described (Wei Biyan 1984). Rape victims may be treated as 'broken shoes', blamed by their husbands for having led their assailants on, often with tragic consequences. An example of the 1950s revealed how a woman waited for five years for her case against her assailant to be resolved, while her husband persisted in his conviction that her loose morals were to blame for her suffering (Bai Ruifang 1956). Another woman was so tormented by her husband's belief that she had been responsible for being raped that, in desperation, she resorted to killing the assailant (Wang Yanming 1988, 59). The similarity in reports of such cases decades apart suggest that changing social and sexual values have not yet seriously disturbed traditional values associated with women's purity.

Editorial commentaries on such cases frequently focus on the injust-ice of the views surveyed, particularly when sexual abuse and rape are involved. Men who feel humiliated by the fact that their wife did not bleed 'on the night of the honeymoon' are invariably told that attaching such importance to hymeneal blood indicates unreasonable and 'partial' (*bu gou quanmian*) demands for proof of female purity (Wu Zhangming, Zhu Xiaolan and Lang Ying 1990, 106). In any case, the woman may not be to blame, so husbands should be sympathetic, and should remember that anxieties about a wife's pre-marital conduct might impair marital happiness (Fang Fang 1987, 123). Such advice could well be read as indirect criticism of the double standard that sanctions pre-marital sexual activity among men but not among women. Suggestions that the hymen can be broken by medical exam-ination, for instance, or by excessive physical exercise, effectively neutralize the potential danger represented by a woman's sexual history; they bring potentially wayward conduct within the boundaries of acceptability. They also offer a convenient escape mechanism for women who might otherwise find it difficult to explain their pre-marital experiences to suspicious husbands. Another, more pragmatic interpretation is that these comments demonstrate an attempt to minimize potential tension and conflict affecting the conjugal relation-ship. It was perhaps no coincidence that, few as they were, the articles of the 1950s that referred to female virginity, hymeneal blood and, by implication, wives' pre-marital sexual experiences appeared at a time when a principal objective of marriage- and family-related work was to boost marital stability. By contrast, more recent preoccupations about female virginity have been set within a context of considerable public exposure to the emotional and sexual difficulties explaining the increase in marital conflict and the divorce rate. This argument by no means denies that women were, and continue to be, victimized in the ways suggested by media reports. However, attempts to assuage what are seen as unnecessary and unjust anxieties about women's pre-marital virginity serve the interests of monogamous order and family stability by devaluing the significance of an aspect of female sexuality still widely considered a threat to successful marriage.

Criticism of men's concerns about hymeneal blood has never obscured the implied immorality of a woman having sex before marriage. The desirability of female virginity before marriage has not diminished as an aspect of the dominant discourse of sexuality, even though some of the specific reasons for warning young people of the perils of sex before marriage may have changed. Recriminations against women who have lost their virginity before marriage or who are suspected of promiscuity continue in both popular and official discourses. Entrenched expectations of female chastity are a function of a prevailing sexual morality which, as Sheridan and Salaff put it, 'denies that women have sexual needs' (Sheridan and Salaff 1984, 124). However, for the purposes of the present discussion, representing 'fallen' women as victims of misfortune and abuse conveniently avoids the difficulties necessarily inherent in formulating other explanations. Representing women as active sexual agents is incompatible with the model of sexual and marital harmony upheld by the dominant dis-course. Containing potentially disruptive expressions of female sexual-ity within the terms of the dominant discourse diffuses their implicit challenge to the subject positions associated with marital stability and satisfaction with which women are encouraged to identify.

## Adultery and the female 'third party'

When women's right to divorce became national law under the 1950 Marriage Law, the government and the All China Women's Federation put considerable efforts into making divorce acceptable to conserv-ative public opinion. Official publications attempted to inspire public support for women's new right by highlighting numerous cases of cruelty to wives and daughters-in-law. Examples of discrimination against divorcées who were forced out of their villages by local prejudice, ostracized by their families and imprisoned (Hua Mu 1953), or of women whose failed attempts to obtain divorce pushed them to commit suicide (Ma Dejie and Liu Xianjun 1950), abounded in the official youth and women's journals. Given that women were both the principal petitioners and the beneficiaries of divorce suits in the early years of the People's Republic, particular attempts were made to convey the idea that freedom of divorce did not mean divorce at will any more than it was a licence for female promiscuity.[2]

Once the initial rush for divorces had freed many women from arranged unions, divorce became much more difficult to obtain. Increasing use was made of mediation to persuade couples that divorce was not in their best interests.[3] 'Trivial' complaints were dismissed, and alienation of affection (*ganqing polie*) was rejected as grounds for divorce, since it indicated an 'exaggerated concern with personal issues at the expense of social order' (Liu Yunxiang 1958). As the initial anti-feudal objectives of the first stage of marriage reform were superseded by other policy priorities, the politically progressive construction of divorce as an instrument of women's emancipation was replaced by a more conservative emphasis on its function as a potentially disruptive factor of social and family life. With the sole exception of the early period of the Cultural Revolution, divorce remained difficult to obtain and rare throughout the 1960s and 1970s; even when disputes were severe, they rarely resulted in divorce (Whyte and Parish 1984, 186–9).[4]

The promulgation of a new Marriage Law in 1981 provoked another dramatic rise in the divorce rate in the early 1980s. Taking advantage of the legalization of 'alienation of affection' as valid grounds for divorce, numerous urban couples filed for divorce. It was reported that in Shanghai the number of divorce applications received by the courts almost doubled in one year (*Zhongguo baike nianjian* 1981, 543; Whyte and Parish 1984, 188). Between 1983 and 1987, figures continued to rise, reaching 1 per cent of the population by 1987 (Sun Wenlan 1991, 2). With extensive publicity given the increasing incidence of divorce and its harmful effects on child development, the 'divorce crisis' became one of the key topics of popular concern. While divorce remains a fairly uncommon occurrence in China, particularly in comparison with societies where the divorce rate is high, the publicity given to it in recent years has contributed to its construction as a grave social problem of contemporary life.

Adultery has consistently been represented as one of the most important causes of divorce ever since the early 1950s. In the so-called period of national rehabilitation between 1950 and 1953, it was commonly treated as a form of feudal abuse on the part of men who callously abandoned their first wives, whom they had married according to parental arrangement, in favour of other, often younger and urban-situated women of their own choice. Until 1953, as Meijer noted, 'divergences from the ordained sexual morality [were] punished as relics of the past in order to protect the future, to safeguard the development of that spiritual progress which [was] needed for the construction of the new socialist society' (Meijer 1971, 100). However, as official policy moved away from the emphasis on releasing women from feudal bonds to the protection and stabilization of marital relationships, 'feudal relationships and feudal remnants' disappeared as the main reason for divorce. Henceforth, 'bourgeois and petty bourgeois perceptions of marriage', including adultery, estrangement on account of the upward mobility of one partner, 'fickle and loose behaviour' (*zhao san mu si*) and 'bourgeois glass of waterism' [were] treated as the 'principal causes of divorce' (Liu Yunxiang 1958).

Xu Anqi, one of the foremost academic authorities on divorce in China, has estimated that some 24 per cent of the divorces obtained through the courts during the first peak in the early 1950s were on the grounds of adultery (Xu Anqi 1990b, 52). However, it is difficult to estimate the exact extent of adultery between the 1950s and the 1970s because of the absence of detailed figures and a lack of legal precision. Although the Marriage Law made no specific reference to adultery, and it was by no means always treated as a punishable offence (Meijer 1971, 94), some legal commentators insisted that 'bigamy and adultery committed after liberation [should] be punished as criminal offences' (Pang Dunzhi 1950, 39–40). Since the late 1970s, adultery has featured prominently in divorce cases brought before the law courts, rising from 19 per cent of all cases in 1981 to 22 per cent in 1987. Even though this signifies more than double the former total of divorces granted on the grounds of adultery, it is a drop in terms of per capita rates (Xu Anqi 1990b, 52; Tan Shen 1993, 9).

Xu Anqi has commented on some notable differences in the characteristics of adultery in the two periods she examined. In the 1950s, divorce plaintiffs cited continued practices of arranged marriage and material constraints, such as separation from spouse because of employment, residential status, imprisonment and poverty, as major factors contributing to adultery. By contrast, 1980s surveys – of course, conducted after the legalization of 'emotional breakdown' as valid grounds for divorce – suggest that 'psychological dissatisfaction' (*xinli xuqiu debudao manzu*) with a marriage partner was much more important, and explained the greater instance of extra-marital affairs between colleagues.[5] By contrast with the common view that adulterous relationships have become more public since the reform period (Li Yuxiao 1985), Xu also suggested that extra-marital affairs in the 1950s tended to be less furtive than in the later period, with many couples openly cohabiting and having children.[6] In her view, greater social tolerance of marital separation in the past fifteen years has reduced women's acceptance of husbands' extra-marital affairs (Xu Anqi 1990b, 53).

While Xu's analysis suggests that the specific characteristics of adultery have changed quite considerably in recent years, the meanings attributed to female gender in representations of the relationships involved reveal considerable similarities across the different periods. As a rule of sexual relations, the model of monogamy upheld by the Marriage Law has been ideally constructed as a signifier of pre-marital chastity as well as sexual exclusivity during marriage, applicable to both women and men. This interpretation was sometimes given a legalistic gloss during the 1950s; a girl who was praised for marrying her first love, despite his lower status and wealth, was told that to have embarked on a 'love relationship' with a second suitor would have violated the monogamous requirements of the law (Wei Hua 1958). As in other aspects of the discourse of sexuality, descriptions of cases of sexual infidelity and adultery have invariably been inscribed with gender differences, sometimes constructed through the gendered use of ideological labels.[7] Accounts of sexual misconduct attribute agency and responsibility differentially depending on the gender of the adulterer, the abandoned spouse and the 'third party'. Criticism of male transgressions is frequently formulated to warn women against men's unscrupulous behaviour as much as to castigate men. Commentaries on male adulterers give greater prominence to their public status – to their professional ambitions and upwardly mobile aspirations – than to their sexual designs. In comparison with the detailed attention given women's sexual misconduct in extra-marital relations, men's sexual misdemeanours are often glossed over, mentioned as an aside at the end of a paragraph. And, whatever the period of publication, stories about male adultery invariably imply some culpability on the part of the wife. A tale from the mid-1950s about a young woman who was repeatedly abused by her corrupt and pleasure-seeking husband devoted considerably more space to criticizing the woman for her mistaken view of love than to the husband for his cruelty (Zhong Dianbei 1955). The dominant message, delivered to 'encourage [the young woman] and other young women like her to struggle', was that, had she been more vigilant against her husband's shallow charms, and had she got to know him better before deciding to marry him, she might have saved herself considerable torment. It was only towards the end of the story that her husband's 'errors' were mentioned, and then only to characterize them as those of a 'cruel and uncivilized' (yeman) person who had 'absolutely no prospects in today's society'. More recent examples have criticized the wives of adulterous men for their failure to behave to their husbands as 'proper' wives should (Liu Xuanda 1992), and have urged wives to show tolerance and understanding in order to encourage their husbands back to the fold (Gao Fang and Zeng Rong 1991, 37–8). Invoking traditional stereotypes of the dominating woman at home and the proverbial 'hen-pecked husband' (*qiguan yan*), criticism of wives could further be interpreted as containing an implicit justification of men's adulterous behaviour; explaining the 'intrusion of a third party' as the result of a husband's dissatisfaction in marriage, which 'occurs, for example, when a wife is garrulous and controlling', or 'lacking in warmth and intimacy', suggests little attribution of responsibility to the man (Su Fu and Huang Yuxian, 1992, 23–4).[8]

The gender imbalance in the allocation of responsibility for adulterous relationships is most evident in the representation of the 'third party'. Media reports about adultery have consistently emphasized the role played by the female 'third party' at the expense of analysis of the causes of marital breakdown. By contrast with the bias towards socio-economic factors in explaining men's involvement in extra-marital relationships, criticisms of the female 'third party's' infringement of the monogamous principle tend to focus on her sexual character. In the 1950s, the mistresses of adulterous men were not infrequently portrayed as scheming sexual trespassers, responsible for leading weak-willed and susceptible men astray and unmoved by the prospect of disrupting happy marriages, as the debate about Luo Baoyi and Liu Lequn revealed (Liu Lequn 1955).[9] The disruption of marriages through the intrusion of the 'third party' was 'invariably the fault of the woman', so one commentator thought, as if the male adulterer had only a minimal role to play (Li Ruolin 1956, 37–8). Along similar lines, a more recent report commented that although both parties involved in adulterous affairs share responsibility, many women and men assume that 'triangular relationships' are created by the intervention of a calculating woman (Mei Yu 1992, 22). A survey carried out in Shanghai in the mid-1980s indicated that young, unmarried women were more likely to become 'third parties' because 'young women lack social experience, have rich emotions, and do not have the kind of family restrictions that married women have' (*Jiefang ribao*, 8 June 1985).[10] 86.1 per cent of the respondents in another Shanghai survey conducted in 1986 felt that the intrusion of the 'third party' was immoral and should be legally punished (*Minzhu yu fazhi*, January 1986, 27–8). As a further suggestion put it, 'the third party, also known as the "foot that digs a hole in the wall" [*wa qiang jiao*, i.e., undermines], . . . harms other people's interests and constructs her own happiness on the basis of someone else's misery. This is why everyone looks on such a person as wicked and low-down good-for-nothing' (*quede shaocai mei chuxi de xiajianpi*) (*Funü zhi you (xia)* 1991, 44).

Almost exclusively identified as female, the 'third party' has, for decades, been constructed as the single most important – and dangerous – threat to marital and familial stability. As the female who transgresses the normative boundaries of sexual propriety, the 'third party' appears as an evil-doer, the creator of chaos and the cause of misery to all those who come into contact with her. She represents transgression of the incontrovertible boundary between the permissible and the forbidden. Such a woman's failure to conform to the attributes of dependence and responsiveness associated with monogamous marriage transforms her into the self-seeking and perverse agent of others' suffering. The dominant discourse has no option but to marginalize her outside the parameters defining the socially and morally acceptable woman. She therefore becomes a woman beyond redemption; she ceases to be a woman, according to the normative standards inscribed in female gender. A woman's loss of virginity before marriage may be explained away by representing her as a victim; but the active and autonomous expression of sexuality implicit in the figure of the adulteress is inconsistent with the feminine standards of passivity and responsiveness projected by the dominant discourse. Within the context of the present discussion, female agency thus denotes anything from potential threat to the established order to chaos. As Lynda Nead put it, in analysing representations of female sexuality in painting, while 'woman as victim could be accommodated within the code of respectability . . . woman as offender transgressed that code and was defined as sexually deviant' (Nead 1988, 56).

Recent representations of women in adulterous relationships are not mere repetitions of those of former years. The range of articles and letters published in the press about adultery reveal a significantly greater diversity of opinions than in the pre-reform period. The following is an appropriate example. In response to a young woman's anguished request for advice about what to do since she had fallen in love with a married man, an editorial comment in *Zhongguo funü* started with 'I can fully understand the pain and conflict you are going through . . . and I am sure that you are a good, self-respecting young woman' (Ling Ya 1985). The editor then went on to question the man's motives in embarking on a relationship with her: 'has he thought about the consequences of this relationship for you? Has he thought about how, in the context of today's moral outlook, such an improper relationship may put a girl in an unbearably humiliating position? If he really loves you, then he should control himself. Since he is unwilling to take on any responsibilities for you, my view is that he is selfish and self-seeking . . . And in any case do you really love him?' Extra-marital sexuality is no longer constructed as a unitary site of evil, necessarily associated with female deviance, and condemned beyond the boundaries defining acceptable sexual practice. Considerably more attention is now given to examining couples' experiences of marital conflict, such as incompatibilities in character and personality, sexual dissatisfaction or professional frustration. The tone of language used in relevant texts is simultaneously less didactic and more tolerant than before; no longer are editorial comments formulated simply to condemn the parties involved. However, greater lenience in tone should not be mistaken for a fundamental difference in approach. A persistent attachment to monogamous marriage as the only legitimate sexual relationship continues to shape dominant approaches to extra-marital affairs; standard reports continue to represent adultery as immoral and irresponsible conduct. Current approaches thus manifest a tension between a basically unchanged construction of sexual morality and marital harmony and recognition that changing circumstances and aspirations signify very real dilemmas for ordinary women and men.

Some recent discussions about extra-marital relationships signify a further departure from earlier representations in that they explicitly contest the assumption of female guilt. The above example indicates an uncustomary focus on the married man's responsibility in becoming involved with a woman. Another case, of a woman who after twelve years of marriage and two children fell in love with a younger man, met a not unsympathetic response when it was published in a magazine debate about the 'third party' (*Funü zhi you* (*xia*) 1991, 42–3). The woman in question had initially followed her mother's advice to marry a man she did not know, in order to avoid being sent down to the countryside during the Cultural Revolution. When years later she fell in love with another man, she was disowned by her family and shunned by neighbours and friends. Such a response, some contributors to the debate felt, was unreasonable given the woman's history. Moreover – though the focus may be on warning the women rather than reprimanding the men – numerous cases describe young women being cheated into affairs with married men. The sympathy and tolerance shown the female 'third party' in these examples may be uncommon, but they nevertheless question the conventional double standard of sexual morality according to which women are censured for activities for which men hold just as much responsibility. By extension, they also challenge the familiar representation of female conduct as the fulcrum of sexual morality, responsible for sustaining marital harmony by conforming to the sexual and gender attributes defined by the dominant discourse of sexuality.

## The unnatural woman

'As they reach the age of leaving home, girls inevitably start to think about marriage' (Tian He 1991, 9); 'marriage is the road that everyone must travel' (*hunyin shi rensheng bi jing zhi lu*) (Xiao Hua 1986). The naturalized representation of marriage as a relationship rooted in biological need coincides with the almost universal practice of marriage in contemporary China. Zeng Yi has estimated that in the late 1980s some 98 per cent of women were married between the ages of 25 and thirty (Zeng Yi 1991, 25). And Li Yinhe noted in her analysis of a survey of unmarried persons conducted in Beijing, 'without asking or knowing why, it is always assumed that as soon as they grow up men and women will marry, to the point that there is almost no alternative' (1991, 69). The near universality of marriage and reproduction is further assumed in explanations that treat the exceptions to the rule as unfortunate responses to unfortunate circumstances. 'In real life, some women devote themselves entirely to their work, and consciously choose to lead a single life, without a family. There are also some women who marry but who don't want children. In fact this is a choice that they are compelled to make. In renouncing family life and children, these women also reject sexual love and maternal love, which creates an enormous gap in their emotional life' (Li Xiaojiang 1986). The portrayal of marriage as a naturalized state logically marginalizes sexual identities and choices that do not conform to it. The absolute authority enjoyed by the model of monogamous marriage denies legitimacy to all sexual practices that challenge it. All sexualities – male and female, heterosexual and homosexual – that depart from the sexual, reproductive and social practices inscribed in the dominant model are thus logically forced into categories of abnormality or deviance, ranging from the improper or odd to the perverse.

Female celibacy and the 'third sex' featured prominently in debates about women's emancipation and family reform between the May Fourth period and the mid-1930s.[11] While mainstream media opinion tended to construct female celibacy as a violation of female nature, some commentators welcomed it as a progressive alternative for women oppressed by patriarchal demands of marriage and childbearing. However, after 1949, those aspects of the debate that had been sympathetic to women's objections to marriage were eclipsed by new claims that free choice of partner eliminated the need for further resistance to marriage. Henceforth, official rhetoric celebrated socialist monogamy as an emancipatory experience, severed from the exploitative structures and pressures of the feudal family. Combined with the construction of marriage as a fundamentally biological union, this meant that public discussion about alternatives to marriage was effectively silenced. Indeed, during the 1950s, the few references to 'staying single' or 'celibacy' (*dushenzhuyi*) that appeared in the press seemed to be made to reinforce the naturalized construction of marriage and procreation. Readers of the time were told in unequivocal terms that 'celibacy is wrong'; the new 'freedom of love', Wei Junyi explained, did not mean 'freedom to remain single' (Wei Junyi 1950).

Any idea that antipathy to marriage might be a positive step is effectively invalidated by the view that singleness is the result of failure to find an appropriate partner. In her Beijing survey, Li Yinhe found that the reason the majority were unmarried was failure to find an appropriate spouse and not lack of desire to marry (1991, 69–85). The following autobiographical description testifies to the same conclusion.

> We, older spinsters, have missed out on marriage and love, and live in loneliness and solitude, subject to disdain from all around. People around us don't treat us as ordinary people, with feelings and needs like everyone else. Whenever I am off work, or particularly happy, or put on some new clothes, there are always suggestive comments. If you are single, you can't even guarantee that your own needs and interests are protected. For example, allocation of housing is always based on the male. We still live eight women to a room in the work dormitory; some of the younger women workers get married in order to obtain proper housing. (Xiao Hua 1986)

The Beijing singles club, set up in 1991 by Wang Xingjuan, is specifically oriented to introducing potential marriage partners to each other, despite its low success rate – of the reported 90 per cent of members looking for partners, only seven couples married in two years (*Renmin ribao*, 13 April 1993). And while this same report noted that the club provides a congenial atmosphere in which women and men need not feel 'guilty' about being single, women who show little interest in pairing off with a potential partner may be discouraged from further attendance.[12]

Two main categories have dominated discussion about single persons in recent years. The first, characterized as the 'over-thirty-year-old

old maids' (*sanshi duo sui de lao guniang*), made particularly prominent headlines during the early to mid-1980s when, on account of demographic as well as social factors, large numbers of women of marriageable age found themselves unable to find a partner.[13] Mostly well educated and from an urban background, many women in this category had spent their youth engaged in political activities only to find themselves looking for a partner when it was too late, or having to put up with men of inferior education and status (Zhang Ping 1992, 105–7). A number of reasons are given for this. Men tend to marry women a few years younger than themselves, and the baby boom of the early 1950s created a surplus of women born between 1946 and 1955 over the numbers of slightly older men. Greater numbers of men of roughly the same age cohort stayed in the countryside at the end of the Cultural Revolution and married rural women. A third view is that the increasing tendency for rural men to look for urban wives exacerbates further the difficulties already faced by better-educated women (Si Wuliu 1992).

The focus on the 'old maids' has overshadowed attention to the other main category of single persons, whose situation is in many ways more serious. The numbers of unmarried men are far higher and represent a social problem of far greater dimensions. Invariably from poor rural districts, in social contexts where the gender imbalance in population distribution may be extremely high, and often with some physical or mental deformity, these men are possibly the least marriageable in contemporary China. The trade in women between regions and localities is in significant part sustained by the needs of this group of men, for whom the purchase of a bride may represent the only means of finding a wife and producing offspring. Given the social, material and legal difficulties confronted by this group, why has the public eye focused so prominently on the single women?

The gender differences inscribed in representations of single women and men give gender-specific meanings to singleness. Media discussion about single men and women is tinged with pity and sympathy for a category of people who find themselves single through no fault of their own. However, many accounts also suggest that single women are by no means simply unfortunate victims of circumstance (Xiao Hua 1986). Advice to older unmarried women to refrain from being too rigid and unyielding in selecting a partner implies what one writer called a 'pickiness' that seems not to be characteristic of men (Tang Liqin, quoted in Honig and Hershatter 1988, 107–8). The assumption that marriage is desirable at any cost, and that singleness can never be on account of positive choice (Si Wuliu 1992), transforms a woman's decision not to marry into the expression of some irregularity. Articles about educated and socially well-placed women who remain single frequently imply some mental or biological condition. They may even imply perverse sexual interests. Tang Liqin described her own experience in just such terms. 'They say that I am a "high-priced girl", that I am old, psychologically abnormal, physiologically incomplete, possessed of a shameful secret that cannot be told ...' (Honig and Hershatter 1988, 107–8). The figure of the single woman is also widely represented as a threat to marital and family stability. Married women fear that single women might steal their husbands; single women also find it difficult to find good female friends, because they represent too much of a threat to the norm (Yu Yan 1993).

Occasionally, articles put a more positive gloss on representations of the single woman. A 35-year-old woman who chose to remain single described her struggle to remain content and happy against the prevailing view that something must be wrong with her. Her message was that rejection of marriage did not necessarily bring with it a life of solitude and despair (Shang Zisong 1992). The editorial commentary accompanying another article offered explicit support to women who chose not to marry, and suggested that single women should be accorded the same treatment in housing allocation as married people. Indeed the author of this article maintained that, in view of the extent of the pressures and stigma they endured, single women deserved special treatment in such material matters (Xiao Hua 1986). Li Yinhe also argued that women who decide not to marry or not to have children should be accorded the same kinds of privileges, particularly in housing, as couples who sign the single-child pledge (Li Yinhe 1991, 85).[14] Moreover, the discrepancy between women's hopes for marriage and their actual experience of marital conflict may make staying single an attractive option for many, another commentator argued. At least staying single reduces the obligation on women to spend time 'doing things for other people' (Tian He 1991). Again, as Tang Liqin proposed,

there is no need to advocate being single. It should be like a religious belief – not promoted, but with freedom of belief [guaranteed]. If a person is willing to remain single, is it like graft or embezzlement, posing a potential social threat? And under present national policy of fewer and better births, how does it impair the national economy? Looked at from this angle what is reproachable about not marrying unless one finds an ideal mate, remaining single all one's life? I go so far as to feel quite at ease about doing so. Perhaps this will be seen as the reflection of psychological abnormality, but I hope I can gain social recognition and support. (Honig and Hershatter 1988, 107–8)

However, such views are not prominent in the press. Although newspaper articles may from time to time make comments to the effect that 'modern society no longer "forces" people into marriage . . . it is simply a question of different choices in life style (*shengcun fangshi*)' (*Renmin ribao*, 13 April 1993), the overriding bias in contemporary representations of single people in China indicates otherwise. The biologized construction of women as wives and mothers cancels out the possibility of constructing celibacy or childlessness as an acceptable option. While this argument applies as much to men as it does to women – marriage is, after all, as natural for men as it is for women – the very particular attributes associated with the single woman imply that she represents a distortion of 'normal' female sexuality. Described as a 'rootless cloud' (*wugen zhi yuncai*) (Yu Yan 1993), the woman who chooses to remain single necessarily challenges the naturalized construction of female sexuality in that she represents the wilful violation of female nature and of the gender attributes associated with it. In not conforming to the gender requirements of the marital relationship, the single woman questions the gender distribution of power – the entire gender hierarchy – inscribed in the relationships invoked by marriage and reproduction. At root, she questions the bases of patriarchal authority.

## Homosexuality

Official discourse between the 1950s and the 1970s was totally silent about homosexuality. The official journals of the women's and youth organizations contained no mention of homosexuality. Though subsequent publications have occasionally included references to, for example, the 'old style' male prostitute, homosexual practice in the early years of the People's Republic was assumed not to exist (Wan Ruixiong 1990, 107). Silence, however, did not signify the absence of opinion about homosexuality. The Communist Party's effective monopoly over the printed word gave the moralistic condemnation of homosexuality prevalent in China since the early years of this century the 'sanctified station of common sense and convention' (Hinsch 1990, 168). As more recent discussion has revealed, official silence masked a widespread view of homosexuality as a violation of the natural heterosexual order, a sexual perversion caused by sickness or psychological abnormality. In a context characterized by popular and official evasion of public discussion about homosexuality, homosexuals have become 'spectres' (*youling*) floating around in contemporary Chinese society (Wan Ruixiong 1990, 103).

Official recognition of the existence of homosexuality in recent years has been hesitant, to say the least. Government treatment of homosexuality as more than a simple matter for the police and labour camps to deal with has come about largely under pressure from the health authorities, and in response to the growing awareness of the need to implement preventive measures against the spread of sexually transmitted disease and AIDS.[15] Indeed, many, arguably most, recent media references to homosexuality in Chinese publications have occurred in contexts associated with AIDS and sex education. With few exceptions, homosexuality is identified as a perversion of nature. 'Homosexuality is an inverted and alienated kind of sexuality, it is abnormal and perverse . . . It goes against nature, inverts right and wrong, and invokes chaos whether in physiological, psychological, moral or social terms' (Wan Ruixiong 1990, 126–7). Public debate about homosexuality is still very circumscribed and popular opinion still condemns it as a sickness or a perversion. Many people surveyed reportedly have never heard of homosexuality; others think that it is either rare or nonexistent in contemporary China (Li Yinhe and Wang Xiaobo 1992; Hinsch 1990, 163). Some psychiatrists also argue that Chinese men are less prone to homosexual attraction than Westerners. The continuing absence of well-informed and sympathetic information about homosexuality sustains homosexuals' vulnerability to abuse of various forms. Chinese law makes no specific mention of homosexuality, but personal accounts of homosexuals testify to brutal treatment, including being beaten up by police in public places and being subjected to aversion therapy in jail. While a 1994 report suggested that there are many male homosexuals in China, they continue to be the frequent target of abuse and punishment (*CND*, 19 December 1994).[16]

The discrimination against homosexuals appears in clear relief when set against the homosexual tradition in China and the relative tolerance shown homosexuals at different moments of the country's dynastic history.[17] Literary sources from as early as the Zhou dynasty document famous homosexual relationships and practices among the social elite. Evidence for the middle imperial period – the Northern and Southern dynasties – also indicates that male homosexuality was widespread, even if not always socially acceptable. By the late Qing dynasty, however, rigid antipathy to homosexuality accelerated, banishing the former relative tolerance to total obscurity. In Hinsch's view, initially encouraged by stringent Neo-Confucian approaches to family relationships and responsibilities, the break with 'the homosexual tradition' resulted principally from the assimilation of Western concepts of biological science into China in the late nineteenth and early twentieth centuries. One effect of the reformist commitment to Western science and technology during this period was the adoption of new conceptions of sexual morality, including a moralistic condemnation of homosexuality as a form of sexual pathology (Hinsch 1990, 162–91). The CCP's subscription to a similar view was overdetermined by its status as the inheritor of this 'reformist' tradition, and by its ideological indebtedness to the rigid approaches to sexuality of Stalinist Russia.

The status of lesbians in China is no better. The literature on the marriage-resistance practices in southern China in the late nineteenth and early twentieth centuries suggests that some women were involved in lesbian relationships, though, according to Janice Stockard, lesbianism was not a major reason for the popularity of sworn spinsterhood (Stockard 1989, 40–1, 71n). However, the separation of lesbianism from the homosexual tradition and the lack of many references to it in traditional sources complicate attempts to assess its status in the imperial period (Hinsch 1990, 173–8). In the contemporary period, even less has been written about lesbianism than about male homosexuality. At least two accounts have testified to women's almost total reluctance to acknowledge their lesbianism, even when anonymity and protection of information was guaranteed. Both Li Yinhe and Fang Fu Ruan have recounted their difficulties in obtaining information about lesbians in contemporary China. In neither of the studies they conducted did lesbians make any response to the advertisements for assistance, either in the form of letters or stories or in contacts for interviews. Both Li and Ruan attributed this to the fact that lesbians were 'even more closeted than gay males' (Ruan 1991, 140). However, by contrast, Dai Wei wrote that 'there is not so much antipathy to lesbianism because it constitutes less of an open threat to public morals, and is therefore less offensive' (Dai Wei 1991, 437).

In recent years, a handful of Chinese researchers have begun to investigate various aspects of homosexuality, in significant part to expose the discrimination homosexuals suffer and to plead openly for greater tolerance. Gay clubs have been established in some of China's larger cities, at least one – Man's World, in Beijing – reportedly with governmental support. Wan Yanhai, a researcher at the National Health Education Institute in Beijing, set up an AIDS hotline in 1993, and has put considerable work into training counsellors to distribute information and advice to gays about AIDS prevention and safe sex (Wu Wen 1993, 41). Occasional articles and academic surveys appear demanding greater tolerance and respect for homosexuals in China. However, with very limited access to information, advice and support, few outlets for social activities, and living in constant fear of discovery, homosexuals are effectively denied a voice in public discourses about sexuality. At best, they are talked to, or talked about; the potential for misrepresentation and distortion of their experience as homosexuals – even in texts which are explicitly supportive of homosexuals' rights – is thus enormous. Personal informants well acquainted with the gay scene in Beijing have commented that, while they welcome the publication of Li Yinhe and Wang Xiaobo's *Tamen de shijie* (Their world) in 1992 – the first book published in the People's Republic of China which makes a case for equal rights for gays – it is far from describing the lived experiences and sufferings of gays in China. As its title suggests, it represents homosexuality as a 'phenomenon' distanced from dominant heterosexual culture and objectified for the purposes of study.[18] Other observations about homosexuality reveal a similar tension, between sympathetic demands for tolerance and recognition on the one hand, and a persistent attachment to the view of homosexuality as a deviant or diseased state on the other. Liberal scholars working on sex education and other sex-related issues continue to present homosexuality as a sickness, despite their demands for recognition of homosexuals' rights. A recent article published in *Minzhu yu fazhi* (Democracy and the legal system), for example, introduced homosexuals as 'deviants' (*pianli zhenghuanzhe*) at the same time as it demanded that lawyers, medical specialists and social scientists alike acknowledge the existence of homosexuality without discrimination (Wu Wen 1993). A review of Li Yinhe's work by one of China's most prominent feminist scholars categorized the sexual preferences of homosexuals as an 'addiction' (Tan Shen 1993, 34).

The condemnation of homosexuality as an 'extraordinary phenomenon [which] violates the laws of human physical and psychological development, and inevitably therefore is subject to the penalties of nature' (Li Wenhai and Liu Shuyu 1992, 204) is the predictable consequence of a naturalized view of heterosexuality and sexual difference. Sexualities that do not conform to the characteristics essentialized by the biological construction of sexuality cannot be explained in the terms legitimated by the dominant discourse; the only possible way of explaining them is by marginalizing them beyond the boundaries of the practices and attributes endorsed by the dominant discourse – by resorting to categories such as deviance and perversion. Naming homosexuality thus appears as another means deployed by the dominant discourse to reinforce its own authority.

One of the modes of constructing homosexuality as deviant behaviour is by feminizing the figure of the male homosexual through references to dress, make-up and bodily gestures. A rare reference to homosexuality during the 1950s and 1960s described how a notorious 'old style' (*lao zige*) male prostitute in the Hankou region used to walk along the street with feminine gestures, 'as if he were bringing the role of Huadan into daily life' (Wan Ruixiong 1990, 107).[19] Another reference noted that male homosexuals are always easily identifiable because of their appearance (Wan Ruixiong 1990, 104). Li Yinhe also commented on the common assumption that homosexuals are effeminate, and therefore easily distinguished from 'real' men. The idea that homosexuality is in some sense a result of transgressing gender boundaries is also explicit: 'homosexuality is an inversion of nature because it is associated with confusing gender boundaries in a child's upbringing, between the "strong masculine spirit" (*yanggang zhi qi*) of the male and the "soft, feminine beauty" of the female' (Wan Ruixiong 1990, 132). It is clearly linked with an abnormal identification of the gender attributes and (hierarchical) relationships implicated in the essentialist construction of heterosexuality. Henrietta Moore has argued that the inscription of gender difference within masculinities and femininities invariably denotes hierarchies of power (Moore 1994, 56). Using this analysis, the feminization of the homosexual is an obvious mode of denying the male homosexual full value as a man. It serves to identify the perverse nature and the dubious gender status of the homosexual, reinforcing his status as 'something-less-than-a-man'.

A common association between homosexuality and crime is another means of reinforcing the deviant status of homosexuals. 'Homosexuality is a behavioural and pyschological abnormality' which may 'lead to theft, prostitution and murder' (*Renmin jingcha* (People's police) 1989, 11–12). 'In common with most countries in the world, China treats homosexuality as criminal behaviour. It offends public morals, and should therefore be subject to legal investigation' (Dai Wei 1991, 464). This approach was specified in 1987 when in Shanghai it was stipulated that 'homosexuality constitutes a crime because it offends public morals and harms the physical and psychological health of minors. . . . Prevention is the best approach to adopt, otherwise, if it becomes established, it will be difficult to control' (Dai Wei 1991, 464–5). In this light, homosexuality appears as a malignant growth which, uncontrolled, will attack the bodies and minds of a healthy, law-abiding generation of youth.

The physical isolation of homosexuals from healthy social circulation, represents attempts to preserve the pure public from contamination. In so far as AIDS is represented as an effect of the 'open-door' policy, homosexuality is constructed as a phenomenon associated with China's modernization. Through its links with AIDS, homosexuality serves as a reminder of the dangers of intimate contacts with the foreigner as well as of the fate awaiting the morally degenerate. Whether represented as physically diseased, mentally sick or sexually perverted, the homosexual – like the prostitute – becomes a polluting agent, a major channel through which the evil and corrupt outsider seeks to penetrate Chinese society. Homosexuality symbolizes the negative potentialities of 'progress' as well as the malicious influence of the foreign other.

The condemnation of homosexuality beyond the boundaries defining acceptable sexual behaviour constitutes a physical and discursive violence against homosexuals. Despite Li Yinhe's argument that homosexuality is not treated with the same severity as other instances of 'improper' pre- or extra-marital sexuality, because of its dissociation from reproduction (1992, 155), personal testimonies of homosexuals tell of extreme vulnerability to social abuse and discrimination as well as formal penalization. The fact that there are no laws about homosexuality is no impediment to the use of the police and legal apparatus to punish those considered guilty of offending public morals. Gays in China conduct their lives in fear of legal prosecution and social persecution, frustration and often self-recrimination, unable to 'come out' even with closest friends. Most find themselves in unsatisfactory marriages sooner or later, not only for appearances, but also because, according to Li Yinhe, many themselves identify their own sexuality as abnormal, unnatural and 'inappropriate as the basis for mature adult life' (Li Yinhe and Wang Xiaobo 1992, 99). The contrasts between the dangerous and demonic qualities attributed to homosexuality by public discourses and the social and psychological conditions characterizing most homosexuals' existence could hardly be greater. The violation of gay and lesbian rights in China through the denial of social and discursive spaces permitting the expression of homosexual identities thus penetrates even the subject positions with which homosexuals themselves identify.

The increase in information about and for homosexuals in recent years in China is without doubt the consequence – in part at least – of a more tolerant editorial climate. That materials demanding recognition of gays' rights – few though they are – are now publicly available is in itself evidence of this. However, the concurrence between the official references to homosexuality and the often alarmist publicity about AIDS and sexually transmitted diseases suggests other factors at work. The government's interests in preventing the spread of practices deemed responsible for the moral and physical degeneration of the population are explicit. They are implicit in the persistent attachment to biological essentialism that underwrites the absolutist status of heterosexuality in official and popular discourses. Public recognition of the existence of homosexuality does not signify its affirmation as a legitimate and ordinary form of sexual identity, but the inevitability of naming something in the attempt to control it.

In many ways, representations of 'abnormal' sexualities in China since 1949 have changed very little. Potential challenges to the hegemony of the dominant discourse of monogamous sexuality are consistently marginalized as deviant, abnormal or sick. While the terms used since the mid-1980s to discuss 'peripheral' sexualities are less rigid and uniform than in the earlier discourse, the construction of 'the other' as a source of danger, disease and chaos has not fundamentally been disturbed. The motivation for what is prevalently represented as deviation from the moral and sexual norm is trivialized by pejorative references to the depraved individualism of Western capitalism. No matter what the circumstances, all subject positions and choices that contest the dominant model of sexual relations are treated with suspicion, and any potential value they might have is dismissed by mere invocation of the term 'bourgeois behaviour'. The dominant discourse cannot accommodate 'deviant' or 'abnormal behaviour', or any actions that cannot be interpreted according to the terms it legitimizes. It can therefore continue to criminalize 'deviant' behaviour, as is evidenced by the continuing representation of adultery and homosexuality as illegal acts. Moreover, the persistent interest in categorizing modes of sexual behaviour as 'right' or 'wrong', or as 'legal' and 'illegal', means that, with few exceptions, the very real tensions and conflicts experienced by ordinary women and men in their sexual and marital relationships are largely ignored. The priority the dominant discourse gives to maintaining monogamous marriage as the site and pivot of all sexual activity and experience is overriding. This leaves no discursive space for women – or men – to choose difference, whether this means simply not marrying, having a lover outside marriage, or rejecting heterosexuality. In fact, it leaves no alternatives for representations of a woman's sexual fulfilment except in the subject positions identified by the status of wife and mother. The possibility that women may prefer to live separate lives, removed from the dominance of the male drive, cannot be contained within a discourse which naturalizes monogamous marriage as the only legitimate form of adult existence.

The materials analysed in this chapter represent women as victims or villains, indicating a similar duality to women's 'nature' as that inscribed in the 'virgin-whore' metaphor. Women are empowered to activate and restrain men's powerful sexual urges, and are charged with guaranteeing standards of sexual morality by regulating their own. The attribution of misery and suffering to women who deviate from normative sexual morality has consistently offered a means of reinforcing the desirability of respectable sexual behaviour. Associating harm with women's sexual transgressions, with the feminization of male conduct, or with celibates' transgressions functions as a kind of sanction against unacceptable practices. The more radical the departure from the normative standards of marriage, the more dire the consequences. Again in Lynda Nead's words, 'the sharpening of the demarcations between the married and the unmarried worked to produce a norm of respectable sexual behaviour and to define extra-marital sex as illicit and deviant' (Nead 1988, 49).

The state's concerns in discussing specific aspects of extra-marital sexuality have been qualified by emphases and tendencies that explained sexual transgressions in women and men in gender-specific ways. All sexual activities not bound by the parameters of legally recognized marriage have consistently been represented as immoral and harmful, in social, psychological and sometimes physical terms. Displays of female sexuality outside the proper boundaries of marriage are represented as the source of disorder and danger. In this light, autonomous female sexuality, mediated neither by patriarchal control associated with marriage nor by the demands of reproduction, constitutes a threat to the model of sexual and marital harmony upheld by the dominant discourse. Uncontrolled, female sexuality is replete with hidden and potentially dangerous powers. Men's sexual misdemeanours, by contrast, are explained not as a consequence of uncontrolled sexuality, except in the case of rape, but as the result of changing socio-economic status, professional circumstance or political power. In this reworking of the male/public–female/private dichotomy, the meanings invested in female sexuality serve to underwrite the normative standards of the dominant discourse of sexuality in ways that cannot be applied to male sexuality. Identifying women's sexual transgressions by reference to categories such as victim or deviant 'third party' aims to contain the extent of sexual deviancy by associating it with pain and evil. It also offers a convenient technique for explaining women's deviation from the norms of marital procreative sex.

The attribution of responsibility to women for patrolling standards of sexual behaviour before marriage has been a constant theme in representations of sexuality since 1949. During marriage, this responsibility grows, commensurate with women's powers to disrupt the conjugal unit. Just as women emerge as the agents of sexual morality and familial harmony, so violating this role by becoming the adulteress or remaining single may destroy the structure on which that harmony rests.[20] It is precisely because women are attributed with the responsibility for regulating the sexual order through regulating their own behaviour that they are empowered to threaten the values of the discourse.[21] Attributing suffering to women's pre- and extra-marital sexual activity therefore has a further purpose. It can minimize the potential threat to the discourse's standards imposed by empowering women as the mediators of sexual morality.

Concerns about the loss of virginity may be interpreted in the same light; the premium the dominant discourse continues to attach to female purity may be associated with the aim of protecting the patriarchal order from contaminating influences. As Mary Douglas has argued, a concern to protect the body – in this case the female body – from sexual contact in all but highly regulated contexts may represent preoccupation with the vulnerability of the social unit (Douglas 1989, 115). By extension, practices and discourses to protect women from sexual contact may express cultural perceptions of the boundaries of familial and social identity. Female chastity thus becomes associated with protecting the group from contaminating influences.[22]

Such ideas are echoed in contemporary representations of female sexuality not so much with specific reference to requirements of female virginity and chastity but to the expectations of women's sexual behaviour, constructed as the axis of appropriate and inappropriate conduct. Female sexuality defines both the general standards of sexual morality demanded of the group and the sexual conduct and attitudes excluded by the discourse. Controlled, it represents social and moral order, while unfettered and autonomous it represents danger, disruption and chaos. The contrasts between the different modes of female sexuality – between the extremes of pollution and purity – define the boundaries of acceptable sexual behaviour in general. Whether by confirmation or negation, the dominant discourse of sexuality constructs female sexuality as the principal agent of sexual order.

Representations of homosexuality confirm the destabilizing potential attributed to female sexuality. The greatest danger of homosexuality lies in its power to contaminate through its association with disease and degeneration. Arguably, however, the representation of homosexuality as an abnormal feminization of male sexuality signifies a distance from the categories associated with normative masculinity. In drawing attention to the feminine attributes of the male homosexual, the dominant discourse subsumes homosexuality under the broad category of the female. The use of feminine constructs to describe homosexual behaviour implies a link between the gender specificity of homosexuality and its endangering properties. It suggests another mode of reinforcing the representation of the female as a potential threat to established sexual and moral order.

# 9 Conclusions

The production of an official discourse of sex after the establishment of the People's Republic in 1949 identified sexuality as a site of political control. It signified the formulation of new techniques to supervise the healthy socialist development of China's youth, and to bring individual sexual behaviour into line with the principles upheld by the party ideologues and their advisors. This project of regulation, however, was more than the control of already predetermined sexual entities. Explanations of biological structures and the inscription of definitions of 'correct' and 'incorrect' conduct in them constructed particular kinds of sexual and gendered subjects; the discourse created its own audience as particularly gendered persons. Through its institutionalized power to monopolize all public references to sexual matters, the official discourse established the only terms that ordinary women and men could use in their public positioning of themselves.

The extent of the changes in Chinese society over the past fifteen years makes it impossible to explain the discursive similarities between the pre- and post-Cultural Revolution periods by simple reference to the continuing interests of party-state authority in controlling young people's lives. The entire context of the discussion about sexuality has changed. The 'explosion' of sexually explicit material since the early 1980s and the transformation of sexual practices among urban young people denote the emergence of what could be called a new sexual culture in China's towns and cities. The 1950s discourse aimed to establish standards of health and behaviour to ensure sustained participation in the economic and social development of the new state;

since the 1980s, public discourse has sought to control crime, the abuse of women and children, the spread of sexually transmitted disease and, of course, population growth. In contrast with the 1950s, official agencies no longer act alone in generating and controlling this dominant discourse. The availability of popular materials alongside those published by official agencies gives to the discourse a status and a readership that it did not enjoy in earlier years. As a result, the representational terrain is much greater than before, generated through an unprecedented range of forms, from the commercialized images of the eroticized female body to those of the responsive, supportive and self-sacrificing wife. The interests of medical experts and state officials, as well as commercial agencies keen to respond to consumer demand, come together in transmitting such images.

The regulation of sexuality provides a powerful means of ordering marital, household and familial, and social relationships. A 'techno-logy of sex', to use Foucault's formulation, created through a variety of medical, pedagogical, social and political discourses, constructs sex as 'a matter that require[s] the social body as a whole, and virtually all of its individuals, to place themselves under surveillance' in the interests of marital, family and social welfare (Foucault 1984, 118). The state's continuing identification of sexuality as a site of intervention sustains the possibilities for shaping sexual and gender relationships to suit the interests of central policy. Ordered and stable household relationships, premised on the conjugal couple and responsive to state interests, are as essential to the success of current policies as they were to the success of economic transformation in the 1950s. The shift in central policy orientations to the problems of migration and fertility control, social welfare, sexual violence and sexually transmitted disease has not modified the importance of the conceptual link between household/family stability and social order. Despite the apparent withdrawal of the state from issues of 'private' concern, and evidence that the state has neither the capacity nor the interest to intervene directly in the management of daily life, its intervention in women's sexuality, under its policy of population control, is at a scale unprecedented in history.[1]

The exclusion from public discourses of references to sexuality during the Cultural Revolution highlights both the contrasts and the continuities between the pre- and post-Cultural Revolution periods. The modes of representational practices were particularly different. The discursive closures of the earlier discourse, identified through the prevalent use of oppositional categories of 'right' and 'wrong', 'correct' and 'incorrect', 'socialist' and 'bourgeois', served to reinforce clear ideological and moral principles associated with the collectivist orientation of the times, as well as to ascribe fixed gender attributes to biologically defined sexual differences. The images and texts they deployed belonged to a discursive strategy – formulated consciously and unconsciously – which operated through associating boundaries with danger and chaos. Areas of knowledge which eluded explanation within the terms of the discourse were simply excluded from it. Hence, silence reigned over homosexuality. The creation of what Jeffrey Weeks called a 'single uniform sexuality' could not absorb contesting sexualities which subverted its terms (Weeks 1981, 10). The generation of discourses of different registers in recent years has diluted such uniformity. The neat ideological categories of the former period have given way to shifting meanings and significations, derived from the commercial reorientations of the reform programme as much as from the ideological revisions of the party. Contestation of dominant positions thus no longer appears simply as a means to reinforce the values and practices of the dominant discourse.

However, this analysis has shown that the overlaps and intersections between the different discourses foreground a number of fundamental assumptions about the sexual and gender ordering of society. The construction of sexuality as a combination of natural drives and responses has not been substantially challenged, though many of the terms used to describe it have changed. The dominant categorization of 'science' as the privileged agent responsible for the definition of biological truth, and often popularly equated with notions of rationality and modernization, has not been disturbed. The scientific views of the experts continue to be located within an episteme that does not question the scientificity of gendered categories of strength and drive, weakness and passivity. What is presented as 'scientific fact' conveys moral and social as much as medical and biological concerns, naturalizing women's responsibilities to their reproductive, nurturing and responsive role.

This study has argued that, through its representations of the gender characteristics associated with the female, the official and dominant discourses of sexuality have constructed women as the main agents responsible for patrolling general standards of sexual morality and family order. Conforming to the biologically based principles of appropriate gender conduct, the 'ideal' woman is fixed in the private sphere of responsive wifely concerns and maternal cares. Her expression of sexual desire is a conjugal responsibility, necessarily contained by the marital relationship. Outside this context, her sexuality becomes a source of potential danger, contamination and chaos.

The full significance of this gender focus becomes apparent only when looked at in conjunction with the denial of female autonomy and the marginalization of women whose sexual behaviour does not conform to the discursive standards. The representation of female sexuality as a naturally responsive complement of the powerful male drive, invariably oriented to the needs of procreation, ignores the female subject as an autonomous site of pleasure. Women's sexual regulation before marriage is associated not principally with women's own interests but with the need to protect her virtue and energy for the inevitable advent of marriage and childbirth. Requirements of pre-marital propriety are conveyed through suggestions that the major responsibility for exercising self-restraint lies with women. During marriage, women's sexual responsiveness, conjugal service and self-sacrifice are demanded in the name of marital satisfaction and familial harmony. The selfless wife, endlessly sensitive to her husband's sexual and domestic needs, is the protectress of moral and bodily boundaries from disruption and chaos. Alongside requirements of sexual restraint after and outside marriage, in particular to suppress her potential to become the iniquitous 'third party', the representation of women's sexuality is inseparable from assumptions of dependency and self-denial.

At a time of widespread abuse of women's basic rights to existence, sexual violence against women, and the sale of women into marriage and prostitution, the idea of sexuality as a site for the generation of gender hierarchy is gaining some currency. As aspirations in love and marriage change, many women no longer accept the representation of sexuality as a harmonious balance of complementary functions and characteristics. In looking at female sexuality from new perspectives in which conflict is prominent, women are contesting the privileged authority the dominant discourse enjoys to define differences between legitimate and illegitimate, normal and abnormal modes of sexual and gender conduct. Recent calls to recognize the category of rape within marriage challenge the idea that women are biologically constructed to respond to the dominant male (Sun Shaoxian 1991, 25). Women's rejection of the view that their sexuality is passive, slow and responsive opens up the discursive space for ideas about women's sexual auton-omy and subjectivity. Those who condemn discrimination against the 'third party' or the 'old maid' subvert the idea of 'woman' as complete only when associated with the strong male in marriage.

Such challenges to the dominant view are not easy to find either in the media or in other social discourses; the voices articulating them are far from taking centre stage. Despite the abundance and diversity of sexual representations publicized since the early 1980s, neither pop-ular nor official texts have seriously begun to treat sexuality as a gender issue affecting power relations between women and men. The view that nature subjects women to lives dominated either by male or reproductive concerns continues to permeate official and unofficial approaches to women in diverse contexts, from education and employment to childbirth. Whether transmitted by medical experts trained to interpret science or by popular advice-givers committed to gender and sexual harmony, the dominant public approaches to sexuality still propagate women's subordination as a natural condition of their existence.

The overlap between the 1950s discourse and recent representations does not simply signify the rehearsal of the same themes by different agents. The 1950s discourse emphasized the public or social importance of women's sexual and gender concerns; the market orientation of social and economic reform in recent years has contributed to the 'reprivatization' of such concerns. The ideological parameters of the earlier period meant that the naturalized gender hierarchy of the sexual discourse could coexist – albeit uneasily – with messages of empowerment to women. In the later period, the association between, on the one hand, a naturalized view of gender hierarchy and, on the other, the representation of woman as a sexualized object in the privatized world of male fantasy and desire has eclipsed these empowering messages. While the diminished authority of state agencies has permitted challenges to the dominant discourse in spaces not directly controlled by the state, the rejection of the collectivist view has simultaneously reinforced the image of the dependent woman responsible to her husband through her sexual and reproductive functions.

If under collectivist ideology, as Li Xiaojiang argues, the rhetoric of male–female equality prevented women from asserting themselves, then under the reprivatization of love and sexuality the continuing attachment to socio-biological constructions effectively legitimizes women's lack of autonomy. Women have started 'a life of self-mastery' (Li Xiaojiang 1986) through the spaces – limited though they are – now available to them. But until individual voices are joined by the official architects of policy on women as well as the editorial boards of popular magazines in seriously challenging this dominant discourse, the assumption that women's gender subordination is biologically determined will continue to shape views and policies about women in a variety of contexts. The belief in an originating gender hierarchy fixed by nature will continue to hamper identification of women's autonomous needs and requirements. Without substantial challenges to these views, they will also continue to limit the possibilities women can explore to reposition themselves as sexual and gendered persons.

# *Notes*

## Chapter 1 Discourses of Sexuality Since 1949

1 For a lucid analysis of the discursive links between sexuality and modernity, and the ways in which human sexuality came to symbolize progress, see Dikötter 1995.

2 This discussion about pre-twentieth-century marriage and family structures is necessarily limited, and oversimplifies many important issues. Recent scholarship has begun to reveal significant variations in marriage practices, including matters concerning women's inheritance and the mechanisms of women's challenges to patriarchal controls of marriage. For further discussion, see Watson and Ebrey 1991 and Ko 1994.

3 A classic of the Chinese Communist Party's cultural canon, *The White-Haired Girl* was first performed in the CCP-controlled liberated area of Yan'an after 1939. It told the story of a young peasant girl who was forced to become a slave in the local landlord's house because her father was unable to pay his rent. Raped and abused by her new master, she fled to the hills, where she gave birth to a baby and her hair turned white. She was eventually found by the communist guerrillas and returned home with them to liberate her village and punish her assailant. For an account of the impact of the play on its audience in Yan'an, see Belden 1973, 282–4. Meng Yue discusses the play as an example of the CCP's erasure of the theme of sexuality and its transformation into that of class (1993, 118–36).

4 Friends of the Red Guard generation have told me that, though there was not a great quantity of such works, they circulated at high speed among enormous numbers of people, with groups of young people gathering round to listen as someone read out loud in dormitories at night. An article in *Qingchun chao* (Tide of youth) provides an introduction to some of the

better-known examples current between the late sixties and early seventies (A Xiangzhai, *Qingchun chao* 4, 1993, 29).

5 I thank Professor Pan Suiming (People's University) for this information. In a stimulating discussion about the erasure of public sexual discourses during the Cultural Revolution, Professor Pan noted that sexual abuse and rape of women was widespread during the peak years of Red Guard activity, and that a classified document about the need to control sexual violence against women was issued at the highest levels of the party. Neither he nor other scholars I have asked have been able to trace this document.

6 Thanks to an anonymous referee of my article 'Defining Difference' (1994–5) for this formulation.

7 The *'wan, xi, shao'* policy was implemented between 1971 and 1979, when it was taken over by the more stringent 'single-child policy'. 'Late' referred to encouraging women and men to marry at the appropriate rather than the legal age of marriage, namely mid-twenties for women and late twenties for men; 'more spaced' referred to long birth intervals of three to four years between children; 'fewer' meant no more than two children per couple in the cities and three in the rural areas. See Zeng Yi 1991, 5–6.

8 These comments come from personal interviews conducted in spring 1993 with graduates of psychology from a university in Beijing and with a psychology lecturer in Shanghai.

9 For a preliminary example of how relatively liberal values have been applied to an unchanged definition of sexual difference, see Li Xingchun and Wang Liru 1991, 103–12, and Yan Ruizhen and Li Peifang 1989.

10 Wang Wenbin, Zhao Zhiyi and Tan Mingxin 1956. A new edition of this was written in 1980 by Tan Mingxin, the sole surviving author; by August 1980 there had been four reprints totalling 2.3 million copies.

11 You Tong, 'Duiyu dangqian lihun wenti de fenxi he yijian' (Analysis and ideas about current divorce problems), was first published in the *People's Daily (Renmin ribao)*, 13 April 1957. It was continued in *ZGFN* 8, 1957, 16–17, and published again by the Falü chubanshe, 1958, 1–10.

12 I wish to thank Jiang Hong, a former graduate student of the City University, London, for helping me clarify some of these ideas in a discussion about the mechanisms and procedures of censorship in China since the late 1980s.

13 As Liu Binyan pointed out in a recent article, press freedom depends on the political climate rather than on formal controls. See Liu Binyan 1992, 15.

14 The most recent and largest of these is Liu Dalin's *Sexual Behaviour in Modern China*, 1992, based on a nationwide survey conducted over a period of two years.

15 These brief comments about readers' tastes are based on discussions I have held over the years with Chinese women and men of different ages: university undergraduates, scholars and researchers in women's studies, writers and journalists, and other professionals. As far as I know, there is no publicly available analysis of readers and readership patterns of these kinds of journals.

16 This observation comes from my visit to the hotline in Beijing in April 1993, when I was able to listen to some of the conversations between the hotline's volunteers and young women calling to seek advice about sexual matters.

17 Other references warned against the deceptive nature of beautiful women. A poem by Lan Li (1958), for example, entitled 'Jiao guniang' (Lovely girl), described the evil thoughts of a pretty girl.

18 Contributors to the debate about women, the family and sexuality, such as Havelock Ellis, Ellen Key, Morgan, Frazer and Malinowski, were all known during the May Fourth period, but in the absence of further research it is impossible to assess the extent to which the early CCP leaders responsible for woman-work were familiar with their views. See Lang 1968, 113–14.

19 Personal communication. This informant further noted that the free-choice principle was welcomed by young people in his village, amongst whom he counted himself, as a sign of liberation from parental control rather than as an indication of the importance of love and compatibility.

20 Some criticisms of the term seem as much for tactical reasons as for any other, to identify easily the fact of the differences between the Chinese women's movements and the Western. However, in a conference in Beijing on Chinese Women and Feminist Thought hosted by the Chinese Academy of Social Sciences in June 1995, many of the Chinese women participants indicated a series of negative associations with the term 'feminism', in particular the idea that it was an expression of the individualistic tendencies of Western ideologies and of attempts to assert power over men.

21 Some of the most prominent examples of writers engaged with such issues are Dai Houying, Wang Anyi, Can Xue, Zhang Jie and Zhang Xinxin. In social science and historical research, Li Xiaojiang's repeated insistence on the right and need of women to represent themselves continues to have immense influence in social sciences and historical research. Tani Barlow discusses this process through identifying the different ways in which the terms for 'woman' – 'funü', 'nüxing', 'nüren' – have positioned women as political subjects (1994, 339–59).

22 In an interview in April 1993, Tao Chunfang of the Beijing Women's Federation commented along the same lines that discrimination against women in employment is, fundamentally, caused by economic scarcity rather than notions of gender hierarchy. The tenacity of this view testifies to the continuing influence of Marxist theories concerning the origins of socio-economic exploitation.

## Chapter 2 The Scientific Construction of Sexual Difference

1 The Law of the People's Republic of China for the Protection of Minors was passed in September 1991 and came into effect in January 1992. For more discussion, see Palmer 1995, 115–18, 129–31.

2 Personal communication from Dr Geng Wenxiu, of the Psychology Department, Huadong University, Shanghai.

3 Medical opinion in the 1950s argued that, since the reproductive organs were not fully developed, children did not experience sexual desire (Wang Shancheng 1956).

4 For further discussions about the research methods and processes, and the bureaucratic obstacles Liu Dalin had to overcome in order to complete his survey, see the special report 'Dalu shouci "xing wenming" diaocha' 1991.

5 Personal communication from a former student of psychology at Beijing's People's University.

6 Many parts of this section are based on my article 'Defining Difference': Evans 1994–5.

7 See article 5 b) and c) of the 1950 Marriage Law of the People's Republic of China. The reference to impotence as a reason against marriage was eliminated from the 1980 Marriage Law. We can see similar eugenic concerns in recent birth-control policy, for example, with the discouragement of individuals with hereditary diseases from procreating to ensure the birth of non-defective babies. See Banister 1987, 222–6. For a discussion about the recent draft law on eugenics and health protection (before it came into effect in June 1995 under the revised title Maternal and Infantile Health Care Law), see Croll 1993–4.

8 It is significant that only when the government began to introduce a birth-control policy after 1955 was publicity given to the notion of an 'appropriate' as opposed to a 'legal' age of marriage.

9 In the West, this view was modified in the 1960s as a result of medical observations of the absence of ill effects of sexual intercourse during pregnancy and menstruation. 'Most instructors of obstetrics now teach that intercourse is permissible . . . during the entire pregnancy period until labor begins . . .' (Romney et al. 1981, 867–8). For a brief survey of the taboos on sexual intercourse during menstruation and pregnancy in the twentieth century, see Rusbridger 1986, 128–33. Chinese experts still recommend abstention from sexual intercourse during menstruation and during the first and last three months of pregnancy, and for six to seven weeks after parturition. For example, see Wang Peng 1993, 119–20. See also below, Chapter 5.

10 Sexual segregation was one of the greatest barriers to successful implementation of the free-choice principle of marriage after 1950. The popular notion that freedom of marriage was little more than an invitation to female promiscuity prevented young people from engaging in ordinary social contact. See, for example, Hu Yaobang 1953.

11 For a discussion of the scientific constructions of sex during the Republican period, see Dikötter 1995. The most influential of the Western writers about sexual matters during the Republican period was Havelock Ellis, whose view of sexuality as a harmonious balance between male and female rooted in natural causes coincided neatly with traditional Chinese approaches. For discussion of Ellis's views, see Weeks 1981, 147–53; and Jackson 1987.

12 Van Gulik described one of the aims of sexual intercourse, as understood during the later Zhou period (770–220 BC), in similar terms: 'the sexual act was to strengthen the man's vitality by making him absorb the woman's

*yin* essence, while at the same time the woman would derive physical benefit from the stirring of her latent *yin* nature' (Van Gulik 1974, 46).

13 The asymmetry in representations of male and female desire was also apparent in the subtitles of various works. An obvious example was the absence of reference to 'Xing de xingfen' (Sexual excitement), a subsection of the part entitled 'Nanxing xingxian de shengli' (The physiology of the male sex glands), in the equivalent section on female sexuality in Wang, Zhao and Tan 1956, 12–14.

14 A gloss on the term *xingyu wangsheng* (excess of sexual desire) defined it as the 'excessive frequency, speed and intensity of sexual excitement' (Wang Peng 1993, 85). Another use of the same term to refer to the intense character of male sexual desire did not carry the same pejorative implications, implying definite gender differences in characterization of sexual desire. See *Xinhun weisheng bi du* editorial group 1984, 28–9.

15 See, for example, discussion about how to make a couple's sex life harmonious in Gao Fang and Zeng Rong 1991, 35–7. See also the characterization of the male as 'strong and powerful' and the female as 'relatively weak' in Li Xingchun and Wang Liru 1991, 109.

16 In this essay, Jackson argued that the basically biological explanations of the male drive were used by Havelock Ellis and other sexologists to legitimize fundamentally discriminatory gender relations.

17 Theodore H. Van de Velde, *Ideal Marriage*, 1930, quoted in Grossman 1984, 195. Van de Velde's (1873–1937) works, which were extremely influential in Europe, stressed the contribution of sex to establishing a good marital relationship.

18 Between the May Fourth period and the 1930s, the issue of female celibacy was widely debated on the one hand as an example of women's resistance to the Confucian system of marriage, and on the other as an unacceptable inversion of women's sexual nature. For more details, see Clarke 1988.

19 For a historical survey of homosexuality in China, see Xiao Mingxiong 1984 and also Hinsch 1990.

## Chapter 3 Advice to Adolescents

1 Between the 1950s and the late 1970s, the mixed social life of young people in the rural areas was considerably circumscribed by customary rules of sexual segregation, which effectively sustained the older generation's control over marriage procedures (Croll 1981, 32–9). Margery Wolf also described 'modern' practices of sexual segregation in *Revolution Postponed* (1985, 164–6).

2 Rural surveys carried out in China between the 1930s and the 1940s showed conflicting views about the age of marriage. In his surveys in north China in the early 1930s, James Lossing Buck found that 81% of women were less than twenty when they first married (1937, 381). By contrast, Martin Yang's study of Taitou between the 1930s and the 1940s concluded that the average age of marriage for women was twenty (1948, 113). Zeng

Yi's findings suggest that, in 1949, women's average age at first marriage was just over eighteen and a half (1991, 27).

3 Between the early 1960s and 1988 the average age of female puberty had dropped one year, to 13.4; by the time of Liu Dalin's survey of 1989–90, it had dropped further, to 13.04 (Liu Dalin 1992, 36).

4 For more discussion about how these 'menstrual monitors' are organized, see Whyte and Parish 1984, 161.

5 Emily Martin points out that English-language scientific texts continue to represent menstruation as a pathology, with the repeated use of terms like 'degenerate', 'decline', 'lack', 'weakened', 'loss' and so on. However, she sees 'no reason why menstrual blood itself could not be seen as the desired "product" of the female cycle' (1989, 52–3), particularly in social and demographic contexts where women spend most of their time not intending to have children (pp. 46–53, 110–12). For an earlier discussion about Western feminist attempts to celebrate menstruation, see Sayers 1982, 115–20.

6 The view that young women should rest during menstruation in order to conserve their energies for the strengthening of their reproductive capacity was also current in the Western medical paradigm that informed the Republican discourses of sexuality. See Ehrenreich and English 1979, 99–104.

7 Jeffrey Weeks noted how, in Britain in the 1930s, circumcision was similarly thought to be a remedy for masturbation, which would promote 'greater capacity for labour, a longer life, less nervousness . . .' (1981, 51).

8 A large clitoris was commonly thought of as a manifestation of perverse masculine tendencies in a woman, presumably owing to the representation of the clitoris as a female penis (Dikötter 1995, 75–6).

9 For a new analysis of the hermaphrodite in China, see Frank Dikötter, 'Monstrous Conception: Medical Knowledge, Foetal Health and the Regulation of Reproduction in China 1550–1995' (forthcoming).

10 A 1995 Amnesty International report on Women in China announced that, according to the official legal press, more than 33,000 women were 'abducted and sold' between mid-1993, when a major crackdown against trafficking in women and children was launched, and early 1995 (AI 1995, 3). Official Chinese statistics estimate that the national rate of female illiteracy dropped from 45.23% in 1982 to 31.9% in 1990. However, they also reveal that the rate of illiteracy in 1982 among girls of fifteen in the rural areas was ten times as high as the male rate; that between 1982 and 1990 female illiteracy as a percentage of the total rose from 69.2% to 73.49%, and that in the same period the differential between urban and rural rates of illiteracy among girls increased considerably while among boys it remained stable. Figures for attendance at primary school and lower middle school in Yunnan Province for 1987 show that there is a consistently higher rate of non-attendance among girls, reaching 22.3% for the eight-year-old cohort and 31.4% for the thirteen-year-olds (Zheng Xiaoying 1995, 23–35).

## Chapter 4  Pre-Marital Preoccupations

1 Personal communication from an editor of the Zhongguo funü chubanshe (Chinese women's publishing house) in Beijing in April 1993.
2 For more detailed analysis of the various patterns of courtship as a pre-marital ritual and as a function of the new model of marriage, see Croll 1981, 41–59.
3 Many articles pointed to this function of sexual segregation during the early 1950s as part of the publicity accompanying the new Marriage Law. For a typical example, see 'Guanche hunyin fa, fandui fengjian canyu sixiang' (Implement the Marriage Law and oppose the remnants of feudal thought) 1951, 14.
4 Many cases cited as proof of local officials' culpability ended in the suicide of the young women involved. See, for example, Meng Changqian 1950; Hou Ding 1951; 'Guanyu "Yu Zhangquan ganshe lian'ai ziyou bichu renming" de fanying' 1951. For further discussions about related kinds of conflicts between young women and their parents that ended in suicide, see Yang 1959, 36–9, 79–82.
5 Lei Jieqiong's use of the term 'matchmaker', moreover, does not include introduction by a third person (usually a colleague or a friend), or by relatives. A survey of Huangchuan County, Henan Province, revealed that, in the period 1979–86, 39.6% of all marriages were through the match-maker, 37.6% through third-party introductions, 6.9% through relatives' introductions, and only 15.8% through direct acquaintance, 'the model of modern marital behaviour' (1994, 174–5). In Shanghai during the same period, 73.7% of marriages were through third-party introductions, while only 14% were through direct acquaintance (p. 175).
6 According to Amnesty International, 33,000 women were abducted and sold between mid-1993, when a major crackdown against human traffick-ing was launched, and mid-1995 (AI 1995, 3). Over the last few years, since news about the abduction and sale of women has hit the headlines, considerable information has accumulated about the networks of traf-fickers and kidnappers established on an inter-regional basis, about the numbers of women 'liberated' from their abductors, about the prices girls and young women fetch in the 'flesh markets', and about the different responses of women and local populations to the phenomenon. Since most of it, however, corresponds with specific regions and localities, and since there are no available detailed figures for its national distribution, it is difficult to formulate a comprehensive view of the operation and its effects. For further discussion, see Chapter 7.
7 Rather than imply that rural marriage practices fit in with a uniform pattern, Harrell has suggested that they be characterized according to a number of hypotheses: first, that following economic reform, the age of marriage would generally fall; second, that marital practices that encour-aged village endogamy as a strategy of mate choice during the Cultural Revolution would give way to a return to pre-communist practices dis-couraging intra-village marriage; third, that with the disappearance of the radical ideology associated with Mao's late years, uxorilocal marriage would decline in many areas where it was not traditionally a favoured

practice; and fourth, that as the government's attack on 'feudal customs' weakened, bride-price and dowry would increase 'for the simple reason that families now have more surplus wealth than ever to invest in signs of social status' (Harrell 1992, 325). For further discussion about the effects of post-1978 reforms on rural marriage practices, see Davis and Harrell 1993 and Lei Jieqiong 1994.

8 This comment comes from a personal informant, a man brought up in a village in northern Jiangsu Province in the 1950s, who witnessed many intergenerational arguments about marital arrangements. The same informant also noted that 'love' was an empty word for most of the peer group with whom he grew up.

9 The most frequent example was of '*danshi*' (but), which invariably introduced a section or paragraph which negated or minimized the importance of the preceding statement. For example, 'love is an important matter, but it isn't the only matter of importance to us' (Song Tingzhang 1955, 2–3).

10 Cai Qun further pointed out that some readers felt that references to tenderness between a couple, or even to a mother's longing to see her son, indicated 'not entirely healthy emotions' (*ganqing bugou jiankang*). From a somewhat different perspective, Esther Cheo Ying also commented on the correspondence between the increasing political controls and the moral constraints on social and sexual conduct of the early 1950s. See Cheo Ying 1980, 73.

11 The use of romantic imagery to define the individual's relationship to the state has a long tradition in China, as part of a literary convention which often idealized the individual's attachment to the state. The most famous example of this, of course, was Qu Yuan (340–278 BC), poet and exiled loyalist of the state of Chu, who cast himself in the role of the rejected lover of his king.

12 Xia Hong provides a brief analysis of the 'realist tradition' and its Cultural Revolution developments in Semsel 1987, 35–41. With specific reference to the revisions of 'The White-Haired Girl', Meng Yue examines the ways in which the erasure of Xi'er's body and sexuality served the party's interests by transforming her from an oppressed women into an oppressed class (Meng Yue 1993, 120–3).

13 Cusack's 'Model Married Couple', 1985 (1958), 156–8, describes the political ideal of the time. Yu Luojin's two famous short stories, 'A Winter's Tale' and its sequel 'A Spring Fairy Tale', were originally published in *Xinhua yuebao* 9, 1980, 94–127, and in *Huacheng* 1, 1982, 141–222, respectively. For more on Yu Luojin, see Honig 1984, 252–65.

14 Gittings 1990 contains good accounts of the political positions represented both by the Democracy Wall movement and the official Anti-Spiritual Pollution campaign (pp. 164–70, 193–205).

15 The proverbial 'glass of waterism' was a term of criticism used by communist writers to point to practices invariably associated with women's sexual promiscuity. It derived from a criticism made by Lenin of Alexandra Kollontai, who, in his eyes, was guilty of suggesting that sexual relations should be as easy as 'drinking a glass of water'. See Zetkin 1953, 13. For more discussion about Kollontai's views, see Porter 1980, 432–3.

16 The Shanghai court asserted in 1950 that sexual intercourse between
   unmarried people was an offence. See Pang Dunzhi 1950, 68.
17 In a personal interview, a psychology lecturer in Huadong University
   pointed out that, although university regulations do not specifically prohibit sexual relations among students, requirements that visitors leave
   rooms and that lights be out by a certain time clearly imply as much.
18 The author of this article noted that these figures were on the conservative
   side, and that the real figures were probably more like 25 to 30 per cent for
   men and 20 to 25 per cent for women.
19 Chapter 7 discusses recent eugenicist policies in China in greater depth.
20 For discussion about recent approaches to the dowry and bride-price, see
   Siu 1993.
21 Chinese Academy of Social Sciences, Demography Department, 1993,
   reported in Amnesty International 1995, 2.
22 I listened to this phone call during a visit I made to the Beijing women's
   hotline offices in April 1993.

## Chapter 5  The Monogamous Ideal

1 For example, Pang Dunzhi (1950, 68) noted that, in 1950, the Shanghai
   court asserted that sexual intercourse between unmarried people was an
   offence.
2 According to 1990 census, the figures for unmarried women and men were
   41.21% and 62.52% respectively for the 20 to 24 age group in 1990,
   4.3% and 16.71% for the 25 to 29 age group, and 0.65% and 7.18% for
   the 30 to 34 age group. In comparison with 1982 figures, the 1990 figures
   signified an increase in numbers of women who were married under the
   legal age of 20, and a drop of 15% in numbers of unmarried women under
   the age of thirty (Zheng Xiaoying 1995, 135).
3 Two of the men, both friends of mine, of this age group who talked with
   me about their choice of partner told me that they considered looks to be
   the most important factor, despite the ideological rhetoric of the time. One
   of them further told me that, when he selected his prospective wife, he
   somehow imagined that love and intimacy would inevitably develop. A
   few years of marriage made him realize that this was not the case, and he
   decided to divorce.
4 Various writers have associated the marital difficulties of the Cultural
   Revolution generation with the pressures to conform to rigid political
   criteria and practices in both selecting and living with a spouse. For a good
   example, see Zhang Xinxin 1989, 59–66. Li Yinhe also pointed out that
   the high rate of divorce among the Cultural Revolution generation in the
   early 1980s was on account of similar reasons (1991, 183).
5 Esther Cheo Ying, for example, made it clear that women often thought
   that sexual intercourse was unimportant, if not totally undesirable (Cheo
   Ying 1980, 72–5, 130–1). See also Xu Anqi's comments on pages 171–2.
6 In their study of family-planning policy and practice in four counties,
   Kaufman, Zhang, Qiao and Zhang found that in all four counties by far
   the most frequently used method of contraception was sterilization, followed (in some cases a long way after) by the IUD (1989, 716). They also

found that sterilizations and IUD insertions peaked in 1979–80 and 1983 (p. 722), lending support to the argument that coercive methods were being used to achieve birth-control objectives.

7  Zeng Yi (1991, 6) noted that births to women aged 20 to 29 accounted for 80% of all births in China at the time of writing.

8  The Law on Maternal and Infantile Health Care, previously named the Draft Eugenics Law, went into effect on 1 June 1995. For further discussion, see Chapter 6.

9  Tuberculosis was commonly associated in the 1950s with women's sexuality, according to Liang Zhao (1957, 25).

10  A 1987 survey of four counties in Fujian and Heilongjiang revealed a contraceptive prevalence rate for 1986 of 91 to 98%. See Kaufman, Zhang, Qiao and Zhang 1989, 716. They attributed the differential between these and the official figures to the possibility that the 'non-eligible' women ('newly married and waiting for the first birth, breast-feeding, pregnant or infertile') were omitted from the lists they used to select their sample, or that some women may not have answered honestly.

11  The Marriage Law of the People's Republic of China, Chapter III, Article 12, states that 'husband and wife are in duty bound to practise family planning'.

12  While men used condoms in three of the four counties Kaufman, Zhang, Qiao and Zhang surveyed, it was the least favoured method (1989, 716). Male sterilization was also uncommon and was not used at all in the two Heilongjiang counties of the sample.

13  Mu Aiping 1995, 179. According to Mu Aiping's findings, the average incidence of abortion for the decade in question was 0.46 per woman, in contrast with Susan Greenhalgh's 0.14 per cent (1992). Mu Aiping explains this discrepancy with reference to Greenhalgh's sample, which covered all women married during 1971 and 1987, while her own focused on women who were between 30 and 39 years old in 1990.

14  It is not possible here to give an adequate analysis of the use of these techniques as violations of women's human rights. But one informant, an anthropologist who recently returned from a fieldwork trip in a village in Gansu Province, mentioned to me that the local birth-control personnel made no attempts to disguise the fact that they often used surprise techniques and considerable pressure to make women 'agree' to having an abortion. In response to the anthropologist's request to go along with them on one of their 'visits', they said 'no', since her presence would embarrass them too much and prevent them from carrying out their work effectively. Another Chinese anthropologist in a personal interview told me that she had come across many instances of forced abortion by induction among women who were already between six and seven months pregnant. In these cases, the aborted fetuses were nearly all born alive. Both these informants referred to makeshift clinics where abortions were performed. One – in a local school – came to my informant's attention when she noticed a queue of very pregnant women lined up outside.

15  Chapter 6 discusses the implications of this and related advice about 'reproductive hygiene' in greater depth.

16 Contemporary texts describe the menopause as a reversal of puberty in very similar terms to those used in the medical texts of the Republican period. See Dikötter 1995, 46–8.

17 The 'prettification' campaign coincided with the 'Five Goods' movement of the mid-1950s, which aimed at giving housework a new status – 'some justification in terms of production, the great status-giver of the new society' – to compensate for the fact that it was no longer deemed desirable, or economically possible, to provide all women with work. See Davin 1976, 152.

18 Chapter 8 contains an analysis of representations of the 'adulteress'.

19 Li Xiaojiang and others have pointed out that the reluctance of enterprise managers to employ young married women or to pay out maternity leave benefits has been but one aspect of the government's implicit encouragement to women to withdraw from the urban labour force in order to resolve growing problems of unemployment (Li Xiaojiang 1994; Tan Shen 1993).

20 In the course of many discussions I had with academics and Women's Federation representatives about women, marriage and the family between March and April 1993, repeated reference was made to this soap as evidence of the popularity of the image of the gentle supportive wife. Lisa Rofel argues that, far from being simply a popular form of entertainment devoid of politics, 'Yearning' represents a 'hegemonic' cultural form which contains significant political meanings (1994, 292–302).

21 'Socialist androgyny' was the term Marilyn Young used recently in a conference on 'Chinese Women and Feminist Thought' to categorize the imagery associated with women during the pre-reform period when feminist (and feminine) issues were legitimized only when they fitted in with broader concerns.

22 Ning Lao T'ai-t'ai subscribed to the same values when she said, 'If a good woman goes out, she must not go in gay clothing. She must wear a black coat and a black shirt and have a black veil across her face . . .' (Pruitt 1967, 177–8).

23 For a list of titles of the most popular women's magazines published between the early 1980s and 1990, see Ma Youcai 1992, 393–419.

## Chapter 6   Healthy Bodies

1 To persuade readers of the benefits of such techniques, a number of stories related the experiences of model midwives who had helped eliminate unhygienic methods of parturition and neo-natal care. For example, 'Youxiu de baojianyuan Zhu Xiujun' (The outstanding health worker Zhu Xiujun) (1953, 20–1) told of an illiterate model housewife who overcame local superstition and introduced new childbirth methods into her village. Qie Ning, in 'Mofan jieshengyuan Chang Xiuhua' (Chang Xiuhua, the model midwife), related the story of a young midwife who confronted local fear and suspicion in order to eliminate unhygienic methods of childbirth (1953). Other articles provided information about new methods of medical intervention to assist childbirth. See, for example, 'Dali tuixing "wutong fenmian fa" ' (Put energy into encouraging painless methods of

childbirth), which introduced advanced Soviet methods of childbirth (1952).

2 References to 'fetal education' in the biography of 'The three mothers of the Chou family' in the *Lie nü zhuan* included the comment that 'a woman with child should be careful about things that affect her. If she is affected by good things, the child will be good; if she is affected by evil things, the child will be evil' (O'Hara 1971, 23). Charlotte Furth examined both the medical views about fetal education and the moral importance attached to mothers' ritual conduct during pregnancy as a vital aspect of the new-born baby's health and welfare. She suggests that the moral aspects of fetal education were to regulate the emotions of women – particularly the 'internal heat' of anger or sexual excitement – to prevent miscarriage or difficult delivery as much as to ensure a healthy baby (1987, 14–18).

3 References during the 1950s to the month of confinement made no comment about its traditional association with notions of female uncleanliness after childbirth. For a discussion of the one-hundred-day taboo on intercourse after childbirth, see Furth 1987, 12–15, 22.

4 I would like to thank an anonymous referee of my *SIGNS* article for pointing out this distinction.

5 In her article on the Draft Eugenics Law, Elisabeth Croll (1993–4) suggested that the term was principally interpreted to refer to the social measures taken to reduce disabilities, rather than its more usual implied sense of controlled breeding associated with Hitler's experiments in fascist Germany.

6 See the article from the New China News Agency (May 1995) on the new Law for Maternal and Infantile Health Care. Raymond Whitaker noted Li Peng's statement in *The Independent on Sunday* (10 April 1994) while the law was still at its draft stage.

7 The second clause of article 6 of the Marriage Law states that 'anyone who suffers from a severe sickness medically considered to be inappropriate for marriage' should not be permitted to marry; this includes 'VD, idiocy, and any physiological defects which inhibit sexual behaviour, including mental illness'.

8 The legal age for marriage as set down in the 1980 Marriage Law is 22 for women and 25 for men. However, throughout the period between the mid-1950s and now, the appropriate age for marriage has encouraged the later ages of 25 for women and 27 for men.

9 For a few of the many available English-language analyses of China's population policy and implementation since the 1980s, see Banister 1987; Kane 1987; Zeng Yi 1989; Greenhalgh 1990, 1993.

10 See, for example, Mosher 1994, and below, note 13.

11 Such pressure has been the subject of vast numbers of articles in the Chinese official and popular press in recent years, the main objective of which has been to point out the illegality of such acts, as well as to encourage readers to think more positively about the prospect of a daughter. Official figures from the 1982 and 1990 censuses reported a rise in sex ratios at birth from 108.4 (1982) to 111.75 (1990) males for every 100 females (Kane 1995, 200). China's 'missing girls' have been the subject of extensive international debate, with varying stress on the

function of female infanticide (Aird 1990), death from neglect and the use of abortion in the fertility-control programme (Zeng Yi 1989). The use of ultrasound techniques to identify the sex of the fetus has been banned, except for medical reasons, by the Law for Maternal and Infantile Health Care. A few localities have pioneered programmes to enhance women's status – and therefore the status of the new-born daughter – through giving girls preferential treatment in access to schools, but reportedly with very limited effects.

12  For example, Wu Zhangming, Zhu Xiaolan and Lang Ying 1990, 114–32, contains an entire section on 'Planned births' which includes such information.

13  There have been a number of eyewitness reports of the family-planning 'task forces' mode of operation. One, written by a woman who accompanied such an operation in the outskirts of Beijing in April 1991, was published in *The Independent* under the pseudonym Liu Yin on 11 September 1991. Her account coincided with the official publication of figures demonstrating a 1.48% population growth rate, in comparison with the 1% target announced by the government for the same year.

14  In a historical survey of sexually transmitted disease in China, Frank Dikötter similarly pointed out that medical responses to venereal disease have long been structured by 'cultural variable and social attitudes' (Dikötter 1993, 341–5).

15  Frank Dikötter, in the same article, pointed out that during the social disintegration of the Cultural Revolution the incidence of STDs may have risen markedly in certain regions, but in the absence of adequate data it is impossible to make any informed assessment (p. 345).

16  Both these examples come from personal conversations with a prominent social scientist from one of Beijing's universities, who has in recent years engaged in research about various aspects of sexuality in contemporary China, including homosexuality and the transmission of sexually transmitted diseases.

17  This formulation is inspired by Susan Sontag's categorization of AIDS as a metaphor for invasion by the 'dreaded foreigner'. See Sontag 1989.

## Chapter 7 Sex and the Open Market

1  For a brief review of the literature on the different kinds of monetary transaction that marked the entry of wives, concubines and maids into a household in the Hong Kong region in the early part of this century, see Watson 1991b, 239–41. Jaschok and Miers 1994 examine the particular case of 'minor marriages', a 'despised form of marriage' in which a little girl was transferred from her natal home to the household of her future husband without her parents incurring the expenses of a dowry, and the *mui tsai*, young girls who were sold as domestic slaves. Helen Siu's study, based on fieldwork in the Pearl River delta, focuses on the changes in marital payments between the early twentieth century and the post-Mao period (1993, 165–88).

2 Though the collective economy of the rural sector considerably reduced the economic functions of the domestic group, the organization of production and distribution and the uneven distribution of welfare and health services maintained the economic interdependence of the generations within the household. This contributed to maintaining the authority of parents in the procedures of marriage. See Croll 1981, 150–6.

3 Some analyses of the 1980s suggested that one of the most significant effects of rural reform was the restoration of the economic interests maintaining the controls exercised by the male head of the household over family members and interests, including marriage. See for example Croll 1987 and Davin 1988. This view has been modified by more recent arguments concerning the increased economic autonomy and ability to pursue their own interests gained by women, including unmarried women, in the commodity economy (e.g., Judd, 1994). An interesting parallel to this latter argument has been made by Gates (1993, 251–73) in her argument that women's ownership of capital within the sphere of kinship has increased their decision-making power, and that such women have 'actively sought to limit their childbearing' (p. 257).

4 The sale of daughters as concubines and as maids (Watson 1991b, 231–55), into the despised 'minor marriages' and as domestic slaves (*mu tsai*) (Jaschok and Miers 1994) represented some of the alternatives available to families who could not sustain the appropriate bridal costs.

5 Between 1982 and 1987 Zeng Yi noted that 0.2% and 0.1% respectively of women between the ages of 45 and 49 were single. For every cohort of women since 1982, 97.5% have been married by the age of 35, and for most cohorts the figure has exceeded 99% (Zeng Yi 1991, 25).

6 A recent Reuters report said that Qingyuan City officials had organized a major search and rescue operation to locate young Vietnamese women who had been sold as wives in villages in Yangshan County, Guangdong Province: 68 women were reportedly found, aged between 16 and 38, several of whom had just had babies (*CND*, 11 August 1995).

7 Quoting from the September 1991 'Decision of the Standing Committee of the National People's Congress Regarding the Severe Punishment of Criminals Who Abduct and Traffic in or Kidnap Women and Children', Amnesty International noted that 'purchasing does not itself constitute a crime because purchasers who "do not obstruct the woman from returning to her original place of residence according to her will" ... shall be exempted from being investigated for criminal responsibility' (Amnesty International 1995, 3).

8 This figure was from a report in the *Legal Daily* (*Fazhi ribao*), quoted by Reuters, 13 January 1995. Given the fact that many abductions and sales are never reported, and that there is no national collation of relevant statistics, all such figures are likely to be conservative.

9 This genre of such writing, known as *fazhi wenxue* (legal literature), provides a common outlet for sensationalist and pornographic materials, often exploited by ordinary publishing companies for profit.

10 Elisabeth Croll noted that, in the villages she visited, the bride-price was rarely less than 1000 yuan (1994, 169).

11 A recent article based on fieldwork conducted in China noted that the economic transactions involved in the sale of a daughter are by no means always recognized as such, and that marriage under such conditions is not necessarily seen by the young woman involved as an abuse of women's rights (Guo Yuhua 1993).

12 It is not my intention in this section to provide a comprehensive analysis of prostitution. For this, the reader should consult Gail Hershatter's forthcoming book *Dangerous Pleasures*. See also Shan Guangnai 1995.

13 Various personal informants have noted that the lack of information about prostitution during the Cultural Revolution corresponds more with the representation of the latter as a period 'when sex did not happen' than with the lived experiences of women and men of the time.

14 For details of the Shanghai campaign to eradicate prostitution, see Hershatter 1992.

15 All citizens were classified as belonging to a specific social and residential category in 1949 in order to facilitate identification of targets for punishment as well as control of mobility.

16 These descriptions abound in a series of interviews Liu Xiaocong held with prostitutes sent to reform through education camps (Liu Xiaocong 1991).

17 Although this view is quite widely held, it has been openly subjected to criticism on the grounds that it ignores the progressive contribution notions of 'sexual liberation' made in European history. See 'Dui xing jiefang de zai renshi' (Re-evaluating sexual liberation), in *Qingshaonian tantao*, 2, 1989, quoted in Wang Xingjuan 1992, 424.

18 The first case of such a prosecution was reported in the *Beijing Evening News* and *AP* on 23 November 1992.

19 Lin Chongwu wrote in 1936 that 'the harm of prostitution is none other than its being a site of the spread of disease, which has serious consequences for the strength or weakness of the race'. Quoted in Hershatter 1994, 159.

20 Launched in August 1989, the campaign against the 'six evils' targeted pornography, prostitution, gambling, drugs, abduction and selling of women and children, and profiteering from superstition.

21 A group of women friends laughed at the idea that *Raise the Red Lantern* was an allegory of the events and consequences of the massacre of 4 June 1989. When I mentioned this analysis when we met in Beijing one evening in April 1993, they simply said that, unless a film was overtly political, all the censors were worried about was sex.

22 For more discussion about rape in contemporary Chinese society, see Honig and Hershatter 1988, 276–86, 299–303.

23 An article in the legal journal *Minzhu yu fazhi* published an account of a woman who drowned herself after her husband reviled her for being raped. See Lin Wanxiu 1985.

24 For an example of this approach, see Zhou Daoluan 1981.

25 Liu Dalin pointed out that, although in only 3% of the couples interviewed in his nationwide survey had a partner been coerced into having sex, this still represented several million people. See *Zhongguo dangdai xing wenhua* (Sexual behaviour in modern China), 1992b, 425.

## Chapter 8 Sexualities under Suspicion

1 The *Time* article also appropriately pointed out that this publication served erotic interests as well as those it ostensibly set out to warn against.

2 Evidence from the law courts suggested that, until the conclusion of the provincial campaigns to implement the Marriage Law in late 1953, most divorces were sought and granted on what were described as anti-feudal grounds. Meijer (1971) does not give any figures but suggests that men were more often cited as the guilty party in cases before 1953. Figures from the old liberated areas indicate that 60–90% of cases were initiated by women. See Zhongyang renmin zhengfu fazhi weiyuanhui, 1950, 38.

3 For more discussion about mediation in domestic conflict, see Palmer 1988, 75–7; 1995, 122–4.

4 After the peak of more than 1.15 million divorces in 1953, numbers settled down to about 400,000 per year until the early 1980s. See Sun Wenlan 1991, 1–2.

5 Xu Anqi notes that, in one district surveyed in 1955, the parties to divorce who cited material reasons for engaging in extra-marital relationships constituted 67 per cent of the total of adultery cases, while only 5% of the total cited psychological or emotional factors. The latter had risen to 46% by 1985 (Xu Anqi 1990b, 53).

6 Xu Anqi argues that this was owing to the combination of a generally 'thin grasp of legal understanding', and the greater tendency to look for new partners to satisfy 'physical need' (*shengli xuqiu*). She notes that illegitimate births occurred in 13% of adulterous relationships, not including the offspring of concubines.

7 For further discussion about the deployment of ideological labels to inscribe gender differences into sexual behaviours and attributes, see Evans 1991, 186–90.

8 It is significant that various women's magazines have recently carried a number of debates advising women what to do in the event of discovering their husbands' extra-marital liaisons. See, for example, the many queries about husbands' affairs received by the women's hotline in Lou Jingbo 1992, and Wu Jian 1992. An article suggested that the escalating incidence of adultery was an expression of the greater social mobility and increased opportunities for meeting people in contemporary society. See Han Lu 1993, 56–7.

9 Starting with an autobiographical piece by Liu Lequn, the wife abandoned by Luo Baoyi, a debate entitled 'Why did our marriage break down?' was published in consecutive issues of *Zhongguo funü* in 1955 and 1956 to air readers' views about the sources of marital conflict.

10 This approach is very similar to that of an article published in 1956 entitled 'Disanzhe you xingfu ma?' (Can the third party find happiness?, Zhu Zhixin 1956. According to this, young girls often cause pain and suffering to others by 'unconsciously putting themselves in the role of the third party' and 'by disrupting harmonious families'.

11 For a detailed analysis of the debate carried in *Funü zazhi* (Women's journal), see Clarke 1988.

12 Personal communication from a female former member of the club.

13 For further discussion about this category, see Honig and Hershatter 1988, 105–10. Evidence of the particular difficulties faced by such women comes from the figures attending the Beijing singles club, where in 1992 60 per cent of the 145 members were women. It is significant that all applicants must have received higher education, and the minimum age is 27 for men and 25 for women. See *Renmin ribao*, 13 April 1993.

14 According to Li Yinhe, writing in 1991, local officials in Hubei Province had already decided to put forward such a proposal (pp. 148–9).

15 See Carrie Gracie's article in *The Guardian*, 22 February 1993. Evidence from human rights organizations indicates that aversion therapy techniques are still used on homosexuals in China and that, although no laws deal specifically with homosexuality, many homosexuals are arrested and given lengthy prison or labour camp sentences.

16 This report erroneously noted that 'the first book on Chinese gays' was about to be published in Hong Kong, written by Fang Gang, a young newspaper editor in Tianjin.

17 For an analysis of the homosexual tradition in China, see Hinsch 1990 and Xiao Mingxiong 1984.

18 Personal informants have also noted that, in its structure and language, the book still treats gays as a strange and abnormal phenomenon, despite its overt support for their cause.

19 Huadan is the lead female role played by a man in traditional Chinese opera. In Chen Kaige's recent film *Farewell my Concubine*, it was represented as a role permitting the expression of ambiguous sexual desires and fantasies.

20 Studies of female virginity in other cultures have drawn similar conclusions. For example, in her work on female virginity in Naples, Victoria Goddard wrote that 'women had the capacity to provoke crises in the system precisely through their sexuality' (Goddard 1987, 190).

21 Gary Seaman also discussed the potential of female sexuality to destroy the political unity of the community. His analysis, however, focused on the polluting powers of menstrual and birth blood rather than on representations of women as agents of sexual morality. See Seaman 1981, 381–96.

22 Tien Ju-k'ang argued that signs of female chastity, including female suicide, were particularly praised during moments of crisis and change in late Ming and early Qing China precisely because of their association with the preservation of standards of social morality at times when the latter was under threat. See Tien Ju-k'ang 1988, 126–35.

## Chapter 9 Conclusions

1 A special issue of *Modern China* on 'Public sphere/civil society in China?' (19, 2, 1993) discusses historical and contemporary perspectives on civil society on China, without, it should be noted, engaging with issues of gender.

# Bibliography

A Che (1995), 'Bu xiang zuo "qingren" ' (I don't want to be a 'lover'), *NYZX* 5, 36.

A Xiangzhai (1993), 'Wenge zhong de "dixia" aiqing wenxue' ('Underground' love literature in the Cultural Revolution), *Qingchun chao* 4, 29.

Ah Cheng (1990), *Three Kings*, trans. with an introduction by Bonnie S. McDougall. London: Collins Harvill.

Ahern, Emily M. (1976) 'The power and pollution of Chinese women', in Arthur P. Wolf, ed., *Studies in Chinese Society.* Stanford, CA: Stanford University Press, 269–90.

Aird, John S. (1990), *The Slaughter of Innocents: Coercive Birth Control in China.* Washington: American Enterprise Institute Press.

Amnesty International (1995), *Women in China.* London: Amnesty International.

Andors, Phyllis (1983), *The Unfinished Liberation of Chinese Women, 1949–1980.* Bloomington: Indiana University Press.

Ayscough, Florence (1937), *Chinese Women, Yesterday and Today.* Boston: Houghton Mifflin.

Baden-Powell, Robert ([1932] 1954), *Scouting for Boys.* London: C. Arthur Pearson.

Bai Ruifang (1956), 'Wode kongsu' (My denunciation), *ZGFN* 8, 2–3.

Baker, Hugh D. R. (1979), *Chinese Family and Kinship.* London: Macmillan.

Banister, Judith (1987), *China's Changing Population.* Stanford, CA: Stanford University Press.

Bao Dongni (1991), *Jiating jiaose* (Family roles), Beijing: Zhongguo huaqiao chubanshe.

Barlow, Tani E., ed. (1993), *Gender Politics in Modern China: Writing and Feminism.* Durham, NC, and London: Duke University Press.

—— (1994), 'Politics and the protocols of funü: (un)making national woman', in Christina K. Gilmartin, Gail Hershatter, Lisa Rofel and Tyrene White, eds, *Engendering China: Women, Culture, and the State*. Cambridge, MA, and London: Harvard University Press, 346–52.

Beijing daxue falü xi minfa jiaoyan shi (1958) (Teaching and research section on civil law, Beijing University law department), 'Dui lihun wenti de fenxi he yijian' (Analysis and ideas about divorce'), *ZGFN* 4, 16–17.

Belden, Jack (1973), *China Shakes the World*. Harmondsworth: Penguin.

Bi Fagui and Deng Zongxiu (1988), *Xing bing fangzhi wenda* (Questions and answers on the prevention and cure of sexual diseases). Guiyang: Guizhou renmin chubanshe.

Bi Shaomin (1993), *Nan nü zhuangyang huichun miaofang babaiba* (Wonderful prescriptions for men and women to restore strength and vitality). Beijing: Zhongguo yiyao keji chubanshe.

Bordo, Susan ([1993] 1995), *Unbearable Weight: Feminism, Western Culture, and the Body*. Berkeley, Los Angeles and London: University of California Press.

Botton Beja, Flora and Bustamante, Romer Cornejo (1993), *Bajo un mismo techo: la familia tradicional en China y su crisis* (Under one roof: the traditional family in China and its crisis). Mexico: El Colegio de Mexico.

'Bu yao gulide jinxing guanyu lian'ai wenti de jiaoyu' (1952) (Don't conduct education about questions of love in isolation from other matters), *ZGQN* 22, 1, 9.

'Bu yao guo zao jiehun' (1957) (Don't marry too early), *ZGQN* 4, 9.

Buck, John Lossing ([1937] 1956), *Land Utilization in China*. New York: Council on Economic and Cultural Affairs.

Butler, Judith (1990), *Gender Trouble: Feminism and the Subversion of Identity*. London: Routledge.

—— (1993), *Bodies that Matter: on the Discursive Limits of 'Sex'*. London: Routledge.

Cai Qun (1953), 'Mantan qingnian zai yuedu zuopin zhong de yixie wenti' (Talking about some problems young people encounter in their reading of literature), *ZGQN* 17, 27–30.

Cameron, Deborah (1988), *Feminism and Linguistic Theory*. London: Macmillan.

Caplan, Pat, ed. (1987), *The Cultural Construction of Sexuality*. London: Tavistock.

Cao Hongxin, Mao Dexi and Ma Zhongxue, eds (1992), *Zhongyi fangshi yangsheng yu xing gongneng zhang'ai tiaozhi* (Chinese medical approaches to preserving health in sexual intercourse and the recuperation of sexual function). Jinan: Shandong kexue jishu chubanshe.

Cao Renlie (1989), *Xing shengli yu xing bing* (Sexual biology and sexual diseases). Beijing: Beijing kexue jishu chubanshe.

Carrithers, Michael, Collins, Steven and Lukes, Steven, eds (1985), *The Category of the Person: Anthropology, Philosophy, History*. Cambridge: Cambridge University Press.

Chen, Jerome (1973), *A Year in Upper Felicity*. London: Harrap.

Chen Benzhen (1956), 'Jing naiqi bu neng canjia zhong laodong' (You must not do heavy labour during menstruation and pregnancy), *ZGFN* 8, 31.

—— (1958), 'Dang diyi ci lai yuejing de shihou' (When you menstruate for the first time), *ZGFN* 8, 23.

Chen Bin (1995), 'Zai tan shouyin, zao xie, "bujie xingjiao"' (Further discussion about masturbation, premature ejaculation and 'unclean sexual intercourse'), *JTYS* 7, 20.

Chen Chunming (1995), 'Zhongguo HIV liuxing chuanbo de tezheng ji qushi' (The characteristics and tendencies in the transmission of HIV in China), *Renmin ribao* (overseas edition), 1 December.

Chen Dong (1954), 'Ruhe zhengque duidai lian'ai wenti' (How correctly to treat the question of love), *ZGQN* 4, 5–6.

Chen Fan, ed. (1990), *Xingbing zai Zhongguo* (Sexual diseases in China). Beijing: Beijing shiyue wenyi chubanshe.

Chen Huilin (1984), 'Jiating shi baoli tequ ma?' (Is the family a special zone of violence?), *ZGFN* 12, 26–9.

Chen Jianwei (1959), 'Lun fengjian jiazhangzhi de pochu' (On the dissolution of the system of feudal patriarchy), *HNRB*, 8 April, 3.

Chen Xianguo (1993), 'Fuqi guanxi ehua de xianzhao yu cuoshi' (Signs of and measures to deal with marital deterioration), *HYYJT* 4, 18–19.

Chen Xueshi and Li Guorong, eds (1992), *Dangdai xinli weisheng* (Psychological hygiene today). Beijing: Zhongguo shehui kexue.

Chen Yan (1986), 'Qinggan xuyao weishi' (Emotions need a bodyguard), *ZGFN* 2, 40.

Chen Yanping (1957), 'Ta rujin shi daxuesheng la' (She is now a university student), *ZGQN* 14, 33.

Chen Ying (1982), 'Chu zai jin tui liang nan zhi zhong de wo' (I, caught between the difficult alternatives of moving on or going back), *ZGQN* 11, 2.

Chen Zhiying, ed. (1993), *Zhongguo funü yu fazhan: diwei, jiankang, jiuye* (Chinese women and development: position, health, employment). Zhengzhou: Henan renmin chubanshe.

Cheng Jinwu (1950), 'Jianli zhengque de lian'ai guan' (Establish a correct perspective on love), *ZGQN* 38, 16–17.

Cheng Xian (1986), 'Chenfu huihen shinian jian' (A decade of sinking in remorse), *Funü shenghuo* 3, 18–20.

Cheo Ying, Esther (1980), *Black Country Girl in Red China*. London: Hutchinson.

Chow, Rey (1993), 'Response', in issue on 'Marxism beyond Marxism' of *Polygraph* [Duke University] 6/7, 209–11.

Chu Zhaorui (1994) 'Zhongguo xingkexue yanjiu ru ri zhong tian' (Research about sex education in China reaches a high point), *NXYJ* 4, 4–8.

Clarke, Laura (1988), 'An "Unnatural State": Views on Celibacy in *Funü Zazhi*', unpublished BA dissertation, Trinity Hall, University of Cambridge.

Conroy, Richard (1987), 'Patterns of divorce in China', *Australian Journal of Chinese Affairs* No. 17, 53–75.

Croll, Elisabeth (1978), *Feminism and Socialism in China*. London: Routledge & Kegan Paul.

—— (1981), *The Politics of Marriage in Contemporary China*. Cambridge: Cambridge University Press.

—— (1987), 'New peasant family forms in rural China', *Journal of Peasant Studies* 14, 469–99.

—— (1993–4), 'A commentary on the new draft law on eugenics and health protection', *China Information* 8, 3, 32–7.

—— (1994), *From Heaven to Earth: Images and Experiences of Development in China*. London: Routledge.

Croll, Elisabeth, Davin, Delia and Kane, Penny, eds (1985), *China's One-Child Family Policy*. London: Macmillan.

Cusack, Dymphna ([1958] 1985), *Chinese Women Speak*. London: Century Hutchinson.

Dai Wei (1991), *Zhongguo hunyin xing'ai shigao* (History of marriage and sexual love in China). Beijing: Dongfang chubanshe.

'Dali tuixing "wutong fenmian fa"' (1952) (Put energy into encouraging painless methods of childbirth), *ZGFN* 8, 6–7.

Davin, Delia (1976), *Woman-Work: Women and the Party in Revolutionary China*. Oxford: Clarendon Press.

—— (1985), 'The single-child family policy in the countryside', in Elisabeth Croll, Delia Davin, and Penny Kane, eds, *China's One-Child Family Policy*. London: Macmillan, 37–82.

—— (1988), 'The implications of contract agriculture for the employment and status of Chinese peasant women', in Stephan Feuchtwang, Athar Hussain and Thierry Pairault, eds, *Transforming China's Economy in the Eighties*, vol. 1: *The Rural Sector, Welfare and Employment*. London: Zed Books, 137–46.

Davis, Deborah and Harrell, Stevan, eds (1993), *Chinese Families in the Post-Mao Era*. Berkeley, Los Angeles and London: University of California Press.

De Lauretis, Teresa (1984), *Alice Doesn't: Feminism, Semiotics, Cinema*. London: Macmillan.

—— (1986), *Feminist Studies/Critical Studies*. Bloomington: Indiana University Press.

Deng Yingchao (1953), 'Xuexi Sulian renmin chonggao de gongchanzhuyi daode pinzhi' (Study the lofty qualities of communist morality of the Soviet people), in *Lun shehuizhuyi shehui de aiqing, hunyin he jiating*. Beijing: Qingnian chubanshe, 1–11.

—— ([1942] 1985), 'Tan nan nü qingnian de lian'ai, hunyin wenti' (On the question of love and marriage for young men and women), in Zhao Chang'an, Lan Wei and Zhang Tianruo, eds, *Lao gemingjia de lian'ai, hunyin he jiating shenghuo* (The loves, marriages and family lives of old revolutionaries). Beijing: Gongren chubanshe, 1–14.

Deng Zhonghua, ed. (1992), *Nüxing xinli* (Female psychology). Beijing: Zhongguo funü chubanshe.

Diamond, Norma (1975), 'Collectivization, kinship, and the status of women in rural China', in Rayna R. Reiter, ed., *Toward an Anthropology of Women*. New York: Monthly Review Press, 372–95.

Dikötter, Frank (1992), *The Discourse of Race in Modern China*. London: Hurst.

—— (1993), 'Sexually transmitted diseases in modern China: a historical survey', *Genitourinary Medicine* 69, 341–5.

—— (1995), *Sex, Culture and Modernity in China*. London: Hurst.

—— (forthcoming) *Monstrous Conception: Medical Knowledge, Foetal Health and the Regulation of Reproduction in China 1550–1995*.

Ding Ling (1950), 'Qingnian de lian'ai wenti' (The question of love for young people), *ZGQN* 39, 10–14.

Ding Wen and Li Ying (1984), 'Lun aiqing' (On love), *Shanghai shehui kexue* 12, 48–50.

Domenach, Jean-Luc and Chang-ming Hua (1987), *Le Mariage en Chine*. Paris: Presse de la Fondation Nationale des Sciences Politiques.

Dong Xijian and Fan Chongyao (1984), *Hunyin jieshao suo neiwai* (Inside and outside marriage introduction bureaus). Hangzhou: Zhejiang renmin chubanshe.

Donzelot, Jacques (1980), *Policing the Family*. London: Routledge & Kegan Paul.

Douglas, Mary ([1966] 1989), *Purity and Danger: An Analysis of the Concepts of Pollution and Taboo*. London and New York: Ark.

Du Min (1984), 'Zenyang cai neng huidao lianren shenbian?' (What do I have to do to return to the side of my beloved?), *ZGQN* 2, 61.

Duan Muchang (1985), ' "Hunwai lian" yu "disanzhe" zhongzhong' (Different kinds of 'extra-marital affairs' and 'third parties'), *Jiefang ribao*, 8 June, weekend supplement 1.

'Dui "lüe lun qiangjian zui" de bu tong yijian' (1981) (Different opinions about 'Brief discussion about the crime of rape'), *MZYFZ* 10, 21.

Edholm, Felicity (1992), 'Beyond the mirror: women's self portraits', in Frances Bonner, Lizbeth Goodman, Richard Allen, Linda Janes and Catherine King, eds, *Imagining Women: Cultural Representations and Gender*. Cambridge: Polity Press and Open University Press, 154–72.

Ehrenreich, Barbara and English, Deidre (1976), *Complaints and Disorders: the Sexual Politics of Sickness*. London: Writers and Readers Publishing Cooperative.

—— (1979), *For Her Own Good: 50 Years of the Experts' Advice to Women*. London: Pluto.

Elvin, Mark (1985), 'Between the earth and heaven: conceptions of the self in China', in Michael Carrithers, Steven Collins and Steven Lukes, eds, *The Category of the Person: Anthropology, Philosophy, History*. Cambridge: Cambridge University Press, 156–90.

Evans, Harriet (1991), 'The Official Construction of Female Sexuality and Gender in the People's Republic of China, 1949–1959', unpublished doctoral dissertation, University of London.

—— (1992), 'Monogamy and female sexuality in the People's Republic of China', in Shirin Rai, Hilary Pilkington and Annie Phizacklea, eds, *Women in the Face of Change: the Soviet Union, Eastern Europe and China*. London: Routledge, 147–63.

—— (1994–5), 'Defining difference: the "scientific" construction of female sexuality and gender in the People's Republic of China', *SIGNS: Journal of Women in Culture and Society* 20, 2, 357–96.

Fan Xing and Jintian Mingyue, eds ([1991] 1992), *Lian'ai xinli* (Psychology of love). Beijing: Zhongguo qingnian chubanshe.

Fang Fang (1987), *Nüxing shengli yu xinli* (Female physiology and psychology). Chengdu: Sichuan renmin chubanshe.

Feminist Review (1987), *Sexuality: A Reader*. London: Virago.

Feng Ding (1958), 'Lun jiazhangzhi he jiating' (On patriarchy and the family), *ZGQN* 23, 16–18.

Feng Lei (1991), 'Yinggai renshi de shehui xianxiang' (A social phenomenon we should acknowledge), *ZGFN* 7, 24.

Feuerwerker, Yi-tsi Mei (1982), *Ding Ling's Ideology and Narrative in Modern Chinese Literature*. Cambridge, MA: Harvard University Press.

—— (1984), 'In quest of the writer Ding Ling', *Feminist Studies* 10, 1, 85–96.

Foucault, Michel (1977), *Discipline and Punish: the Birth of the Prison*. Harmondsworth: Peregrine.

—— (1984), *The History of Sexuality*, Vol. 1: *An Introduction*. Harmondsworth: Penguin.

—— (1987), *The Use of Pleasure: The History of Sexuality*, Vol. 2. Harmondsworth: Penguin.

—— (1990), *The Care of the Self: The History of Sexuality*, Vol. 3. Harmondsworth: Penguin.

Fu Caiying ([1987] 1991), *Sheng er yu nü sanbai wen* (Three hundred questions about having children). Beijing: Jindun chubanshe.

Funü shiyong daquan, ed. (1986), *Funü shiyong daquan* (A compendium for women's use). Shijiazhuang: Hebei renmin chubanshe.

*Funü xin shenghou daquan*, ed. (1987), *Funü xin shenghuo daquan* (Women's new life compendium). Beijing: Nongcun duwu chubanshe.

*Funü zhi you* (Women's friend), ed. (1991), *Funü baike daquan* (Women's encyclopedia), 2 vols. Beifang funü ertong chubanshe.

Furth, Charlotte (1986), 'Blood, body and gender: medical images of the female condition in China', *Chinese Science* 7, December, 43–66.

—— (1987) 'Concepts of pregnancy, childbirth and infancy in Ch'ing dynasty China', *Journal of Asian Studies* 46, 1, 7–35.

—— (1994), 'Rethinking Van Gulik: sexuality and reproduction in traditional Chinese medicine', in Christina K. Gilmartin, Gail Hershatter, Lisa Rofel and Tyrene White, eds, *Engendering China: Women, Culture, and the State*. Cambridge, MA, and London: Harvard University Press, 125–46.

Gao Fang and Zeng Rong, eds (1991), *Jiushi niandai nüxing baishi zhinan* (A comprehensive guide for women in the nineties). Beijing: Nongcun duwu chubanshe.

Gao Guizhen (1953), 'Wo zenyang chengwei guangrong de zhiyuanjun weihunqi' (How I became the glorious fiancée of a volunteer), *ZGQN* 5, 14–15.

Gao Lin, ed. (1991), *Nüxing yu xinxing jiating* (Women and the new style family). Beijing: Zhishi chubanshe.

Gao Yang (1995), 'Lai zi chu'nümo xiufu zhensuo de baogao' (Report from the hymen repair clinic), *DJJK* 6, 14–16.

Gates, Hill (1993), 'Cultural support for birth limitation among urban capital-owning women', in Deborah Davis and Stevan Harrell, eds, *Chinese Families in the Post-Mao Era*. Berkeley, Los Angeles and London: University of California Press, 251–74.

*Gei shaonü de xin* (1984) (Letters to young girls). Shanghai: Shanghai renmin chubanshe.

Geng Wenxiu (1991), 'Dangdai daxuesheng hunqian xing xingwei yanjiu ji xing jiaoyu shexiang' (Research into the pre-marital sexual activities of students today and tentative ideas about sex education), unpublished paper, Huadong shida xinlixue xi (Psychology Department, Huadong Normal University, Shanghai).

Geng Xi (1958), 'Rang qingnian zhuiqiu shenmo yang de aiqing' (What kind of love should young people pursue?), *ZGQN* 16, 31–2.

Gilmartin, Christina K., Hershatter, Gail, Rofel, Lisa and White, Tyrene, eds (1994), *Engendering China: Women, Culture, and the State.* Cambridge, MA, and London: Harvard University Press.

Gittings, John (1990), *China Changes Face: The Road from Revolution, 1949–1989.* Oxford: Oxford University Press.

Goddard, Victoria (1987), 'Honour and shame: the control of women's sexuality and group identity in Naples', in Pat Caplan, ed., *The Cultural Construction of Sexuality.* London: Tavistock, 166–92.

*Gongren ribao* sixiang jiaoyu bu (1983) (Thought and Education Department of the Workers' Daily), *Aiqing, hunyin, daode* (Love, marriage, morality). Beijing: Gongren chubanshe.

Greenhalgh, Susan (1990), 'The evolution of the one-child policy in Shaanxi', *China Quarterly* 122, 191–229.

—— (1992), 'The changing value of children in the transition from socialism: the view from three villages', Research Division Working Papers no. 43. New York: Population Council.

—— (1993), 'The peasantization of the one-child policy in Shaanxi', in Deborah Davis and Stevan Harrell, eds, *Chinese Families in the Post-Mao Era.* Berkeley, Los Angeles and London: University of California Press, 219–50.

Grossmann, Anita (1984), 'The new woman and the rationalization of sexuality in Weimar Germany', in Ann Snitow, Christine Stansell and Sharon Thompson, eds, *Desire: The Politics of Sexuality.* London: Virago, 190–208.

Gu Shi (1983), 'Aiqing zai xiandai shenghuo shang' (Love in modern life), *ZGQN* 3, 30–2.

'Guanche hunyin fa, fandui fengjian canyu sixiang' (1951) (Implement the Marriage Law and oppose the remnants of feudal thought), *ZGQN* 76, 30.

*Guanche hunyin fa yundong de zhongyao wenjian* (1953) (Important documents of the campaign to implement the Marriage Law). Beijing: Renmin chubanshe.

Guangdong sheng funü lianhe hui, Guangdong sheng jiating jiaoyu yanjiu hui, Guangdong kexue yu er shiyan jidi, eds (1986), *Xinhun shenghuo zhidao* (A guide to life for newly-weds). Guangzhou: Xin shiji chubanshe.

'Guanyu xing zhishi de jige wenti' (1956) (Some questions about sexual knowledge), *ZGQN* 13, 27–8.

'Guanyu "Yu Zhangquan ganshe lian'ai ziyou bichu renming" de fanying' (1951) (Response to 'Yu Zhangyan's interference with the freedom of love drove someone to death'), *ZGQN* 66, 17.

Guo Su (1950), 'Wode lian'ai jingguo' (My experience of love), *ZGQN* 38, 18.

Guo Yuhua (1993), 'Yuan dao er lai de xifumen' (Daughters-in-law from distant parts). Beijing: unpublished draft.

Han Lu (1993), Nüshimen, qing duo dian xinli zhunbei' (Ladies, please be a bit more psychologically prepared), *NXYJ* 3, 56–7.

Harrell, Stevan (1992), 'Aspects of marriage in three south-western villages', *China Quarterly* 130, 323–37.

He Yuguang and Huang Jianwei, eds (1986), *Qingnian fufu shouce* (Manual for young couples). Nanchang: Jiangxi kexue jishu chubanshe.

Henan sheng quanguo minzhu funü lianhehui (Henan All China Democratic Women's Federation) (1955), *Ruhe zhengque duidai lian'ai, hunyin yu jiating wenti* (How to treat correctly the question of love, marriage and the family). Zhengzhou: Henan renmin chubanshe.

Hershatter, Gail (1989), 'The hierarchy of Shanghai prostitution 1870–1949', *Modern China* 15, 4, 463–97.

—— (1992), 'Regulating sex in Shanghai: the reform of prostitution in 1920 and 1951', in Frederic Wakeman and Yeh Wen-hsin, eds, *Shanghai Sojourners*. Berkeley: Center for Chinese Studies, 145–86.

—— (1993), 'Prostitution and the market in women in early twentieth-century Shanghai', in Rubie S. Watson and Patricia Buckley Ebrey, eds, *Marriage and Inequality in Chinese Society*. Berkeley: University of California Press, 256–85.

—— (1994), 'Modernizing sex, sexing modernity: prostitution in early twentieth century Shanghai', in Christina K. Gilmartin, Gail Hershatter, Lisa Rofel and Tyrene White, eds, *Engendering China: Women, Culture, and the State*. Cambridge, MA, and London: Harvard University Press, 147–74.

—— (forthcoming), *Dangerous Pleasures: Prostitution and Modernity in Twentieth Century Shanghai*. Berkeley: University of California Press.

Hinsch, Bret (1990), *Passions of the Cut Sleeve: The Male Homosexual Tradition in China*. Berkeley: University of California Press.

Honig, Emily (1984), 'Private issues, public discourse: the life and times of Yu Luojin', *Pacific Affairs* 57, 2, 252–65.

Honig, Emily and Hershatter, Gail (1988), *Personal Voices: Chinese Women in the 1980s*. Stanford, CA: Stanford University Press.

Hooper, Beverley (1985), *Youth in China*. Harmondsworth: Penguin.

Hou Ding (1951), 'Li Ersao gaijia' (Second sister-in-law Li remarried), *ZGQN* 79, 27–8.

Hu Yaobang, 'Qingnian tuan yao jiji canjia guanche hunyin fa yundong' (The Communist Youth League must actively participate in carrying out the Marriage Law campaign), *ZGQN* 4, 2–3.

Hua Ming (1952), ' "Zhenshi de gushi" gaosu wo shenmo' (What "True Story" told me), *ZGQN* 20, 11–14.

Hua Mu (1953), 'Zai guanche hunyin fa yundong zhong qingnian funü yinggai zuo shenmo?' (What should young women do in the campaign to implement the Marriage Law?), *ZGQN* 4, 9–10.

Huang Bingshan, ed. (1990), *Zhongyi zhiliao aisibing* (Chinese medical cures for AIDS). Haerbin: Heilongjiang kexue jishu chubanshe.

Huang Shuze, 'Fandui shu xiong' (Oppose breast-binding), *ZGQN* 4, 23–4.

—— (1955), 'Zenyang cai neng duanjue shouyin de huai xiguan?' (What should I do to get rid of the bad habit of masturbating?), *ZGQN* 13, 38–9.

Huang Xiong, Gu Baoli, Ji Jin'an and Zhao Chengzong, eds (1991), *Renkou yu shengyu* (Population and reproduction). Shanghai: Fudan daxue chubanshe.

Hunan Changsha xian geming weiyuanhui weisheng ju (The Health Bureau for the Revolutionary Committee of Changsha County, Hunan), ed. (1975), *Nongcun funü weisheng* (Hygiene for rural women). Beijing: Renmin weisheng chubanshe.

'Hunyin zhong de xing nüedai' (Sexual violence in marriage) (1992), *JTYS* 4, 27.

Jackson, Margaret (1987), ' "Facts of life" or the eroticization of women's oppression? Sexology and the social construction of heterosexuality', in Pat Caplan, ed., *The Cultural Construction of Sexuality*. London: Tavistock, 52–81.

Jaschok, Maria and Miers, Suzanne, eds (1994), *Women and Chinese Patriarchy: Submission, Servitude and Escape*. London: Zed Books.

Jia Zheng (1987), 'Dang tamen miandui qiangbao de shihou' (When they [women] come face to face with violence), *ZGFN* 3, 26–7.

Jiang Kun and Xue Saiqin, eds (1992), *Funü bing* (Women's diseases). Beijing: Nongcun duwu chubanshe.

Jiang Wenyu (1986), 'Xingxing sese zeou xinli' (The diverse psychology of mate selection), *Nü qingnian* 3, 7.

*Jiankang wenzhai bao*, 14 April 1993.

Jin Ma, ed. ([1986] 1987), *Qingnian aiqing shenghuo* (The love life of young people). Zhejiang: Zhejiang kexue jishu chubanshe.

Jin Ruiying and Shang Shaohua (1980), 'Yichang "jiating jiufen" yinqi de hongdong' (A stir caused by a 'domestic dispute'), *ZGFN* 12, 20–3.

Jin Zhu and Bai Yue, eds (1991), *Lian'ai yu jiaoji yishu* (Love and the art of social communication). Beijing: Beijing chubanshe.

Johnson, Kay Ann (1983), *Women, the Family and Peasant Revolution in China*. Chicago: University of Chicago Press.

Ju Ming (1995), 'Zai "hun qian" de xiao shijie li' (In the small world of the 'pre-marital checkup'), *DJJK* 6, 5–6.

Judd, Ellen R. (1994), *Gender and Power in Rural North China*. Stanford, CA: Stanford University Press.

Jun Qiu (1986), 'Qing bangzhu wo baituo fannao' (Please help me get rid of my misery), *ZGFN* 2, 39–40.

Kane, Penny (1987), *China's Second Billion: Population and Family Planning in China*. Chicago: University of Chicago Press.

—— (1995), 'Population and family policies', in Robert Benewick and Paul Wingrove, eds, *China in the 1990s*. London: Macmillan, 193–203.

Kang Shuhua, Liu Lanpu and Zhao Ke (1988), *Nüxing fanzui lun* (On female crime). Lanzhou: Lanzhou daxue chubanshe.

Kaufman, Joan, Zhang Zhirong, Qiao Xinjian and Zhang Yang (1989), 'Family planning policy and practice in China: a study of four rural counties', *Population and Development Review* 15, 4, 707–29.

—— (1991), 'The quality of family planning services in rural China', revised paper first presented at the annual meeting of the Population Association of America, Baltimore, 30 March–1 April 1989.

Ko, Dorothy (1994), *Teachers of the Inner Chamber: Women and Culture in Seventeenth Century China*. Stanford, CA: Stanford University Press.

Lai Gen (1957), 'Xidi yixia ba, liangxin zhanmanle wugou de ren' (Have a wash, conscience washes filthy people clean), *ZGQN* 22, 31–2.

Lampton, David M. (1977), *The Politics of Medicine in China: The Policy Process, 1949–1977*. Boulder, CO: Westview Press.

Lan Li (1958), 'Jiao guniang' (Lovely girl), *ZGQN* 10, 36.

Lang, Olga ([1946] 1968), *Chinese Family and Society*. New Haven: Yale University Press.

Lapidus, Gail Warshofsky (1978), *Women in Soviet Society: Equality, Development and Social Change*. Berkeley: University of California Press.

Lawrence, Susan (1994), 'China's tough population policy works, but critics say it hurts women', based on *US News and World Report*, 19 September.

Laws, Sophie (1985), 'Male power and menstrual etiquette', in Hilary Homans, ed., *The Sexual Politics of Reproduction*. Aldershot: Gower, 13–30.

Lei Ji (1950), 'Tantan wode lian'ai guan' (Talking about my view of love), *ZGQN* 38, 19.

Lei Jieqiong (1957), 'He nianqing ren tan hunshi' (Talking about marriage with young people), *ZGQN* 4, 24.

Lei Jieqiong (1994), *Gaige yilai Zhongguo nongcun hunyin jiating de xin bianhua* (Changes in marriage and the family in China's countryside since the reform of the economic system). Beijing: Beijing daxue chubanshe.

Lei Jing (1986), 'Hun qian yi fang yinman jingsheng bing shi ke fou lihun?' (Can you divorce if before marriage your partner hid a history of mental sickness?), *ZGFN* 7, 39.

Levy, Marion J. (1949), *The Family Revolution in Modern China*. New York: Atheneum.

Lewis, Jane, ed. (1986), *Labour and Love: Women's Experience of Home and Family, 1850–1940*. Oxford: Blackwell.

Li Dun (1993), *Xing yu fa* (Sex and law). Zhengzhou: Henan renmin chubanshe.

Li Guixia (1993), 'Aiqing shi women ziji de shi' (Love is our own matter), *HYYJT* 4, 19.

Li Ji (1952), 'Guangrong de guniang' (Glorious girl), *ZGQN* 17, 20–2.

Li Jiangtao (1986), 'Yige bei hushile de wenti' (A problem that has been overlooked), *ZGFN* 2, 6–7.

Li Ping, Ou Xiaowei, Hou Hong and Dai Xiaojing, eds (1985), *Daxuesheng de lian'ai guan* (Perspectives of love among university students). Guangzhou: Guangdong renmin chubanshe.

Li Ruifen (1995), 'Wo dui nü'er de xing qimeng' (My approach to my daughter's sexual awakening), *DZYX* 6, 20.

Li Ruolin, 'Lian'ai neng zheiyang ziyou ma?' (Can love be this free?), *ZGQN* 6, 37–8.

Li Shuhuai and Gai Xing (1988), 'Zhi renyuan bixu baohu hao beihai funü mingyu' (Law enforcement – personnel must protect the reputation of injured women), *Fazhi ribao* 8 Jan., 3.

Li Songchen, ed. (1983), *Jiating daode guihua* (Anecdotes about family morality). Beijing: Zhongguo zhantang chubanshe.

Li Wenhai and Liu Shuyu (1992), *Chengren xing jiaoyu zhimi – xing de wujie he duice* (A guide to adult sex education – misunderstandings and ways to deal with sex). Changsha: Hunan kexue jishu chubanshe.

Li Xiangjin (1958), 'Jiesheng yuejing zhi de zhedie fa' (Economical ways of folding menstrual paper), *ZGFN* 11, 24.

Li Xiaofeng (1959), 'He luohou qingnian jiao pengyou yihou' (After making friends with backward youth), *ZGQN* 10, 24.

Li Xiaojiang (1986), 'Nüxing de shenghuo daolu' (Women's road to life), *ZGFN* 3, 30–1.

—— (1989), *Xing gou* (Gender gap). Beijing: Sanlian shudian.

—— (1994), 'Economic reform and the awakening of Chinese women's collective consciousness', in Christina K. Gilmartin, Gail Hershatter, Lisa Rofel and Tyrene White, eds, *Engendering China: Women, Culture, and the State*. Cambridge, MA, and London: Harvard University Press, 360–82.

Li Xiaojiang and Tan Shen, eds (1991a), *Funü yanjiu zai Zhongguo* (Research on women in China). Zhengzhou: Henan renmin chubanshe.

—— (1991b), *Zhongguo funü fenceng yanjiu* (Research on the stratification of Chinese women). Zhengzhou: Henan renmin chubanshe.

Li Xingchun and Wang Liru ([1988] 1991), *Fuqi hexie quanshu* (Encyclopedia of marital harmony). Beijing: Nongcun duwu chubanshe.

Li Yang (1956), 'Chunümo yu aiqing' (The hymen and love), *ZGFN* 11, 12–13.

Li Yinhe (1991), *Zhongguoren de xing'ai yu hunyin* (Sexual love and marriage among the Chinese). Zhengzhou: Henan renmin chubanshe.

Li Yinhe and Wang Xiaobo (1992), *Tamen de shijie: Zhongguo nan tongxinglian qunluo toushi* (Their world: a perspective on China's male homosexual community). Taiyuan: Shanxi renmin chubanshe.

Li Yu-ning, ed. (1992), *Chinese Women through Chinese Eyes*, Armonk, NY: M.E. Sharpe.

Li Yuxiao (1985), 'Lihun shi bu shi dangqian yanzhong de shehui wenti?' (Is divorce a serious problem in contemporary society?), *ZGFN* 10, 18–19.

'Lian'ai fangshi taolun' (1985) (Discussion on forms of love), *Jiating* 5, 24–5; 6, 20–1; 7, 26–7.

Liang Zhao (1957), 'Jihua shengyu bing bu nan' (Birth control is not at all difficult), *ZGFN* 4, 26.

Liao Shijie, You Zhonglun and Tang Xiaoqiang (1982), *Lian'ai shujian* (Correspondence on love). Chengdu: Sichuan renmin chubanshe.

*Lihun wenti xuanji* (Selected essays on the problem of divorce). Beijing: Falü chubanshe.

Lin Chun (1995), 'Gender equality in China: between the state and the market', paper presented to the International Symposium on Chinese Women and Feminist Thought, held in Beijing, 21–24 June.

Lin Dong (1955), 'Deng ni huilai zai jiehun' (Let's wait until you return to marry), *ZGFN* 4, 13.

Lin Qiaozhi (1957), 'Cong shengli shang tan jiehun nianling wenti' (Talking about the age of marriage from a physiological point of view), *ZGFN* 4, 25.

Lin Wanxiu (1985), Qinren zaodao wuren yihou' (After a family member suffers humiliation), *MZYFZ* 4, 40.

Lin Wen (1986), 'Meimei de chu lian' (Younger sister's first love), *ZGFN* 3, 26–7.

Ling Ya (1985), 'Yuan ni jin kuai zhengtuo buxing de qingwang' (I hope you struggle free of your unhappy emotional tangle as soon as possible), *ZGFN* 3, 22–3.

Liu, Lydia H. (1993), 'Invention and intervention: the female tradition in modern Chinese literature', in Tani Barlow, ed., *Gender Politics in Modern China: Writing and Feminism*. Durham, NC, and London: Duke University Press, 33–57.

Liu Binyan (1992),'The future of China', *New Left Review* 194 (July/August), 5–16.

Liu Changqing (1995), 'Nüxing xinggaochao zhang'ai xun yin' (Seeking to explain what stops women from having orgasm), *DZJK* 6, 28.

Liu Dalin (1986a), *Jiating shenghuo guanli* (Management of family life). Shenyang: Lianong kexue jishu chubanshe.

—— (1986b), *Jiating shehuixue mantan* (Talks about family sociology). Jinan: Shandong renmin chubanshe.

—— (1987), 'Xingkexue yu funü jiefang' (Sexology and women's liberation), *Shehui kexue zhanxian* 1, 120–5.

—— (1992a), 'Fa ren shen xing de qingshaonian fanzui' (Juvenile delinquency makes food for thought), *JTYS* 4, 14.

——, ed. (1992b), *Zhongguo dangdai xing wenhua – Zhongguo liangwan li 'xing wenming' diaocha baogao* (Sexual behaviour in modern China – a report of the 'sex civilization' survey on 20,000 subjects in China). Shanghai: Sanlian shudian.

—— (1995a), 'Fuqi jian zenyang fachu xing xihao' (How couples send out sexual signals to each other), *DZYX* 5, 42.

—— (1995b), 'Fuqi xing'ai de kuaile yuanze' (The pleasure principle in conjugal sexual love), *DZYX* 6, 48–9.

Liu Dezeng and Hao Shimin (1950), 'Nü tuanyuan Hao Xiaogai de gushi' (The story of Hao Xiaogai, a female Youth League member), *ZGQN* 33, 33.

Liu Dezhen (1952), 'Wo liang you xinxin jianli yige xin jiating' (We have the confidence to set up a new home), *ZGFN* 1, 31.

Liu Lequn (1955), 'Women fufu guanxi weishenmo polie?' (Why did our marriage break down?), *ZGFN* 11, 6–7.

—— (1958), 'Wo weishenmo tongyi lihun' (Why I agreed to divorce), in *Lihun wenti xuanji* (Selected essays on the problem of divorce). Beijing: Falü chubanshe, 14–16.

Liu Luxian, Liu Nanxian and Huang Canheng ([1990] 1991), *Qingnian nüxing baike quanshu* (Encyclopedia for young women). Changsha: Hunan kexue jishu chubanshe.

Liu Minwen, Zhou Lijun et al., eds (1989), *Nanren he nüren – qinmi de moshengren* (Men and women – intimate strangers). Beijing: Beijing kexue jishu chubanshe.

Liu Xiaocong (1991), 'Maiyin funü xintai lu' (Records of prostitutes' state of mind), *NXYJ* 3, 12–15; 4, 15–17.

Liu Xinwu, Wang Wen et al. ([1979] 1982), *Lian'ai, hunyin, jiating* (Love, marriage, family). Beijing: Zhongguo qingnian chubanshe.

Liu Xuanda (1992), 'En yu ai' (Kindness and love), *JTYS* 4, 28.

Liu Ying and Xue Suzhen, eds (1987), *Zhongguo hunyin jiating yanjiu* (Research on marriage and the family in China). Beijing: Shehui kexue wenxian chubanshe.

Liu Yunxiang (1958), 'Guanyu zhengque renshi yu chuli dangqian de lihun wenti' (On correctly understanding and handling current divorce problems), *Faxue* 3, 55–8.

'Linda zenmo la?' (1954) (What's up with Linda?), trans. from Russian, *ZGFN* 12, 24.

Lou Jingbo (1992), 'Funü re xian, nide SOS' (The women's hotline, your SOS), *NXYJ* 2, 22–3.

Lu Shumin and Tang Jianhua ([1990] 1991), *Funü baojian 365 wen* (365 questions about women's health). Beijing: Zhongguo renkou chubanshe.

Lu Tongling (1995), *Misogyny, Cultural Nihilism, and Oppositional Politics: Contemporary Chinese Experimental Fiction*. Stanford, CA: Stanford University Press.

'Lun shehuizhuyi shehui de aiqing, hunyin he jiating' (1953) (On love, marriage and the family in socialist society), trans. from Russian in *Lun shehuizhuyi shehui de aiqing, hunyin he jiating* (On love, marriage and the family in socialist society). Beijing: Qingnian chubanshe, 12–29.

Luo Hanchao and Lou Youyi (1989), *Xingbing yu xing qiguan pifubing* (Sexual diseases and genital skin diseases). Chengdu: Sichuan renmin chubanshe.

Luo Jia (1955), 'Feizao pao de aiqing' (Soap bubble love), *ZGFN* 4, 8–9.

Ma Dejie and Liu Xianjun (1950), 'Liu Mei weishenmo zisha?' (Why did Liu Mei commit suicide?), *ZGQN* 48, 49.

Ma Li (1991), 'Wo suo lijie de xiandai nüxing mei' (Contemporary feminine beauty as I understand it), *ZGFN* 11, 16–17.

Ma Youcai (1992), 'Hunyin jiating yanjiu de pengbo fazhan' (The flourishing development of research on marriage and the family), in Xiong Yumei, Liu Xiaocong and Qu Wen, eds, *Zhongguo funü lilun yanjiu shi nian* (Ten years of theoretical studies of Chinese women). Beijing: Zhongguo funü chubanshe, 393–419.

Ma Yuan (1993), 'Mistakes', trans. Helen Wang, in Henry Y. H. Zhao, ed., *The Lost Boat: Avant-Garde Fiction from China*. London: Wellsweep Press, 29–42.

MacCormack, Carol P. (1980), 'Nature, culture and gender: a critique', in Carol P. MacCormack and Marilyn Strathern, eds, *Nature, Culture and Gender*. Cambridge: Cambridge University Press, 1–24.

*Marriage Law of the People's Republic of China 1950* (1977). Beijing: Foreign Languages Press.

*Marriage Law of the People's Republic of China 1980* (1982). Beijing: Foreign Languages Press.

Martin, Emily (1989), *The Woman in the Body: A Cultural Analysis of Reproduction*. Milton Keynes: Open University Press.

Mei Yu (1992), 'Yinyang liebian de lüse yaomo' (The green demons of marital rupture), *JTYS* 4, 22.

Meijer, M. J. (1971), *Marriage Law and Policy in the People's Republic of China*. Hong Kong: Hong Kong University Press.

Meng Changqian (1950), 'Yinggai renzhen xuexi hunyin fa' (We must diligently study the Marriage Law), *ZGQN* 43, 40.

Meng Yue (1993), 'Female images and national myth', in Tani Barlow, ed., *Gender Politics in Modern China: Writing and Feminism*. Durham, NC and London: Duke University Press, 118–36.

Meng Yue and Dai Jinhua (1989), *Fuchu lishi dibiao* (Emerging from the horizon of history). Zhengzhou: Henan renmin chubanshe.

Meng Zheyin (1950), 'Wo gaibianle jiu de lian'ai guan' (I changed my old view of love), *ZGFN* 15, 47.

Millett, Kate (1971), *Sexual Politics*. New York: Avon Books.

Min, Anchee (1993), *Red Azalea: Life and Love in China*. London: Victor Gollancz.

*Minzhu yu fazhi* (Democracy and law), ed. (1981), *Hunyin anjian 100 li* (100 legal cases about marriage). Shanghai: Minzhu yu fazhi zazhishe.

Molyneux, Maxine (1985), 'Family reform in socialist states: the hidden agenda', *Feminist Review* 21, 47–66.

Moore, Henrietta (1988), *Feminism and Anthropology*. Cambridge: Polity Press.

—— (1993), 'The differences within and the differences between', in Teresa del Valle, ed., *Gendered Anthropology*. London: Routledge, 193–204.

—— (1994), *A Passion for Difference: Essays in Anthropology and Gender*. Cambridge: Polity Press.

Mosher, Steven W. ([1993] 1994), *A Mother's Ordeal: One Woman's Fight against China's One-Child Policy*. London: Little, Brown.

Mu Aiping (1995), 'Rural Women's Economic Activities and Fertility Behaviour in Selected Areas of China during 1979–1990', unpublished doctoral dissertation, University of Glamorgan.

Mulvey, Laura ([1975], 1989), 'Visual pleasure and narrative cinema', in *Visual and Other Pleasures*. London: Macmillan, 14–26.

'National concern for singles over 30' (1984), *Beijing Review* 27, 30, 8–9.

Nead, Lynda (1988), *Myths of Sexuality: Representation of Women in Victorian Britain*. Oxford: Blackwell.

Ng, Vivien W. (1987), 'Ideology and sexuality: rape laws in Qing China', *Journal of Asian Studies* 46, 1, 57–70.

'Ni xiang zuo ge hao qizi ma?' (1991) (Do you want to be a good wife?), *Funü baike daquan* (xia), 12–19.

*Nineties* Special Supplement for 1991 (1991), 'Dalu shouci "xing wenming" diaocha' (First mainland survey of 'sexual civilization') *Jiushi niandai* 4, 6–10.

Niu Zhi (1951), *Hunyin da geming* (The great revolution in marriage). Guangdong: Nanfang tongsu duwu lianhe chubanshe.

Ocko, Jonathan K. (1991), 'Women, property and law in the People's Republic of China', in Rubie S. Watson and Patricia Buckley Ebrey, eds, *Marriage and Inequality in Chinese Society*. Berkeley: University of California Press, 313–46.

O'Hara, Albert Richard (1971), *The Position of Women in Early China According to the Lieh Nü Chuan 'The Biographies of Chinese Women'*. Taipei: Meiya Publications.

Palmer, Michael (1986–7), 'The People's Republic of China: some observations on family law', *Journal of Family Law* 25, 1, 41–68.

—— (1988), 'The People's Republic of China: problems of marriage and divorce', *Journal of Family Law* 27, 1, 57–79.

—— (1991), 'The People's Republic of China: more rules but less law', in M. D. A. Freeman, ed., *Annual Survey of Family Law: 1989*, 13, 325–42.

—— (1995), 'The re-emergence of family law in post-Mao China: marriage, divorce and reproduction', *China Quarterly*, 141, 110–34.

Pan Suiming (1992), 'Tongnian, xuyao xing jiaoyu' (Infants need sex education), *HYYJT* 4, 30–1.

—— (1993), 'China: acceptability and effect of three kinds of sexual publication', *Archives of Sexual Behaviour* 22, 1, 59–71.

Pang Dunzhi (1950), *Xin hunyin fa jiben renshi* (Basic knowledge about the new Marriage Law). Shanghai: Huaqiao tushushe.

Peng Guoliang, ed. (1993), *Yibai ge nüren tan nanren* (One hundred women talk about men). Changsha: Hunan chubanshe.

Porter, Cathy (1980), *Alexandra Kollontai: A Biography*. London: Virago.

Porter, Roy and Lesley Hall (1995), *The Facts of Life: The Creation of Sexual Knowledge in Britain, 1650–1950*. New Haven, CT, and London: Yale University Press.

Pruitt, Ida (1967), *A Daughter of Han: The Autobiography of a Chinese Working Woman*. Stanford, CA: Stanford University Press.

Qie Ning (1953), 'Mofan jieshengyuan Chang Xiuhua' (Chang Xiuhua, the model midwife), *ZGFN* 6, 24–5.

Qin Zhengru (1953), 'Aiqing' (Love), *ZGFN* 1, 31.

Qing Jie (1986), 'Da jiejie de kaidao' (Older sister helps sort things out), *ZGFN* 5, 43–4.

'Quanguo fulian fandui xuan mei' (1993) (The Women's Federation nationwide opposes beauty contests), *Qingnian shibao*, 30 July, 7.

Quanguo renda changweihui fazhi gongzuo weiyuanhui xingfa shi (The Criminal Law Office of the Legal Work Committee of the Standing Committee of the National People's Congress) (1991), *Guanyu yan jin maiyin piaochang de jueding, Guanyu yan cheng guaimai bangjia funü ertong de fanzui fenzi de jueding* (Decisions on strictly prohibiting prostitution and decisions on strictly punishing criminals who abduct and kidnap women and children). Beijing: Zhongguo jiancha chubanshe.

Rai, Shirin, Pilkington, Hilary and Phizacklea, Annie, eds (1992), *Women in the Face of Change: the Soviet Union, Eastern Europe and China*. London: Routledge.

Ren Fengge and Wu Pingfan (1988), *Hunyin chun qiu* (Spring and autumn of marriage). Urumchi: Xinjiang daxue chubanshe.

Ren Kunru (1951), 'Yansu duidai jiehun he lihun' (Treat seriously marriage and divorce), *ZGQN* 76, 30.

Ren Yuan (1954), 'Zhenshi de aiqing, meiman de hunyin' (Sincere love and a happy home), *ZGFN* 5, 15–16.

Rofel, Lisa (1994), ' "Kewang": funü he tongsu wenhua' ('Yearning': women and popular culture), in Li Xiaojiang, Zhu Hong and Dong Xiuyu, eds, *Xingbie yu Zhongguo* (Gender and China), Beijing: Sanlian chubanshe.

Romney, Seymour L., Gray, Mary Ann, Little, A. Brian, Merrill, James A., Quilligan, E. J. and Stander, Richard W., eds (1981), *Gynaecology and Obstetrics: the Health Care of Women*. New York: McGraw-Hill.

Rougemont, Denis de (1974), *Love in the Western World*. New York: Harper & Row.

Ruan, Fang Fu (1991), *Sex in China: Studies in Sexology in Chinese Culture*. New York and London: Plenum Press.

Rusbridger, Alan (1986), *A Concise History of the Sex Manual, 1886–1986*. London: Faber & Faber.

'Sange shou ru nü qingnian de huyu' (1984) (The appeal of three wronged girls), *ZGQN* 11, 30–1.

Sayers, Janet (1982), *Biological Politics: Feminist and Anti-Feminist Perspectives*. London: Tavistock.

Schafer, Edward (1980), *The Divine Woman*. San Francisco: North Point Press.

Scott, Joan Wallach (1988), *Gender and the Politics of History*. New York: Columbia University Press.

Seaman, Gary (1981), 'The sexual politics of karmic retribution', in Emily Martin Ahern and Hill Gates, eds, *Anthropology of Taiwanese Society*. Stanford, CA; Stanford University Press, 381–96.

Semsel, George, ed. (1987), *Chinese Film: The State of the Art in the People's Republic*. New York: Praeger.

Shan Guangnai (1995), *Zhongguo changji – guoqu he xianzai* (Chinese prostitution: past and present). Beijing: Falü chubanshe.

Shang Fang and Li Yiwu (1991), *Dushen nan nü* (Single men and women). Beijing: Zhongguo huaqiao chubanshe.

Shang Zisong (1992), 'Nanren yan zhong de dushen nüren' (Single women in men's eyes), *NXYJ* 2, 35–6.

*Shanghai dazhong weisheng bao*, 14 April 1993.

Shanghai diyi yixue yuan fushu Zhongshan yiyuan fuchan ke (Department of Gynaecology and Obstetrics of the Zhongshan Hospital, affiliated to the Shanghai Number 1 Hospital) (1974), *Funü baojian zhishi* (Knowledge about women's health). Shanghai: Shanghai renmin chubanshe.

Shao Fuxian (1987), *Dangdai aiqing xinli* (The contemporary psychology of love). Hubei: Hubei renmin chubanshe.

Shao Jun (1993), 'Nüren, geng xuyao sisuo' (Women need to think that much more), *Funü wenzhai jingbian* 3, 45.

Shen Wenjiang, Liu Li et al. ([1986] 1987), *Qingnian weisheng shouce* (A manual for young people's hygiene). Beijing: Zhongguo qingnian chubanshe.

Sheng Ping, ed. (1985), *Xiandai nüxing shenghuo shouce* (A manual of modern women's lives). Beijing: Gongren chubanshe.

Sheridan, Mary and Salaff, Janet W., eds (1984), *Lives: Chinese Working Women*. Bloomington: Indiana University Press.
Shi Fang (1993), *Zhongguo xing wenhua shi* (History of China's sexual culture). Haerbin: Heilongjiang renmin chubanshe.
Shi Li (1988), *Jiaose, kun'gan, zhuiqiu: dangdai nüxing xingxiang tansuo* (Roles, distress, aspirations: exploring images of contemporary women). Beijing: Zhongguo funü chubanshe.
Shi Yubin (1989), 'Xiandai Zhongguo liangxing daode guan de bianhua' (Changing views of sexual morality in modern China), *Shehuixue yanjiu* 2, 72–6.
Showalter, Elaine (1987), *The Female Malady: Women, Madness and English Culture, 1830–1980*. London: Virago.
Shreeves, Rosamund (1992), 'Sexual revolution or "sexploitation"? The pornography and erotica debate in the Soviet Union', in Shirin Rai, Hilary Pilkington and Annie Phizacklea, eds, *Women in the Face of Change: the Soviet Union, Eastern Europe and China*. London: Routledge, 130–46.
Shu Huaimeng (1993), 'Nüren bu laodao cheng ma?' (Is it OK for women not to chatter?), *NXYJ* 5, 61.
Shu Zhe (1995), 'Er nü "zao lian" fumu mo huang' (Don't panic in front of your children's 'premature love'), *DZJK* 7, 25.
Shue, Vivienne (1988), *The Reach of the State: Sketches of the Chinese Body Politic*. Stanford, CA: Stanford University Press.
Si Ren (1986), 'Yige shaonü de zaoyu' (A young girl's bitter experience), *Nüzi shijie* 3, 18–22.
Si Wuliu (1992), 'Hao nanren jiehun, hao nüren danshen?' (Do good men marry and good women stay single?), *NXYJ* 2, 20–1.
Siu, Helen (1993), 'Reconstituting dowry and brideprice in south China', in Deborah Davis and Stevan Harrell, eds, *Chinese Families in the Post-Mao Era*. Berkeley, Los Angeles and London: University of California Press, 165–88.
Snitow, Ann, Stansell, Christine and Thompson, Sharon, eds (1984), *Desire: The Politics of Sexuality*. London: Virago.
Snow, Helen Foster, see Wales, Nym.
Song Chu (1986), 'Shisan, shenmi de nianling: shi tan qingchunqi xing jiaoyu de poqiexing' (Thirteen, a mysterious age: exploratory talks on the urgent need for adolescent sex education), *ZGFN* 7, 30–1.
Song Meiya (1991), 'Yi zhuang zhangfu qiangjian qizi an' (A case of marital rape), *ZGFN* 1, 14–15.
Song Qi (1991), *Zaihun lei* (Tears of remarriage). Beijing: Zhongguo huaqiao chubanshe.
Song Tingzhang (1955), *Zenyang zhengque duidai lian'ai wenti* (The correct approach to the question of love). Shenyang: Liaoning renmin chubanshe.
Sontag, Susan (1989), *Aids and its Metaphors*. Harmondsworth: Penguin.
Stacey, Judith (1983), *Patriarchy and Socialist Revolution in China*. Berkeley and Los Angeles: University of California Press.
Stockard, Janice E. (1989) *Daughters of the Canton Delta: Marriage Patterns and Economic Strategies in South China, 1860–1930*. Stanford, CA: Stanford University Press.
Su Fan (1956), 'Wode jiaoxun' (My lesson), *ZGFN* 3, 31–2.

Su Fu and Huang Yuxian (1992), *Aiqing jiating shenghuo yixue* (Medicine for love and family life). Guangzhou: Huanan ligong daxue chubanshe.

Su Liwen and Lu Qiyi, eds ([1989] 1991), *Funü weisheng baojian* (Women's health and hygiene). Beijing: Zhongguo zhanwang chubanshe.

Su Wen (1957), 'Zhei zhong fengqi shi zhengchang ma?' (Is this common practice proper?), *ZGQN* 2, 40.

Su Yuan (1956), 'Shei shi duoyu de disanzhe?' (Who is the extra third party?), *ZGQN* 7, 39.

Sun Longji (1991), *Zhongguo wenhua de shenceng jiegou* (The deep structure of Chinese culture). Taipei: Tangshan chubanshe.

Sun Shaoxian (1991), 'Guanyu zhangfu qiangjian qizi zui de sikao' (Reflections on the crime of marital rape), *ZGFN* 7, 25.

Sun Wenlan (1991), *Lihun zai Zhongguo* (Divorce in China). Beijing: Zhongguo funü chubanshe.

Sun Yue (1992), Nüxing yu ai (Women and love). Beijing: Zhongguo funü chubanshe.

Symposium: 'Public Sphere'/'Civil Society' in China? Paradigmatic Issues in Chinese Studies, III (1993), *Modern China*, 19, 2.

Tan Shen (1993), 'Shehui zhuanbian yu Zhongguo funü jiuye' (Social transformation and Chinese women's employment), in Chen Zhiying, ed., *Zhongguo funü yu fazhan: diwei, jiankang, jiuye* (Chinese women and development: position, health, employment). Zhengzhou: Henan renmin chubanshe, 337–85.

Tan Zhen (1956), 'Biyun yingxiang jiankang ma?' (Does contraception affect your health?), *ZGFN* 7, 26.

Tang Dao (1986), *Hunyin xinlixue* (Psychology of marriage). Shanghai: Shanghai renmin chubanshe.

Tang Shuhua, Liu Xianpu and Zhao Ke, eds (1988), *Nüxing fanzui lun* (On female crime). Lanzhou: Lanzhou daxue chubanshe.

Tian He (1991), 'Yu Bo Fuwa duihua: guanyu nüxing de fansi' (Conversations with Bo Fuwa: reflections about being female), *NXYJ* 6, 9–12.

Tian Liu (1953), 'Nü qingnian tuan yuan – Xu Lamei' (The female Youth League member – Xu Lamei), *ZGQN* 1, 29–30.

Tien Ju-k'ang (1988), *Male Anxiety and Female Chastity: A Comparative Study of Chinese Ethical Values in Ming-Ch'ing Times.* Leiden: Brill.

Van de Velde, Theodore H. ([1930] 1960), *Ideal Marriage: Its Physiology and Technique.* London: Heinemann.

Van Gulik, Robert ([1961] 1974), *Sexual Life in Ancient China.* Leiden: Brill.

Vance, Carol S. (1984), *Pleasure and Danger: Exploring Female Sexuality.* London: Routledge & Kegan Paul.

Wales, Nym (Helen Foster Snow) (1967), *Women in Modern China.* The Hague: Mouton.

Wan Ruixiong (1990), 'Xing'ai zai da bianzou' (Great changes in sexual love), in Chen Fan, ed., *Xingbing zai Zhongguo* (Sexual diseases in China). Beijing: Beijing shiyue wenyi chubanshe, 101–32.

Wan Zi (1993), 'Tongxinglian xianxiang shi xi' (Explanation and analysis of the phenomenon of homosexuality), *NXYJ* 4, 44–6.

Wang Bao'en (1953), 'Dajia yao zhongshi hun qian jiankang jiancha' (Everyone should attach importance to the premarital checkup), *ZGFN* 3, 38.

Wang Fuling and Song Jie, eds (1993), *Lihun falü zixun* (Advice about divorce law). Beijing: Zhongguo jiliang chubanshe.

Wang Peng, ed. (1993), *Xing zhishi baike* (Encyclopedia of sexual knowledge). Changchun: Jilin renmin chubanshe.

Wang Ranji, Zhang Zhiyou, Cui Jin and Wan Chun (1990), *Qiangjian zui de rending yu fangzhi* (Defining and preventing the crime of rape). Beijing: Zhongguo huaqiao chubanshe.

Wang Shancheng (1956), 'Tan xing shenghuo' (Talking about sexual relations), *ZGFN* 8, 30.

Wang Shuqin, ed. (1993), *Tongsu nüxing yixue* (Popular medical science of female sexuality). Haerbin: Heilongjiang kexue jishu chubanshe.

Wang Wenbin, Zhao Zhiyi and Tan Mingxin (1956), *Xing de zhishi* (Knowledge about sex). Beijing: Renmin weisheng chubanshe.

Wang Xingjuan (1992), 'Guanyu maiyin piaochang wenti de yanjiu' (Research on the problem of prostitution), in Xiong Yumei, Liu Xiaocong and Qu Wen, eds, *Zhongguo funü lilun yanjiu shi nian* (Ten years of theoretical studies of Chinese women). Beijing: Zhongguo funü chubanshe, 420–41.

Wang Yang and Xu Xiaolin (1991), *Nüshi* (Lady). Chengdu: Sichuan renmin chubanshe.

Wang Yanming (1988), *Lianren, fuqi, qing'ai – xiandai hunlian nanti jiexi* (Lovers, spouses and love – an analysis of the problems of modern marital love). Beijing: Nongcun duwu chubanshe.

Wang Youqin (1985), 'Guanyu xing daode de yixie sikao' (Some reflections on sexual morality), *ZGFN* 10, 10–12.

Wang Yuling (1959), 'Wode kunao' (My anxiety), *ZGFN* 22, 18.

Wang Zhen (1986), 'Bu ke hushi qingchunqi de jiaoyu' (We cannot neglect adolescents' education), *ZGFN* 8, 36–7.

Watson, Rubie S. (1991a), 'Afterword: marriage and gender inequality', in Rubie S. Watson and Patricia Buckley Ebrey, eds, *Marriage and Inequality in Chinese Society*. Berkeley and Los Angeles: University of California Press, 347–68.

—— (1991b), 'Wives, concubines and maids: servitude and kinship in the Hong Kong region, 1900–1940', in Rubie S. Watson and Patricia Buckley Ebrey, eds, *Marriage and Inequality in Chinese Society*. Berkeley and Los Angeles: University of California Press, 231–55.

Watson, Rubie S. and Ebrey, Patricia Buckley, eds (1991), *Marriage and Inequality in Chinese Society*. Berkeley and Los Angeles: University of California Press.

Weeks, Jeffrey (1981), *Sex, Politics and Society: the Regulation of Sexuality since 1800*. London: Longman.

—— (1985), *Sexuality and its Discontents: Meanings, Myths and Modern Sexualities*. London: Routledge & Kegan Paul.

—— (1986), *Sexuality*. London: Tavistock.

Wei Biyan (1984), 'Shamo zhong de xiao cao zai panzhe ganlu de zirun' (The sprouts of grass growing in the desert long for moisture of the sweet dew), *ZGQN* 3, 60.

Wei Haibo, Wu Duan, Yu Bin and Zhang Liting (1986), 'Wuhui, daigou, disanzhe: Shanghai shimin daode yishi diaocha zhaji' (Dances, seduction and the third party: notes on an investigation into the moral consciousness of Shanghai citizens), *MZYFZ* 1, 27–8.

Wei Hua (1958), 'Aiqing' (Love), *ZGFN* 7, 18–19.

Wei Junyi (1950), 'Jiehun hui bu hui yingxiang jinbu?' (Does marriage impede progress?), *ZGQN* 50, 43.

—— (1953) 'Yang haizi shi fou fang'ai jinbu?' (Does bringing up children impede progress?), *ZGQN* 21, 13–14.

Wen Bo ([1988] 1989), *Zhongguo ren de hunyin* (Marriage in China). Beijing: Zhongguo shehui kexue chubanshe.

Wen Jianhua et al., eds (1986), *Ai de xuanze: 120 ming nan nü qingnian aiqing de zishu* (Choices in love: love stories of 120 young men and women). Beijing: Zhongguo wenlian chubanshe.

Whyte, Martin King (1992), *From Arranged Marriages to Love Matches in Urban China*. Hong Kong: Hong Kong Institute of Asia Pacific Studies.

Whyte, Martin King and Parish, William L. (1984), *Urban Life in Contemporary China*. Chicago: University of Chicago Press.

'Wo ling you xin huan zenmo ban?' (1991) (I've fallen for someone else so what should I do?), *Funü baike daquan* (xia), 42–3.

'Wo shi zenmo yang bangzhu airen baituo disanzhe de?' (1991) (In what way did I help my husband get rid of the third partner?), *Funü baike daquan* (xia), 15–17.

Wolf, Arthur P., ed. (1978), *Studies in Chinese Society*. Stanford, CA: Stanford University Press.

Wolf, Margery (1985), *Revolution Postponed: Women in Contemporary China*. London: Methuen.

Wong, Jan (1992), 'Trafficking in young women, a sad fact in modern China', *Globe and Mail*, 26 June.

Woo, Margaret Y. K. (1994), 'Chinese women workers: the delicate balance between protection and equality', in Christina K. Gilmartin, Gail Hershatter, Lisa Rofel and Tyrene White, eds, *Engendering China: Women, Culture, and the State*. Cambridge, MA, and London: Harvard University Press, 279–95.

Wu Di (1993), 'Qishi nin bu dong wode xin – zhongxue sheng zao lian riji' (In fact you don't understand my heart – the diary of a middle school student in 'early' love), *NXYJ* 3, 32–4.

Wu Jian (1992), 'Miandui xi xin bu yan jiu de zhangfu' (Facing the husband who likes the new as well as the old), *NXYJ* 1, 48–9.

Wu Jieping et al. (1983), *Xing yixue* (The medical science of sex). Beijing: Kexue jishu wenxian chubanshe.

Wu Wen (1993), 'Zhang Fu, "mei" yu "se" da fanchuan' (Zhang Fu, playing the part of 'beauty' and 'desire'), *MZYFZ* 10, 41–3.

Wu Yi (1956), 'Zai bu neng youyi bu dingle' (You cannot go on having doubts and not making a decision), *ZGFN* 7, 26.

Wu Yuming (1986), 'Yisheng de gaojie' (Doctor's warning), *ZGFN* 5, 42–3.

Wu Zhangming, Zhu Xiaolan and Lang Ying ([1987] 1990), *Hun qian hun hou weisheng sanbai wen* (Three hundred questions about hygiene before and after marriage). Fuzhou: Fujian kexue jishu chubanshe.

Xiang Hua (1980), 'Hunyin, xingfu, jiankang' (Marriage, happiness and health), *ZGQN* 12, 36.

'Xiang xie shenmo banfa lai zengjia xuesheng de jiankang?' (1950) (What methods can we think of to improve students' health?), *ZGQN* 48, 33–4.

Xiao Dong (1981), 'Aiqing bixu shishi gengxin, shengzhang, chuangzao' (Love must constantly be renewed, nurtured and created), *ZGQN* 10, 9.

Xiao Hua (1986), 'Dushenzhe de jiannan' (The difficulty of being single), *ZGFN* 2, 38.

Xiao Mingxiong (1984), *Zhongguo tongxinglian shi lu* (Historical records of homosexuality in China). Hong Kong: Fenhong santong chubanshe.

Xie Bozhang ([1974] 1975), *Qingchunqi weisheng* (Adolescent hygiene). Beijing: Beijing renmin chubanshe.

Xie Juezai (1953), 'Chongqing de aiqing' (Lofty love), *ZGFN* 9, 4.

Xie Zhihong and Jia Lusheng (1989), 'Gulao de zuie' (An ancient crime), *Wenhui yuekan*, 2, 2–15.

*Xinhun weisheng bi du* editorial group ([1982] 1984), *Xinhun weisheng bi du* (Necessary reading for the newly-weds). Beijing: Renmin weisheng chubanshe.

Xiong Xuewu, Liu Gewen, Zhou Guorong, Liu Peiyu, Jiang Guangyin and Jiang Shaochuan (1983), *Jiehun qian hou* (Before and after marriage). Hubei: Hubei renmin chubanshe.

Xiong Yumei, Liu Xiaocong and Qu Wen, eds (1992), *Zhongguo funü lilun yanjiu shi nian* (Ten years of theoretical studies of Chinese women). Beijing: Zhongguo funü chubanshe.

Xu Anqi (1988), *Lihun xinli* (The Psychology of divorce). Beijing: Zhongguo funü chubanshe.

—— (1990a), 'Beidongxing, jueze quan he di manyi' (Passivity, the power to choose and low satisfaction), *Shehuixue yanjiu* 3, 103–9.

—— (1990b), 'Lun disanzhe jieru hunyin jiufen de tedian yu qushi' (The characteristics and tendencies of the intervention of the third party in marital conflict), *Shehuixue yanjiu* 4, 51–6.

Xu Chen and Zhang Kongqian (1987), *Funü gengnianqi yiliao baojian shouce* (Manual for women's health during the menopause). Beifang funü ertong chubanshe.

Xu Hua (1956), 'Bu yao zhao nianling tai xiao de zhongxuesheng tan lian'ai' (Don't go out with under-age middle school students), *ZGQN* 22, 26.

Xu Jimin and Wang Lie, eds (1991), *Aiqing xue* (The study of love). Taiyuan: Shanxi jiaoyu chubanshe.

Xu Jinxun and Fan Dezhen (1987), *Xinhun yu jiankang* (Health for the newly-weds). Shanghai: Shanghai kexue jishu chubanshe.

Xu Linyue (1958), 'Rufang de fayu' (Breast development), *ZGFN* 8, 24.

Xu Mingjiang (1955), 'Tan qingnian tuan zuzhi zai dui qingnian jinxing hunyin lian'ai wenti jiaoyu zhong de jige wenti' ( On some problems in the Youth League's education of young people in issues of love and marriage), *ZGQN* 7, 5–6.

Xu Zhong (1994), 'Xing kuaigan quefa zenmo ban?' (What should you do if you do not find sex pleasurable?), *NXYJ* 1, 53.

Xue Fagui and Deng Zongxiu (1988), *Xing bing fangzhi wenda* (Questions and answers about the prevention and cure of sexual diseases). Guiyang: Guizhou renmin chubanshe.

Ya Ping (1958), 'Xingfu de Daye funü' (The happy women of Daye), *ZGFN* 6, 14–15.

Yan Renying (1955), 'Guanyu "chunümo" wenti' (About the problem of the 'hymen'), *ZGFN* 5, 28.

—— (1958), 'Yuejing bing he jingqi weisheng' (Menstrual sickness and menstrual hygiene), *ZGFN* 11, 23.

Yan Ruizhen and Li Peifang (1989), *Qingshaonian shengli xinli jiankang zhinan* (A guide to young people's physiological and psychological health). Beijing: Xueshu qikan chubanshe.

Yang, C. K. (1959), *The Chinese Family in the Communist Revolution.* Cambridge, MA: MIT.

Yang, Martin (1948), *A Chinese Village, Taitou, Shantung Province.* London: Routledge & Kegan Paul.

Yang Dawen, Zheng Li and Liu Suping (1979), *Hunyin fa yu hunyin jiating wenti jianghua* (Talks about the Marriage Law and marriage and family problems). Beijing: Renmin chubanshe.

Yang Ge (1957), 'Zhao Yiman' (Zhao Yiman), *ZGQN* 1, 20–2; 2, 17–19; 3, 23–5; 4, 23–5; 5, 16–18.

Yang Jianbao and Zhang Zhili ([1989] 1990), *Xing bing zheng zhi* (Symptoms and control of sexual diseases). Beijing: Zhongguo funü chubanshe.

Yang Jiezeng and He Wannan (1988), *Shanghai changji gaizao shi hua* (Talks about the transformation of Shanghai's prostitutes). Shanghai: Shanghai sanlian shudian.

Yang Shouxin, Wu Yaozhong and Zhang Xiyu, eds (1986), *Guniang zui guanxin de 100 ge wenti* (Girls' 100 most important questions). Haerbin: Heilongjiang renmin chubanshe.

Yang Xiong (1992), *Dangdai qingnian wenhua huisu yu sikao* (Recollections and reflections on contemporary youth culture). Zhengzhou: Henan renmin chubanshe.

Yang Yong (1985), 'Jiu weihu hunyin daode wenti fang Lei Jeiqiong dajie' (An interview with Sister Lei Jieqiong on the question of upholding marital morality), *ZGFN* 10, 13–14).

Yang Zi and Zhang An (1992), *Nüxing de meili* (The beauty of women). Beijing: Zhongguo qingnian chubanshe.

Yao Peikuan (1992), 'The study and practice of adolescent sex education in China', *SASS Papers* (4). Shanghai: Shanghai shehui kexue yuan, 443–56.

'Yao shanyu zhengui de aiqing' (1954) (Be true to precious love), *ZGFN* 11, 4.

Ye Tong (1954), 'Yuexi li yinggai zhuyi xie shenmo' (What you should pay attention to in the month of confinement), *ZGFN* 1, 32.

Yi Ming (1995), 'Shengxia jingqi funü yi xu fang shou liang' (Menstruating women must still guard against catching cold in midsummer), *JTYS* 7, 17.

You Tong (1957), 'Duiyu dangqian lihun wenti de fenxi he yijian' (Analysis and ideas about current divorce problems), *ZGFN* 8, 16–17.

Young, Marilyn B. (1973) *Women in China: Studies in Social Change and Feminism.* Ann Arbor: University of Michigan Press.

'Youxiu de baojian yuan Zhu Xiujun' (1953) (The outstanding health worker Zhu Xiujun), *ZGFN* 1, 20–1.

Yu Feng (1955), 'Jintian de funü fuzhuang wenti' (The question of women's dress today), *ZGFN* 3, 31–2.

Yu Jiu (1954), 'Zai tan ruhe zhengque kandai lian'ai wenti' (More on how to approach correctly the question of love), *ZGQN* 7, 14–15.

Yu Minghua (1956), 'Shi shenmo fang'aile qingnian de youyi he aiqing?' (What is it that hinders friendship and love between young people?), *ZGQN* 11, 31–3).

Yu Ping (1957), 'Kunao' (Anxiety), *ZGFN* 3, 14–15.

Yu Ronghe (1981), 'Qingchun jianying' (Adolescent silhouettes), *ZGFN* 2, 42.

Yu Yan (1993), 'Nüren: danshen de kungan' (Women: the misery of being single), *NXYJ* 5, 48.

Zeng Yi (1989), 'Is the Chinese family planning programme tightening up?', *Population and Development Review* 15, 2, 333–7.

—— (1991), *Family Dynamics in China: A Life Table Analysis*. Madison: University of Wisconsin Press.

Zeng Zhaoyi (1952), 'Weishenmo hui liuchan' (Why miscarriages occur), *ZGFN* 12, 38.

'Zenyang renshi biyun wenti' (1955) (How to approach the question of contraception), *ZGFN* 5, 6–7.

Zetkin, Klara (1953–4), 'Liening tan funü, hunyin he xing de wenti' (Lenin's views on women, marriage and sex), *ZGFN* 11, 6–7; 12, 13; 1, 6–7; 2, 13.

Zha Bo and Geng Wenxiu (1992), 'Sexuality in urban China', *Australian Journal of Chinese Affairs* 28, July, 1–20.

Zhang Biao (1991), *Fuqi qingmi* (Conjugal secrets). Beijing: Zhongguo hua-qiao chubanshe.

Zhang Fan, ed. (1952), *Lian'ai, hunyin yu fufu shenghuo* (Love, marriage and conjugal life). Shanghai: Zhanwang zhoukanshe.

Zhang Jiajun ([1989] 1991), *Fuqi bing zhi* (Curing conjugal diseases). Beijing: Kexue puji chubanshe.

Zhang Lihua, Ru Haitao and Dong Naiqiang (1992), 'Jianguo sishi nian funü tushu gaikuang' (A survey of books on women in the forty years since 1949), in Xiong Yumei, Liu Xiaocong and Qu Wen, eds, *Zhongguo funü lilun yanjiu shi nian* (Ten years of theoretical studies of Chinese women). Beijing: Zhongguo funü chubanshe, 592–609.

Zhang Lisheng (1984), 'Yanjiu qingnian ren de xinli' (Researching youth psychology). *ZGFN* 9, 34–5.

Zhang Lixi and Song Hui, eds (1992), *Nüxing xinli* (Female psychology). Beijing: Zhongguo funü chubanshe.

Zhang Mingyuan and Weng Zhonghua (1986), *Nüxing xinli he shengli* (Female psychology and physiology). Hangzhou: Zhejiang renmin chu-banshe.

Zhang Ping (1992), *Kuang fu yuan nü: daling weihun wenti toushi* (Carefree bachelors and worried spinsters: a perspective on the problem of the older unmarrieds). Xi'an: Shaanxi renmin jiaoyu chubanshe.

—— (1993), *Dangjin Zhongguo shehui bing* (Social disease in contemporary China). Unpublished draft.

Zhang Qingyun et al. ([1982] 1984), *Nüqingnian shujian* (Correspondence with young women). Shenyang: Liaoning renmin chubanshe.

Zhang Shuxian and Zhang Hongru (1990), *Jiushi niandai jiating shenghuo guanjian shouce* (A manual of the key to family life in the nineties). Beijing: Xuefan chubanshe.

Zhang Xijun (1957), 'Cong shenglixue jiaodu tan hunling wenti' (Talking about the age of marriage from the biological perspective), *ZGQN* 6, 34.

Zhang Xinxin (1989), 'How come you aren't divorced yet?', in Perry Link, Richard Madsen and Paul G. Pickowicz, eds, *Unofficial China: Popular Culture and Thought in the People's Republic of China*. Boulder, CO: Westview Press, 57–71.

Zhang Yiwen and Wu Yiyong (1990), *Funü gengnianqi* (The menopause). Beijing: Kexue chubanshe.

Zhang Yuan (1995), 'Shenmo shi xing jiaoyu?' (What is sex education?), *Jiankang* 6, 27.

Zhang Zhixin ([1982] 1984), *Aiqing shujian* (Correspondence about love). Taiyuan: Shanxi renmin chubanshe.

Zhang Zhixin and Feng Mingchun (1985), *Daode shujian* (Correspondence about morality). Taiyuan: Shanxi renmin chubanshe.

Zhao Chang'an, Lan Wei and Zhang Tianruo, eds ([1942] 1985), *Lao gemingjia de lian'ai, hunyin he jiating shenghuo* (The loves, marriages and family lives of old revolutionaries). Beijing: Gongren chubanshe.

Zhao Rongfa (1989), 'Huangpai jinggao: tongxinglianzhe' (Showing the yellow card to homosexuals), *Renmin jingcha* 368 (October), 10–15.

Zhao Yiheng (1992), 'Xing jiefang yu Zhongguo wenhua de lijiao xiayan yundong' (Sexual liberation and the Confucian ethics of the nineties), *Minzhu Zhongguo* 2, 71–8.

—— ed. (1993), *The Lost Boat: Avant-garde Fiction from China*. London: Wellsweep Press.

Zheng Hao (1957), 'Cengjing zouguo de wan lu' (The twisted path I once went along), *ZGQN* 2, 33–4.

Zheng Lunian (1987), 'Wushi sui ye meihao' (It's also beautiful to be fifty), *ZGFN* 3, 44–5.

Zheng Xiaoying, ed. (1995), *Zhongguo nüxing renkou wenti yu fazhan* (Problems and development of China's female population). Beijing: Beijing daxue chubanshe.

Zheng Yefu (1994), 'Nan nü pingdeng de shehui sikao' (Social reflections on equality between men and women), *Shehuixue yanjiu* 2, 108–13.

Zhi Xin, ed. (1992), *Xie gei nüxuesheng* (Written to female students). Chengdu: Dianzi keji daxue chubanshe.

Zhong Dianbei (1955), 'Congming xie, jianqiang xie, yiding yao xiang Ma Chengliang shi de e ren zuo douzheng' (Be intelligent and determined, for we must struggle against evil people like Ma Chengliang), *ZGQN* 16, 23–4.

*Zhongguo baike nianjian* (1981) (China yearbook). Beijing: Zhongguo da baike quanshu chubanshe.

*Zhongguo falü nianjian* bianji bu, ed. (1995), *Zhongguo falü nianjian 1995* (Chinese law yearbook 1995). Beijing: Zhongguo falü nianjian she.

Zhongguo funü shehui diwei diaocha keti zu (Group for the Survey of Chinese Women's Social Position), ed. (1993), *Zhongguo funü shehui diwei gaikuang* (Summary of Chinese women's social position). Beijing: Zhongguo funü chubanshe.

Zhongyang renmin zhengfu fazhi weiyuanhui (Legal Committee of the Central People's Government), ed. (1950), *Hunyin wenti cankao ziliao huibian* (Compendium of reference materials on marriage problems). Beijing: Renmin chubanshe.

Zhou Daoluan (1981), 'Lüe lun qiangjian zui' (Brief discussion about the crime of rape), *MZYFZ*, 6 June, 10.

Zhou Efen (1955), 'Youguan yuejing de jige wenti' (Some questions about menstruation), *ZGFN* 2, 25.

Zhu Fengwen (1987), 'Qian tan qiangjian anjian zhengju rending zhong de xinli fenxi' (Brief comments on a psychological analysis of the proof and identification of rape), *Zhongguo fazhi bao*, 21 Oct., 3.

Zhu Keyu (1951), 'Yingxiong de ganxiang, yingxiong de xin' (The thoughts and heart of a hero), *ZGQN* 62, 42–4; 63, 21–2.

Zhu Li (1951), 'Dan niang shi zenyang shenghuo de?' (How did old mother Dan live?), *ZGQN* 67, 30.

Zhu Zhixin (1956), 'Disanzhe you xingfu ma?' (Can the third party find happiness?), *ZGFN* 3, 30–1.

Zong Fuhua and Yang Tong (n.d.), *Nüxing meili de baochi yu chuangzao: dangdai funü shenghuo fangshi* (Preservation and creation of feminine glamour: life styles of contemporary women). Huerhot: Neimenggu renmin chubanshe.

Zui gao renmin jiancha yuan ed. (1991) *Qiangjie zui* (The crime of rape). Beijing: Zhongguo jiancha chubansche.

'Zunzhong aiqing shenghuo zhong de ziyuan yuanze' (1956) (Respect the principle of voluntary choice in love), *ZGQN* 10, 36–7.

# Index